Ideas for China's Future

Weiying Zhang

Ideas for China's Future

Translated by Matthew J. Dale

palgrave
macmillan

Weiying Zhang
Langrun Yuan Area
Peking University
Beijing, China

Translated by
Matthew J. Dale
Cambridge, USA

ISBN 978-981-15-4303-6   ISBN 978-981-15-4304-3 (eBook)
https://doi.org/10.1007/978-981-15-4304-3

This Palgrave Macmillan imprint is published by the registered company Springer Nature Singapore Pte Ltd.
The registered company address is: 152 Beach Road, #21-01/04 Gateway East, Singapore 189721, Singapore

Preface

The basic idea this book tries to convey is: Ideas matter and China needs right ideas to defeat wrong ideas and to guide its future reform.

More than 100 years ago, Irish economist Francis Edgeworth stated: "The first principle of Economics is that every agent is motivated by self-interest." This sentence succinctly generalizes the basic assumption of economics. According to this principle, economists understand every individual's actions as the maximization of personal interests. Social phenomena are the result of games between interests. Social transformation is understood as one interest being victorious over another interest. Or, it is a rational decision made after politicians have analyzed the costs and benefits of a transformation. It should be said that this assumption is true in many circumstances and is a useful tool for the analysis of economic and social issues, but it ignores an important fact. That is, human action is also swayed by ideas, world views, and ideologies. Just as Scottish Enlightenment thinker David Hume believed, even though people are governed by interests, interest itself—and all of humanity's affairs—is governed by ideas.

The influence of ideas on human action comes from the fact that "humans are rational entities." What is a rational entity? It is the human ability to think, have objectives, and make plans. As rational entities, when we do any activity, we must have an adequate reason. This adequate reason is provided by our ideas. If human action is not influenced by ideas, then humans are no different from animals.

Rational people pursue their own interests. However, interests, as they are understood, are formed by ideas. That is to say, what our interests are depend on our thoughts and beliefs. For example, a few decades ago, when farmers were told their interests were in conflict with those of the landlords, and the workers were told their interests were in conflict with those of the capitalists, it was in their interests to exterminate the landlords and the capitalists. They began revolutions.

For a long time, the idea of interests has been defined very narrowly in economics. Economics assumes that each individual will pursue his or her own maximum utility. This utility is often understood as the satisfaction of material desires, but this understanding is very limited. People's interests are not just material interests as traditional economics assumes. Instead, they include many non-material interests, and these non-material interests are more sensitive to ideas. Social relationships are the source of non-material interests. As a social animal, a person's happiness is to a large degree determined by his relationship with others, meaning other's opinion of him. Living in society, we certainly desire the respect of others. If we hope for a good reputation, the things we do must be just and meet other's expectations. Justness is determined by our ideas. In other words, our ideas about justice will certainly influence our actions. Therefore, non-material interests are more reliant on and sensitive to ideas.

Rationality in economics is instrumental rationality. Simply put, instrumental rationality means that individual goals are a given, so rationality means choosing the most effective way to reach that goal, maximize our preferences, and maximize our utility. From the perspective of instrumental rationality, rationality is the slave of desires and emotions; it has no role in setting individual objectives. In real life, making real choices, goal rationality is more important. What exactly should we pursue? What should we not pursue? Humans are social rational entities with many desires. Choosing which desires to satisfy or not is something humans can choose. This is the biggest difference between humans and animals. According to Immanuel Kant's explanation, rationality assists in our selection of goals. Rationality should be the master of desires, not its slave. Morals are preferences that restrict people. The majority of people in society select their objectives according to certain ethical principles. These ethical principles are formed by a person's ideas.

The power of ideas is manifested most obviously in social transformation. In many transformations in the history of humanity, it was not that one type of interest defeated another type of interest; instead, one type of thinking or ideology defeated another type of thinking or ideology. New ideas defeated old ideas, but it could also be said that ideas defeated interests. Many transformations appear on the surface to be victories of interests but are actually victories of ideas. The New Democratic Revolution and Socialist Revolution led by the Chinese Communist Party were not the victory of peasant and workers' interests over those of landlords and capitalists, instead they were the victory of Marxism over other ideologies. An important reason that vested interests can become reformers is the power of ideas. The Chinese Communist Party is seen as the vanguard of the working class, but the main founders of the Communist Party were not born into the working class. Instead, they were the elites of the old system. Why would these people born into the ruling class seek to start a revolution? Because they accepted a new type of idea. This idea was Marxist Leninism.

The planned economy itself is the product of ideas. The successes that China has accomplished over the last 40 years of reform and opening were also the result of ideas defeating interests. After the end of the "Cultural Revolution," Deng Xiaoping initiated market-oriented Reform and Opening because he had new ideas. He believed that the planned economy could not solve China's problems. The common people needed more liberty to direct their own initiatives. The market was to play a role. China's experiences over the last 40 years have proven that the advances and regressions of reform actually have all been related to the soundness of ideas. China's future reforms—especially political system reforms—to a large degree will still be determined by the kind of ideas and leadership to come about.

Where do ideas come from? They come from the market of ideas! The so-called market of ideas is the equal and free competition of viewpoints, beliefs, theories and proposals. To a large degree, the last forty years of reform were the result of competition in the market of ideas. Without the Great Debate on Truth Criterion or the Thought Liberation Movement, Deng Xiaoping's reforms could not have happened. Without broad and thorough debate amongst economists, the "Socialist Market Economy" would not have been set as an objective of reform. Without debate, the "Rule of Law Country" ideal could not have been established. Only a free market of ideas can create new thoughts and ideas about future reform.

While China has made great progress in both economic and social development since the beginning of reform and opening, there is still a long way to go to become a liberal society. The ideas of Deng Xiaoping and Jiang Zemin previously were shared among China's leadership. It is a pity that these ideas have regressed (although implicitly) for at least a decade under the flagship of the "China Model." As a result, reforms in many respects have moved backward, instead of forward. Particularly in the past few years, political and ideological correctness have replaced practical and pragmatic philosophy. The Party has topped everything. The government has become more powerful and interventionist. The state sector has regained momentum to expand recklessly. Private entrepreneurs have become less and less confident. The movement toward the rule of law has been reversed. Political democratization now cannot even be publicly mentioned. The market for ideas is almost completely closed down. While "deepening reform" is still an official slogan, real reform is dead.

All these regressions have worried me and many others a lot. I have written dozens of essays in the past decade to call for getting back on the liberalization track. While many of my essays are not easy to publish in China, quite a few of my fellow Chinese can still read and appreciate them, thanks to new Internet self-media. I write because I deeply believe right ideas will eventually triumph over wrong ideas and vested interests. I am just uncertain how long it will take. So, I hope to propose ideas for China's future.

This book is a collection of some selected essays I wrote over the last few years (one exception is Chap. 15 which was written in 2003). Even though each essay appears as an independent chapter, all of them develop around "ideas for China's future" as a main theme. The writing time of the original version of each chapter is noted for the reader to have a good sense of the social and economic background when the contents were written. I hope that this book will lead the reader to have a deeper understanding of the important ideas in China's economic reforms over the last 40 years, and the possible path of future reform. Certainly, I also hope more and more Chinese people will accept my ideas. For any social transformation, in the short term, perhaps the ideas of political leaders are crucial, but in the long term, the ideas of the common people are more important.

I am very grateful to Matthew Dale for his industrious and excellent work in translation of this book.

Beijing, China
10 December 2019

Weiying Zhang

Contents

PART I

The Market and Cooperation

CHAPTER 1

Interests and Ideas in Economics

People's viewpoints influence their understanding of their own interests. Human cognition is limited and viewpoints can be incorrect, so humans will make decisions that are disadvantageous to personal interests.

The duty of economists is to change people's viewpoints via their own research, causing people to better recognize their fundamental interests.

The progress of ideas starts from a small group of people. If there is no true tolerance for the ideas of a small group of people, our society cannot possibly progress.[1]

* * *

Economics is generally understood as the study of interests. Economists believe human action is swayed by interests and rational people understand their own interests. Each person pursues his or her own interest, so all actions can be reasonably explained by "interests." This is something I learned from economics over a long period of time. However, there was

[1] The original version of this chapter was written in December 2013 as the keynote speech to the NetEase Annual Economists Conference.

W. Zhang, *Ideas for China's Future*,
https://doi.org/10.1007/978-981-15-4304-3_1

always something that baffled me: If this is the case, why do we need economists? That is to say, since with or without economists each person's individual actions would be the same—no better and no worse—what do we want economists to do?

If economists cannot make society better, then perhaps our use of society's resources is pointless. This economic assumption cannot explain why humanity makes as many mistakes as it does. This includes the fact that over a long period of time, one-third of the world's population chose a type of economic system called "central planning." This system brought tremendous hardship to those living under it. We do not even have a way to explain some basic issues within economics. For example, according to the Rational Expectations School, any expected economic policy will not succeed. If this is true, then every government official should also have rational expectations, so if they expect a policy will not work, why would they still set policies? This has perplexed me for a very long time.

Over the last few years, I have recognized more and more it is not only interests that sway human action, but also thoughts, ideas, and ideologies. That is to say, when people chose to do something, they are not only influenced by interests, but what they believe in or do not believe in. More precisely, people understand their own interests via their own viewpoints. However, people's knowledge is limited, so viewpoints can be mistaken, thus causing them to make disadvantageous decisions.

This of course is not a new viewpoint of mine. Actually, more than two hundred years ago, Scottish Enlightenment thinker and economist David Hume said that even though men be much governed by interest; yet even interest itself, and all human affairs, are entirely governed by opinion.[2] John Maynard Keynes has a very famous quote:

> *The ideas of economists and political philosophers, both when they are right and when they are wrong, are more powerful than is commonly understood. Indeed the world is ruled by little else. Practical men, who believe themselves to be quite exempt from any intellectual influence, are usually the slaves of some defunct economist. Madmen in authority, who hear voices in the air, are distilling their frenzy from some academic scribbler of a few years back. I am sure that the power of vested interests is vastly exaggerated compared with the gradual*

[2] Hume, D. ([1742] 1987). "Whether the British Government Inclines More to Absolute Monarchy, or to a Republic." in E. F. Miller (ed.) *Essays, Moral, Political and Literary*, Part I, Essay VII. P.51. Indianapolis: Liberty Press.

encroachment of ideas. … But, soon or late, it is ideas, not vested interests, which are dangerous for good or evil.[3]

In *Money, Method, and the Market Process*,[4] Ludwig von Mises, who stood opposed to Keynes in economics, wrote: "Everything that men do is the result of the theories, doctrines, creeds, and mentalities governing their minds. Nothing is real and material in human history but mind." (p. 289) He also wrote: "It is generally believed that the conflict of social doctrines is due to the clash of group interests. If this theory were right, the cause of human cooperation would be hopeless." (p. 298) In *Human Action*,[5] Professor Mises wrote:

Action without thinking, practice without theory are unimaginable. (p. 177)

Human action is directed by ideologies. Thus society and any concrete order of social affairs are an outcome of ideologies … Any existing state of social affairs is the product of ideologies previously thought out. Within society new ideologies may emerge and may supersede older ideologies and thus transform the social system. However, society is always the creation of ideologies temporally and logically anterior. Action is always directed by ideas; it realizes what previous thinking has designed. (pp. 187–188)

In *Constitution of Liberty*,[6] F. A. Hayek made the following comment:

The belief that in the long run it is ideas and therefore the men who give currency to new ideas that govern evolution, and the belief that the individual steps in that process should be governed by a set of coherent conceptions, have long formed a fundamental part of the liberal creed. (p. 178)

I cited these famous economists to explain human action is not only swayed by interests, but also by ideas. This is the reason many actions based on interests wave the banner of ideas. If we acknowledge this point, then economists have ample scope for their abilities. Simply put, human

[3] Keynes, J. M. (1936). *The General Theory of Employment, Interest and Money*. P.400. London: Macmillan.

[4] Ludwig von Mises. (1990). *Money, Method, and the Market Process*. Selected by Margit von Mises and edited with an introduction by Richard M. Ebeling. Auburn, Ala: The Ludwig von Mises Institute, Norwell, MA: Kluwer Academic Publishers.

[5] Ludwig von Mises. (1999). *Human Action*. Auburn, Alabama: Mises Institute.

[6] F. A. Hayek. (2011 (1960)). *The Constitution of Liberty*. Chicago: University of Chicago Press.

progress was driven by new ideas. The duty of economists is to change people's viewpoints through scholarship in order to allow people to understand their own true interests.

For example, above I mentioned a third of the world's population chose to live under the awful centrally planned economy for that long of a period. It was not because they did not care about their interests, it is just that they did not understand their true interests. They incorrectly believed that the planned economy could bring them the greatest benefit, but now we know that this is a terribly mistaken idea. Precisely this kind of mistaken idea has led to tremendous disasters in human history.

Since the beginning, economists have worked to change people's viewpoints. More than two hundred years ago, Adam Smith led us to understand that the market is humanity's most effective system of cooperation. If we have a true private property system and free competition, self-interested human behavior is not bad for society. The main contribution to society of Chinese economists over the last 30 years was to lead China towards accepting the market economy ideas that Adam Smith proposed over two hundred years ago. Chinese economists broke apart our blind faith in the people's communes and the planned economy. They ended our belief that the egalitarian system of iron rice bowls and communal kitchens was good. Chinese economists also led the masses to believe in free competition, free prices, private property, and entrepreneurship; all of which are vital to the progress of any economic system. This propelled our reforms, causing the Chinese economy to achieve rapid development.

For economists to accomplish this task, they must have a true spirit of independence. Just as Mises said, even though humanity can cooperate, only individuals can think, society cannot. Humanity's new ideas have always started within a small group of people. We could also say that a type of viewpoint or idea is new because the vast majority of people do not acknowledge it. Most people think according to traditional ideas.

In *Human Action* (1990), Professor Mises criticized faith in the masses to do the right thing. He wrote this belief "is no better founded than was belief in the supernatural gifts of kings, priests, and noblemen. Democracy guarantees a system of government in accordance with the wishes and plans of the majority. But it cannot prevent majorities from falling victim to erroneous ideas and from adopting inappropriate policies which not only fail to realize the ends aimed at but result in disaster. Majorities too may err and destroy our civilization. The good cause will not triumph merely on account of its reasonableness and expediency." He explained further, "civilization improves and society and state render men more satisfied," only when the majority "will finally espouse policies reasonable and likely to attain the ultimate ends aimed at." (p. 193).

Therefore, only when an economist maintains his independent spirit and free mind are his ideas worth paying attention to. Only then can he possibly make a contribution to the progress of humanity. In economics, monopolies are a very important idea. The Anti-Monopoly Law is a major part of the body of laws. Previously, I have published articles to argue that anti-monopoly laws conflict with true competition.[7] The reason for this is related to economists' incorrect definition of competition and monopoly. I have also said that we only need to oppose one kind of monopoly, and that is the government-enforced monopoly. Free markets will not create sustained, true monopolies. However, here I must emphasize one monopoly that we must oppose. That is the monopoly of ideas. It is a type of idea that guides everything, reigns over everything; it causes us to have no way to compete with it, nor propose any idea different from it. I believe that this type of monopoly of ideas does disastrous harm to humanity. It obstructs the appearance of new ideas, thus it smothers the spark that lights the development and progress of human civilization. When freedom of thought exists during an era, humanity will attain great progress. If thought is not free, humanity's pace of progress will stagnate.

Today, we absolutely face this kind of problem. Thankfully, even people that live in the unfree world can enjoy the technology and ideas created by the free world.[8] This is the benefit that economic globalization and the Internet has brought us. We must not forget that the progress of human ideas started with a small number of people. If we cannot truly tolerate the ideas of a minority, our society cannot truly progress. China's history has many examples to prove this point. Two thousand years ago, when Confucius was alive, his ideas were not accepted by the sovereigns of each kingdom, nor were his ideas accepted by the masses. Fortunately, at the time, the rulers of each kingdom did not try to muzzle him, so his ideas could still be spread. In the end, they became the cornerstone of Chinese culture. During the time of the First Emperor of Qin, the Burn Books and Bury Scholars Movement began, which led to a catastrophe. We ought to remember that period of history.

[7] Weiying Zhang. (2015). *The Logic of the Market: An Insider's View of Chinese Economic Reform*. Chapter 4. Washington, DC: The Cato Institute.

[8] This point is made by F.A. Hayek in the *Constitution of Liberty*. See p. 100–101.

satisfied. Only when the minority will finally espouse policies now liable and likely to attain the ultimate ends aimed at [illegible]

[illegible]

CHAPTER 2

The Institutional Foundation of Human Cooperation

The more widespread human cooperation is, the more rapid human progress will be. In order to cooperate, humanity has created various institutions, such as private property rights, the rule of law, social norms, and ethics.

Why does humanity need government? It is needed for us to escape the prisoner's dilemma and cooperate better. However, after government exists, it often becomes a force that damages liberty, injures human safety, and destroys cooperation.

How can we restrain government? The only effective way is to lock power in a cage. That cage is constitutionalism and the democratic system.[1]

* * *

[1] The original version of this chapter was written in May 2013.

W. Zhang, *Ideas for China's Future*,
https://doi.org/10.1007/978-981-15-4304-3_2

All of Humanity's Progress Has Come From Cooperation

What is studied in economics? Traditionally, it studies resource allocation and market equilibrium. I believe that this definition is misleading. What does economics truly research? It researches how rational people cooperate with one another.

All of humanity's progress has come from cooperation. Two thousand years ago, Master Xun asked: "Human strength is not as great as an ox, nor can humans walk fast like a horse, so how are humans able to utilize oxen and horses?" His answer was that "*rén néng qŭn*," meaning humans can mutually cooperate. Species like ants and bees also have "division of labor" and "cooperation," but it is based on instincts, not rationality. Therefore, the way of life for animals over the last few thousands or tens of thousands of years has not changed, except for their domestication by humans. Human cooperation, by comparison, is mainly based on rationality. It is action with an objective. The way of life for people today and ten thousand years ago is different. Ten thousand years ago humans led a hunter-gatherer existence, but today we have entered the Information Era.

It could be said that the more wide-spread the scope of human cooperation is, the more rapid human progress will be. People that are alive today cooperate on a global scale. Almost anything we use was the result of cooperation between all of humanity. Nothing is made in a single location, and it is not possible for a single person to create everything. For example, perhaps a laser pointer is made in China, but the technology came from America. There are many stages of production required to produce something, all of them requiring computerized controls. The microchips a computer uses were designed in America, and probably produced in Taiwan using components from Japan and Korea. Everything's value chain is spread over the globe. This is the reason humanity has achieved such great progress over the last two hundred years.

Two difficulties face human cooperation. The first is what economists call the "Prisoner's Dilemma" and what social psychologists call the "Cooperation Dilemma." This is a problem created by human's selfish nature. The other difficulty for human cooperation comes from humanity's ignorance. We often want to do good things or help others, but the result can be bad, or even be a deadly mistake. Parents love their children, but many children's misfortunes are caused by their parents. Why? Because humanity's knowledge of itself and the environment is very limited.

Sometimes we do not even know our true interests. This is a reflection of our ignorance. The planned economy is a classic example of this. In the beginning, we mistakenly believed that a centralized authority could know the needs of every person and the endowments of society's resources. With a unified production and distribution plan (the so-called top-level plan), we could avoid the faults of the market economy and allow every person to live better. Today this idea seems very naïve, but a few decades ago, we were that naïve. This was not caused by our lack of people with an education in economics. To the contrary, at that time, some of the best economists in the world believed in the planned economy. In the 1930s, Oskar Lange, a well-known University of Chicago economist, declared he proved the planned economy was workable under the neoclassical paradigm. Later, many people approved of his theories. Even great economists like Paul Samuelson and Joseph Schumpeter did not dare to question the theoretical validity of the planned economy.[2]

Ignorance and the "Prisoner's Dilemma" have brought about many difficulties—and even disasters—to humanity. However, humanity is continuously learning and progressing. Many of humanity's institutional arrangements were created to decrease human ignorance and resolve the "Prisoner's Dilemma" faced by human cooperation.

The Prisoner's Dilemma: A Contradiction Between Individual Rationality and Collective Rationality

Below, I use a simple game to explain the "Prisoner's Dilemma."

Imagine society is formed by two individuals, Mr. Jia and Mr. Yi. Each of them has two options. The first is to respect the other person's rights and property. The second is to disrespect the other person's rights, such as engaging in theft. In this case, society faces four possible outcomes. (1) If both people mutually respect each other's property, then each person has a return of two points. (2) If both people disrespect each other's property by stealing from each other, then neither of them has any points. (3) If Mr. Jia respects property rights but Mr. Yi does not, then Mr. Jia has negative one point, but Mr. Yi has three points. (4) Or, if Mr. Jia steals but Mr. Yi

[2] For the debate on feasibility of the socialist planned economy, see Jesus Huerta de Soto's *Socialism, Economic Calculation, and Entrepreneurship*, published in 2010 by Edward Elgar.

respects property rights, then Mr. Jia has three points, but Mr. Yi has negative one point. It is easy to see from each individual's perspective the best result occurs when he (or she) chooses to steal when his (or her) partner respects property rights. The second-best result is when both people mutually respect each other's property rights. The third best result is when everyone steals. The worst result is when the individual respects property, but the other person steals. Therefore, from an individual's perspective, regardless of whether other people respect property or not, his or her best option is to disrespect property rights. The result is that both people do not respect property rights, so they both have zero points. In reality, if both people respect property rights, each of them could be better off by receiving two points. This is the so-called "Prisoner's Dilemma," which is also known as the contradiction between individual rationality and collective rationality. Individual rationality leads to choosing theft, but collective rationality leads to respecting property.

The conflict between collective rationality and individual rationality can be understood as *ex ante* rationality and *ex post* rationality. Before the decision, each person has an incentive to respect property rights if the other party also makes the same decision. However, *ex post*, each person has a motivation to behave opportunistically. There is no incentive to fulfill the commitment, even if the other party chooses to respect property rights. The issue now is how to resolve the contradiction between *ex ante* rationality and *ex post* rationality, or the contradiction between collective rationality and individual rationality. Rationally, if we are equal with everyone else, how can we benefit ourselves by stealing from others? Only if every person respects property rights can all persons benefit themselves. This creates the need for institutions as the rules of the game. If an institution can guarantee for each individual the *ex ante* rational choice is also the *ex post* rational choice, we have resolved the Prisoner's Dilemma. In Game Theory terminology, institutions are a "commitment" made between people.

Immanuel Kant had this to say about creating institutions to resolve the Prisoner's Dilemma: "Given a multitude of rational beings who, in a body, require general laws for their own preservation, but each of whom, as an individual, is secretly inclined to exempt himself from this restraint: how are we to order their affairs and how establish for them a constitution such that, although their private dispositions may be really antagonistic, they may yet so act as a check upon one another, that, in their public relations, the effect is the same as if they had no such evil sentiments."[3]

Social Cooperation Requires Rules of the Game

Humanity has created institutions and methodologies—called "rules of the game"—to resolve the difficulties it faces from cooperation in real life. Of course, just as F. A. Hayek pointed out, these institutions and methodologies are certainly not collectively designed, but instead evolved over a long period of history.[4] These institutions and methodologies can be separated into different categories. Here I will discuss a few of the most important ones.

The first is the property rights system. It is the most important system humanity has created to overcome the Prisoner's Dilemma. David Hume believed it was the first among the three fundamental laws of nature.[5] With the private property system, property rights are effectively protected, so the game changes. Property rights are natural rights, and existed before governments did. I will now explain two very interesting, real-world examples.

In a fishing village on the coast of Yorkshire, England, a lot of wood floats in from other places. After the tide goes down, it becomes un-owned property. How do the local fishermen allocate this wood? It is an issue of defining property rights. Throughout the ages, fishermen have upheld a rule that whoever gets to the shore first, and places a marker on a piece of wood, owns that piece of wood. People can no longer take whatever they want. This is not legislation initiated by government, but all fishermen respect this rule.[6]

In a village on the Yellow River in my hometown of Wubao County in northern Shaanxi, when the Yellow River flows heavily, a lot of peat floats down from upstream. The locals call this "river coal (*hétàn*)." After the

[3] The quotation is cited from Jeffrie G. Murphy's *Kant: The Philosophy of Right*, p. 94, published by Mercer University Press, 1994.

[4] See F. A. Hayek, *Law, Legislation and Liberty*. London and New York: Routledge, 2013.

[5] Hume's three fundamental laws of nature are that of the stability of possession, of its transference by consent, and of the performance of promises. David Hume, *Treatise of Human Nature* (Book 3, Part 2, Section 6). Cited from F.A. Hayek. 2011 (1960) *The Constitution of Liberty*, p. 226. Chicago: University of Chicago Press.

[6] R. Sugden, 1989, "Spontaneous Oder." *Journal of Economic Perspective*, 3(4): 85–97.

flood, the river coal is stranded on the shore so the villagers vie with each other to "dredge river coal." It is an important part of their livelihood. Their respect for the rules are the same as the fishermen in Yorkshire: Whoever places something of their own, such as a straw hat, clothing, shoulder poles, or gunnysacks, on unclaimed river coal, owns it. No one else will dispute it. To get more river coal, some people are even immodest enough to take off their underpants.

These two areas are far apart; one is on the coast of England and the other on the bank of the Yellow River in northwest China. Residents of these two areas have probably never interacted with each other, but their rules of the game are the same.

This is the "possession rule," or the first-on rule of property rights, meaning the first person to occupy something owns it. Are there universal values? I believe this is a universal value, because it is respected by people all over the world. It not only deals with the basic standards of interpersonal relationships, it also deals with the basic standards of international relations. Today there are discussions about national sovereignty. Although there is no multinational world government, countries can recognize and respect each other's sovereignty because humanity holds this type of universal value. We Chinese say that the Diaoyu Islands are ours. Why is it ours? Because "since ancient times" it was ours, meaning we occupied it first. If we do not recognize universal values, international territorial disputes cannot be resolved, nor is international cooperation possible. I will emphasize the private property rights system is the most important institution humanity has invented to resolve the Prisoner's Dilemma. Without this institution, humanity would descend into "a war of all against all" as Thomas Hobbes discussed.

In modern society, property rights are often protected by a country's laws. Laws themselves are set to adjust expectations and promote cooperation. If a transaction is beneficial to both parties, but one party is opportunistic and does not pay or produces counterfeit goods, what should be done? Contracts are a commitment made by both parties to cooperate. For example, when a company lists on the stock market, equity rights are distributed. This benefits all stakeholders, because it allows a more efficient allocation of resources and more people can share in the creation of wealth. This kind of cooperation requires everyone to respect property rights, but if after the fact someone engages in embezzlement or corruption, what should be done? We have a series of laws on corporate governance structures. These laws help resolve the Prisoner's Dilemma of those involved. If a person manages an enterprise but is corrupt, or does not service the interests of shareholders, shareholders can take legal proceedings against that person. If that person fears legal proceedings, he will work diligently. Therefore, the law itself is an important system for resolving the Prisoner's Dilemma.

Social norms are another system that promotes interpersonal cooperation. The law is set by a concentrated structure of authority, and forcefully enforced by the state. If the courts judge a person to be guilty, but the person does not comply, the courts can enforce their decision by force. Conversely, social norms do not have centralized organizations for formulation and enforcement. They evolved from the countless repetitive games of countless participants, and each of us are their enforcers. If, for example, someone spits in public, it violates social norms. Each of us has the power to stop this kind of behavior that violates social norms. Of course, there is also a problem of the second-order Prisoner's Dilemma: If you stop a person from spitting in public, and that person takes revenge on you, what should be done? Because of this concern, many people look the other way.[7] Social norms do not have the backing of state power. Only when a norm becomes commonly acknowledged by everyone, meaning everyone believes they should respect it or will be condemned for it, can it be enforced. Speaking for the majority of people, given that other people respect a norm, not only is respecting it the best choice for each individual, but also condemning and punishing other people that do not respect it is also optimum. At that point, we could say that social norms reached a "Nash Equilibrium." If most people expect that other people will respect a norm, and any violations of that norm will be condemned by the majority, the minority's violation of that norm will not damage the constraints of social norms.

There is not a clear division between laws and social norms. The "*li* (etiquette)" in China's traditions is a combination of laws and social norms. It is an important system for overcoming the cooperation

[7] For the detailed discussion of the second-order prisoner's dilemma, see R. Ellickson, 1991, *Order without Law: How Neighbors Settles Disputes*, p. 237 (Cambridge MA: Harvard University Press); R. Ellickson, 1999, "The Evolution of Social Norms: A Perspective from the Legal Academy. (*Working Paper No.* 230, Yale Law School, Program for Studies in Law, Economics and Public Policy); R. McAdam, 1997, "The Origin, Development and Regulation of Norms." *Michigan Law Review*, 96(2): 238–433; Weiying Zhang, (2018), *Game Theory and Society*, Chapter 6. London and New York: Routledge.

difficulties faced by Chinese. Most etiquette came from society, and was mostly enforced by society, but some of it was enforced by the government, such as the flogging of un-filial sons.

Ethics and morals are also an important system for the promotion of social cooperation. In some circumstances, morality and ethics are the internalization of laws and social norms. They are the result of being taught at a young age. There are many opportunities to cheat people in everyday life. Perhaps we do not cheat people because we fear the punishment of the law, or because we worry about the condemnation from public opinion. No matter what the case, there are always situations where cheating others disturbs our conscience. This is the role morals play. Acting according to morals and ethics is not irrational, because morals are themselves the product of rationality—although not rationally designed, as argued by Hayek.[8] It is not possible for an irrational person to truly have morals.

Human Cooperation Requires a Limited Government

Why does humanity need government? To escape the Prisoner's Dilemma and better cooperate. The basic function of government is to protect the safety of individual life and property, as well as the equal liberties of individuals. Only when safety and liberty are effectively guaranteed can humanity possibly cooperate. However, on the other hand, once government exists, it often becomes a force that damages liberty, safety, and cooperation. Why? The government is also managed by people, but they are different from common people because they have a monopoly on the legal use of force.

In the Chinese mind, the government is a "superhero." Like god, it is not self-interested, but is all-knowing and all-powerful. In reality, no such government as this exists under the heavens. Governments in all countries are operated by people. Even if these people are called kings, emperors, governors-general, politicians, or bureaucrats, they are like us in that they have a self-interested nature, are ignorant, and make mistakes. They will also make deals that hurt others and benefit themselves. The difference between them and those of us that live in the market is they can legally force us, in the name of government, to do things we are not willing to do.

[8] F.A. Hayek, 1991 (1988) *The Fatal Conceit*, Chapter Four. Chicago: University of Chicago Press.

The government's income does not come from prices, instead it comes from taxes. Taxes are collected forcefully, no matter whether we are satisfied with the services provided by government or not. This is different from the purchases we make in the market. In the market, any forceful buying or selling done against the wishes of individuals is illegal. Because of this reason, the government easily becomes a force for the destruction of cooperation. Therefore, the means of restraining government is a significant matter.

How can government be restrained? We know that in the past we mainly relied on god, religion, and individual morality, but when these failed to obstruct the lawlessness of the rulers, people rose up to overthrow the old government and establish a new government. The greatest progress human thought made over the last five hundred years was to recognize that emperors, kings, and government officials are also self-interested, so relying on god and individual morality was not an effective means to restrict them. The only effective way is to lock power in a cage. That cage is constitutional government and the democratic system.

What is so-called constitutional government? It is when any ruler must act in accordance with the constitution and the law. Authority cannot overreach the law. Alternatively, all government power must be explicitly conferred by the law. Democracy refers more to the election of government leaders by the public, meaning "power is granted by the people." We should not believe that the majority is always correct. The majority can also make mistakes and act in a way that threatens human cooperation. If a democratic system does not have constitutional restraints, it can become majority despotism. This is the lesson we learned from Adolf Hitler. If a country does not have constitutional government and the rule of law, it cannot truly have a democratic system. Democracy must start with a constitutional government.

Constitutional government is also necessary for other systems. Most ancient Western thinkers opposed democracy but advocated constitutional government. In Aristotle's political science, monarchy and aristocracy are also constitutional governments. He believed that the law should be the supreme ruler. If the power of the monarchy is not restrained by law, the monarch will become a tyrant. If the power of the aristocracy is not restrained by law, the aristocracy will become an oligarchy.

Montesquieu, in *The Spirit of Laws*, advocated "the separation of powers," meaning the power of the monarch must be restrained by law. He praised the constitutional monarchy of Great Britain at the time, but not modern democracy.

Restrictions on government must first start by establishing constitutional government and the rule of law. This was the history of Great Britain, and also the experience of most Western countries. The establishment of England's constitutional government started in 1215 with the Magna Carta and was essentially complete by the Glorious Revolution in 1688. Great Britain's democracy started in 1832 with the First Reform Act, which expanded the electorate from the nobility to the middle class. It was basically completed in 1928 when universal suffrage was expanded to all adult female citizens. The process took 96 years. Not only does the democratic system require constitutional government, monarchy also requires constitutional government. This is a basic historical fact.

Some believe constitutionalism will weaken the strength of government. This is incorrect. In reality, the strongest governments are constitutional governments. Since governments have existed, humanity's greatest game has been the game between the common people and the government. Even under a despotic system, the common people can choose to not cooperate (passive resistance). A government that has not gained the trust of the common people cannot possibly be a strong government. How can the government gain the common people's trust? Spoken words carry no conviction; it can only use systems to restrain itself. Constitutional government and democracy are like a commitment to the common people by the government. With this commitment, the government cannot do whatever it pleases, so the common people will have more trust in the government and be more willing to cooperate with the government.

The history of Great Britain has clearly illustrated this point. Before the Glorious Revolution, the government's public debt hovered around two million pounds for a long time. It was not that the government did not wish to borrow more money. Instead, the king always repudiated debt, and the creditors were helpless, so people with money were not willing to loan it to the government. Constitutional government was implemented after the Glorious Revolution. The power of the king was restrained by parliament. If the king did not carry out his word, the parliament could dispose of him. People's trust in government increased, so it was no longer difficult for the government to borrow money. The scale of government debt continuously increased. In 1697, it reached £16.7 million, then it reached £54 million in 1720, and by 1790 it had reached £244 million. Within the span of 100 years it had increased 120 times. Without this kind of financial support, Great Britain could not have achieved hegemon status in Europe.[9] This is the power of constitutional government.

Overall, only a constitutional and democratic government can gain the trust of the citizens, and only a government that has gained the trust of the citizens can be a truly strong government. Looking over the world, which countries have the strongest governments? They are all governments in countries that have implemented constitutional government and democracy, because they can gain the trust of the common people.

Under constitutional government and democracy, people abide by the law based on their respect for the law, not because they fear the law. People believe that the law is fair and just, so it should be abided by. Therefore, the law set by the government can be better enforced, and people are more willing to cooperate with one another. Under unconstitutional systems of government, most people believe the law serves special interests and is a tool the ruler uses to enslave the people. Even though there are serious consequences for breaking the law, people still will seek out every opportunity to evade the law. In that kind of society, how can people have a better spirit of cooperation?

[9] D. C. North and B. R. Weingast, 1989, "Constitutions and Commitment; The Evolution of Institutions Governing Public Choice in Seventeenth Century England." *Journal of Economic History*, 49: 803–832.

CHAPTER 3

The Market as the Most Effective System of Cooperation

The market and liberty are actually the same thing. If a person supports market economics, he should also approve of humanity's freedom to choose. Therefore, I say that the market is liberty, and liberty is the market.

Under the planned economy, Chinese all lived in a "Prisoner's Dilemma." The market-oriented Reform and Opening was done in order to escape the Prisoner's Dilemma and promote interpersonal cooperation.[1]

* * *

The Market Economy as Cooperation Between Strangers

In order to cooperate, humanity has created many institutions. We call these institutions "rules of the game." Here we will specifically discuss a very important system. That system is the market economy. It is the system studied most by economists.

[1] The original version of this chapter was written in 2014.

W. Zhang, *Ideas for China's Future*,
https://doi.org/10.1007/978-981-15-1304-3_3

People have many misunderstandings about the market system. Some people believe the market allows people to pursue their own private interests no matter whether other people live or die. This idea is completely incorrect. What is the true function of the market? It allows humanity to cooperate better! At this point, it is also the most effective system to promote human cooperation. Today, thanks to the power of the market, human cooperation has become as wide-spread and as penetrating as it is so that every product we enjoy is the result of global cooperation. This was unthinkable two hundred years ago.

Cooperation in the market economy is not simply mutual assistance, but instead is mutual dependence. In the market economy, each person is only one node in a complex division of labor chain. Without any one of them, the others cannot move forward. As each person specializes on one matter, it can be done better. This is the benefit brought about by specialization and the division of labor. Master Xun explained this reasoning two thousand years ago. He said: "The perfection of the Hundred Skills is required just to nurture the needs of a single individual. Yet even the able find it impossible to be universally skilled, and it is impossible for an individual to hold every office. If people live in alienation from each other and do not serve each other's needs, there will be poverty."[2] It is precisely the market economy that allows large-scale division of labor to be possible. Only then can humanity enjoy the benefits that it brings. Two hundred years ago, British economist Adam Smith said that division of labor and specialization happen only because of the invisible hand of the market.

Cooperation also exists in traditional societies, but it is only between acquaintances, such as members of a village or family. The market economy has expanded cooperation to encompass strangers. Cooperation between strangers guides all of society. This is what Hayek's extended order of human cooperation means.[3] In the market economy, the vast majority of people we transact directly or indirectly with—even more than 99%—are people we have never met and do not know where they live. If a person goes to the supermarket, he knows which company produced a product, but does not know the owner or the employees. These unknown

[2] Master Xun, *On Enriching the State*, Volume 10.1. English translation cited from page 121 in *Xunzi: A Translation and Study of the Complete Works*, Books 7–16, Volume 2 (1990), by John Knoblock.

[3] F. A. Hayek, 1988. *The Fatal Conceit: The Errors of Socialism*, p. 11–15, edited by W. W. Bartley III. Chicago; University of Chicago Press.

people produce based on self-interest, but they must provide products that benefit others and satisfy others before they can make money. The market is a marvelous mechanism. Can anyone think of any other system that can turn cooperation into a global process? The places with higher degrees of marketization have more advanced products, more rapid progress, more new products, and more wealth.

The reason the market system can increase human cooperation to such a high degree is because it effectively resolves the issues of "ignorance" and "shamelessness." I have said before that there are two reasons for man-made calamities.[4] The first is ignorance. The second is shamelessness. A combination of the minority's shamelessness and the majority's ignorance often leads to humanity's largest disasters.

What is shamelessness? It is the harming of other's interests to the benefit of one's own interests. What is the logic of the market? To make oneself happy, first others must be made happy. If others are not happy, oneself cannot be happy. This is the reason, in the market system, pursuit of individual interests will not turn into shameless behavior. Market competition is competition to create value for others. For example, if someone wants to be an entrepreneur, but product quality and customer service are bad, consumers will not pay for those goods and services, so the entrepreneur cannot make money. If employees are not happy, an enterprise cannot do well. Competition makes each person happy because the prerequisite for each person to be happy is the creation of value for others. I discuss this point because it has another major significance. In the freely competitive market, every cent a person earns relies on personal qualities, represents contributions made to others, and of course also involves some luck. We know whether or not a person is happy is not entirely determined by money, but also where that money comes from. Speaking for the vast majority of people, income from personal qualities and hard work brings about much more happiness than income from other's charity. The people that live off state welfare are not happy, because their income was not earned from personal qualities. The free market gives each person the opportunity to fairly compete. It allows each person to participate in the creation of wealth and means each cent earned was the result of personal effort, so people are happier.

[4]Weiying Zhang, 2017, *The Road Leading to the Market*, Chapter 2 "Why do human beings makes mistakes?". London and New York: Routledge.

The market is also an incentive mechanism to reduce human ignorance. Production and interpersonal cooperation require a huge amount of information, such as information on individual preferences, technology, and resources. This information is dispersed amongst many people, so obtaining this information has a cost. Advocates of the planned economy assume that the economy is static, meaning all information exists objectively, people's demands were established early on, and technology and resources are given. Therefore, they believe that the central planning organ can easily accumulate each person's information. This is completely incorrect and is itself a reflection of ignorance. The market transmits information via the price system and competition.[5] This reduces human ignorance. In order for entrepreneurs to earn money, succeed, and achieve their aspirations, they must have a good enough ability and incentive to collect and process all the various information needed to make decisions. Entrepreneurs need true information the most, but government departments do not need true information.

In reality, information is the result of entrepreneurial activity. It is subjective, not something that naturally exists and is objective. The market economy's greatest contribution is the advancement of human knowledge. For example, without entrepreneurs like Steve Jobs and Bill Gates, there would not be a market for personal computers, so how could we calculate the demand for computers? Entrepreneurs judge the value of new products and technologies via their own alertness and imagination. They judge the demands of consumers and measure earnings from different decisions to determine whether or not to act. This avoids the many mistakes human ignorance can lead to.

I also must emphasize the point that the market is the foundation of morality. The market not only is an "invisible hand" transmitting information between participants but is also an all-seeing "invisible eye" that supervises each person's behavior.[6] This is because people engage in repetitive games on the market, not one-time games. The market has a memory. It remembers the good and bad behavior of each person. Game Theory has proven that repetitive games can resolve the Prisoner's

[5] Hayek, F.A. (1945). "The Use of Knowledge in Society." in *Individualism and Economic Order*, p. 77–91. London and Henley: Routledge and Kegan Paul, 1976.

[6] Daniel B. Klein, "Knowledge, Reputation and Trust by Voluntary Means." in Daniel B. Klein (ed.), 1997, *Reputation: Studies in the Voluntary Elicitation of Good Conduct*. Ann Arbor: The University of Michigan Press.

Dilemma that exist in one-time games, leading to interpersonal cooperation. In a free market economy, the most suitable enterprises to survive are certainly the ones that emphasize reputation and consumer trust. This is also the reason people in the market economy have a higher degree of trust. Market-oriented societies have a higher level of morality and a stronger cooperative spirit than other types of societies. An obvious comparison is China and America. Every Chinese person that has visited or lived in America has a deep impression that the degree of trust between Americans is much higher than in China. Why? One of the reasons is that America has a comparatively freer market system.

Liberty, Private Property, and Entrepreneurship as the Foundation of the Market

For the market to have this effect, it must be established on a foundation of liberty, private property, and the entrepreneurial spirit.

Liberty is the first foundation. Liberty means that each of us can do what we are best at so we can best exert our abilities in the division of labor. It is also liberty that allowed us to create many new ideas, new technologies, and new products. The consumer can choose what to buy, and the producer can choose what to produce. If we deprive people of the freedom to choose, the market will not exist and mutually beneficial cooperation is impossible. In China, productive activities are heavily restricted and intervened by the government, so we cannot possibly have a truly meaningful market. In reality, the market and liberty are the same thing. An advocate of the market economy should also support humanity's freedom to choose. This is why I say that the market is liberty, and liberty is the market.

Private property rights are the second foundation. Private property rights are a guarantee of personal liberty. Without property rights, people cannot possibly be free. Only when each person's private property rights can be fully guaranteed can people have stable expectations and be willing to exchange. If private property rights are not clearly defined, voluntary exchange and cooperation to create value is impossible. If an economy has a large number of privileged classes, then the government can expropriate private property at any time. If contracts for voluntary exchange are not respected, then people cannot possibly have the incentive to cooperate via the division of labor. Property rights not only apply to tangible property, but also intangible property, such as intellectual property and trademarks. If

McDonald's creates a brand, and then the government decides that everyone can use this brand for free, would McDonald's create that brand? No. Would people that use this brand carefully protect the value of this brand? Also no. Therefore, the property rights system is a foundation for the effective operation of the market. A major reason for the chaos in China's market order is that private property rights are not effectively protected.

The entrepreneurial spirit is the third foundation. The market does not operate by itself. People cause the market to operate. Entrepreneurs are the mainstay of action in the market economy. There are some people who, compared with the average person, have a better ability to judge the future, are more risk-tolerant, and are more imaginative. We call these people entrepreneurs. Entrepreneurs continuously discover what other people need and create things that others are willing to pay for. They make new products that the market is willing to accept. Only through the innovative activities of entrepreneurs can the division of labor be continuously deepened, the value chain continuously stretched, and new industries continuously appear. Without entrepreneurs, the market economy system cannot exist. Since ancient times, humanity has been endowed with the entrepreneurial spirit, but only in the market economy can the entrepreneurial spirit be exerted to the fullest extent to engage in activities that create value. Entrepreneurs not only improve resource efficiency via discovering and correcting market disequilibrium, they also innovate to give us new products, new production methods, and new industries to promote sustained economic development. Entrepreneurs must predict the future, make decisions, and take responsibility for all of their mistakes. The entrepreneurial spirit allows us to obtain the goods and services we like without resorting to administrative commands. Global division of labor and economic integration is also the result of the entrepreneurial spirit.

The Planned Economy Entrapped Chinese into the Prisoner's Dilemma

Why does China need Reform and Opening? Why does the market economy need to replace the planned economy? It is very simple. Under the planned economy, Chinese life was a "Prisoner's Dilemma." The market-oriented Reform and Opening will allow us to escape the Prisoner's Dilemma and promote inter-personal cooperation. The economic success over the last thirty years is the result of cooperation. There was not only cooperation between Chinese, but also between Chinese and people from the rest of the world. Without the latter type of cooperation, we could not have achieved such rapid growth, nor could the standard of living in China have increased so much.

Under the planned economy, both people from the rural and urban areas lived in a Prisoner's Dilemma. I was born and raised in the countryside. From a very young age I knew that if all peasants worked hard, everyone would have enough to eat. But no one worked hard. Everyone was lazy, and what was the result of laziness? Everyone was hungry. The irony is the government forcefully implemented "cooperatization" and "people's communes" to promote cooperation between peasants, but the result was peasants were less and less willing to cooperate after "cooperatization." On the contrary, after implementing the so-called "household production responsibility system," peasants had an incentive to cooperate. Not only did this resolve the issue of peasants feeding themselves, urban residents could also buy fresh produce at the farmers market.

Under the planned economy, people that worked for state-owned enterprises also lived in a Prisoner's Dilemma. The "*tiěfànwǎn* (iron rice bowl)" and "*dàguōfàn* (communal canteen cauldron)" meant that the result of over or under performing was the same. The best way for state-owned enterprise employees to improve their welfare was to be lazy. The result was a general shortage of industrial products.

These of course were not only China's problems, but also the problems of every country that implemented the planned economy system. The experience of the central planning experiment has proven if the private property system is eradicated, then the systemic foundation for human cooperation will also be eradicated. People will be trapped in a serious Prisoner's Dilemma. Our old system in its entirety, meaning the planned economy system before Reform and Opening, objectively encouraged people to think of every way to gain at other people's expense, without working. Without an incentive to work, there is even less of an incentive to innovate, so China fell further and further behind developed countries. At that time, there was also "competition" between people, but it was mainly mutually harmful competition. It was a political struggle, not competition to create value. Of course, we also did not have ideas of fairness and justice, nor even respect for basic human rights. Even a minimum moral standard was unthinkable.

The Reason for China's Social Morals Crisis

The success of the economic aspects of China's market-oriented reforms over the last 30 years has attracted worldwide attention. Regrettably, the level of morality in Chinese society has not increased by the same degree. Of course, I do not agree with the judgment that we are less moral today than we were before Reform and Opening. At that time, indiscriminate arrests, public criticisms, and even murder for political and ideological reasons were seen as normal, or were even cheered on. Today, if someone is in mortal danger and no one else does anything, it is sensationally condemned. This could be considered progress, or we could at least say that our awareness of morality is recovering. Indisputably, our society faces a serious moral crisis. The question to ask is what is the source of the moral crisis? I believe that the answer many people give is incorrect. They view morals as morality itself, instead of seeing the systemic sources of the moral crisis.

It could be said that today's moral issue has both historical and practical reasons. Many of today's ills are an outbreak of problems buried decades ago. It is easy to destroy morals, but reviving them takes a long time, just as the saying goes "sickness comes like a landslide but goes like spinning silk." The most important reason started in the 1950s with the destruction of the private property system. Eradicating the private property system will certainly cause morals to degrade. This is not a new theory; it is a point made 2000 years ago by Aristotle. He said, "We see that there is much more quarrelling among those who have all things in common, though there are not many of them when compared with the vast numbers who have private property." (*Politics*: Book 2) In a society where all assets belong to the commons, generosity is impossible, and no one will show mercy.

The countryside is an example. In traditional villages, what type of person will survive and thrive? A diligent, honest, and kind person. Only those types of people can flourish, and are a model for other peasants. The people that shirk responsibility are not only poverty stricken, they are also looked down upon by others. After the cooperatives and people's communes were established, everything was upended. Diligence was gone, honesty was gone, and kindness was also gone. When I was little, the old peasants were still relatively diligent and honest, but the younger ones shirked responsibility, were lazy, and were dishonest. By the time I grew up, the old peasants also started to shirk responsibility and be lazy.

Why are there so many swindles in today's China? The root cause is private property rights are not respected and the government wantonly intervenes in economic activity. The result is people do not have stable expectations, so they are only willing to engage in one-time games. They only consider short term interests without considering long term interests, entrapping them in a classic Prisoner's Dilemma. When the government can shut down a coal mine at any time, what incentive does the mine owner have to invest in expensive safety equipment? In this situation, the government is the true owner of the mine.

People's moral behavior is related to whether or not society is fair. When a small group of people can obtain vast incomes because of privileges, or when government bureaucrats are seriously corrupt, people think that society is unfair. That kind of society cannot truly be moral. A simple example of this was in the 1980s when it was very common to have a bicycle bell stolen. Imagine there is a very moral person who bought a bell after it was stolen the first time. After it was stolen the second time, he bought another one. What about the third and fourth time? I bet that person would take the bell off another person's bike, or just simply not have a bell, because he believes society is too unfair. Similarly, if a person seeks to do honest business, but then sees someone else making big money by relying on government relationships to get ahold of a piece of land or official documents, while at the same time the original person is being squeezed by government officials, will that person be at ease? In an unfair society, it is too difficult to make people respect a minimum moral standard.

Additionally, people's morals are ruined by serious language corruption caused by ideological controls. Language corruption surreptitiously switches the concept of a word or phrase to provide a legitimate reason for illegitimate behavior. It puts a bad name on good behavior or puts a good name on bad behavior. What are the consequences of language corruption? One consequence is the degradation of morals. Thomas Paine, a thinker during the American War for Independence, said: "When a man has so far corrupted and prostituted the chastity of his mind, as to subscribe his professional belief to things he does not believe, he has prepared himself for the commission of every other crime." (*The Age of Reason*)[7] Human cooperation begins with the expression of language. To act as one

[7] Thomas Paine, *The Age of Reason,* First Part Section 1. Ed. By Kerry Walters. Peterborough: Broadview Press, 2011.

speaks is the minimum moral standard. By breaking through this minimum standard, the psychological wall of morality has been demolished. When a person can tell a lie even they do not believe, his personality is already split, so what psychological barriers can restrain him from doing unethical things? When telling a lie has already become a common part of society's culture, how can a small businessperson that sells fake goods possibly be condemned by his own conscience? Frankly, compared to the outrageous lies told by certain government officials, producing fake goods is nothing.

The moral crisis is also related to the conflict between legality and rationality in our society. In a normal society, legal activities should be rational, and rational activities should be legal. The two should be aligned. Rationality can also be said to be in accordance with the spirit of natural law. It is stipulated by "God," or benefits human cooperation and is generally accepted. Legality is in accordance with the laws and policies stipulated by governments. Only if government laws are in accordance with laws stipulated by God, meaning they accord with human nature, can they benefit human cooperation. However, in China, many laws set by governments do not conform to human nature, do not conform with natural law, and do not benefit human cooperation. This creates a conflict between rationality and legality. Should we act according to rationality or the law? A moral person perhaps will choose to act according to rationality, but at a certain point the conflict between rationality and legality destroys the boundaries of morality. An example of this is rational compensation for doctors, which should be set by the market. Assume a doctor's rational compensation should be five hundred thousand yuan, but the government decides he can only accept fifty thousand yuan. At that point, there is a conflict between rationality and legality. If he is aware that he is being treated unfairly, perhaps he will accept *hóngbāo* (red envelopes filled with cash). However, after he accepts red envelopes, his concept of professional ethics will change. If he can legally be paid five hundred thousand yuan annually, he will feel honored to do a sacred profession with dedication. If he takes money on the side, even if in the end he earns eight hundred thousand or one million yuan, he would feel dishonorable. Being a doctor would not be a sacred profession, and there may be an issue with his professional ethics.

To conclude, China can only become a cooperative society if we establish a market economy based on private property rights. Only then can we have a good social order, a true improvement in the moral standards of

Chinese society, and humanity in our hearts. We can only have a true market economy if we implement the rule of law and democracy. Only with fairness and justice can Chinese live with honor. To complete this kind of reform, we not only need entrepreneurs in business, but also institutional entrepreneurs, who are either the theorists for changing the rules of the game, or politicians firmly dedicated to reform.

CHAPTER 4

The Logic of the Market and the Way of Virtue

The logic of the market is the way of virtue. The market does not require us to become "sages" and harm ourselves to benefit others, but the market will punish "petty men" that harm others to benefit themselves.

A good system can turn petty men into virtuous men and a bad system can turn virtuous men into petty men. Any law or policy that inhibits free competition or suppresses entrepreneurship opens a path for petty men.[1]

* * *

The concept of Confucian virtue is often only discussed among cultural scholars and moral philosophers. As an economist, I find it difficult to discuss this issue, but I am still willing to provide my own thoughts on the subject.

I want to start with humanity's most basic issue. A basic fact of human society is that each person is self-interested and self-centered, but we can only survive and prosper through cooperation. More than two thousand years ago, Master Xun, an ancient Chinese philosopher, asked: If humans

[1] The original version of this chapter was written in August 2016.

W. Zhang, *Ideas for China's Future*,
https://doi.org/10.1007/978-981-15-4304-3_4

are not as strong as oxen or as fast as horses, how can humans control oxen and horses? The answer is humans can cooperate.

Therefore, a basic issue human society faces is: How can self-interested people be made to cooperate? In the history of Western thought, this is associated with the writings of Hugo Grotius, a seventeenth century Dutch natural law scholar. He believed that we pursue our self-interest, pursue our self-preservation, and love to quarrel, yet we also desire friendly social interaction. Even if we do not require mutual aid to obtain the necessities of life, we still desire a social life. These two aspects of human nature have made the question of maintaining social order very clear: How should we live among people who like to quarrel and at the same time have friendly social interactions? In order to advance our desire for friendly social interactions, what type of restrictions should we put on our own inclination to quarrel?[2]

Grotius' conundrum is the concept economists call the "Prisoner's Dilemma." Even though cooperation benefits everyone involved, self-interested people might choose to not cooperate based on considerations of individual rationality. To understand this issue, humanity must have certain commonly respected basic behavioral norms. The basic function of these behavioral norms is to cause self-interested people to undertake reciprocal interactions. Not only should they interact peacefully, but also cooperate in a win-win manner.

We often call these behavioral norms "*dào*" or "doctrine." From the ancient times to the present, great thinkers have "set doctrines under the heavens." This is the case in both the East and the West. However, different thinkers have proposed different doctrines. Confucian "etiquette (*lǐ*)" was a doctrine Confucius set for humanity. A Confucian gentleman *(jūnzǐ)* is a personalization of this etiquette. If a person behaves according to "etiquette," then he or she is a gentleman. Therefore, a gentleman is not a specific person, but instead is a standard and the model for cooperation.

In ancient society, however, because humanity was basically in a zero-sum state (meaning every gain came at someone else's loss), "altruism" and "self-interest" were often antithetical. As a result, the concept of "gentlemanly virtue" turned into the moral preaching of "altruism" that required sacrificing individual interests. Confucian writings state: "The

[2] See J. B. Schneewind, *The Invention of Autonomy: A History of Modern Moral Philosophy*, p. 70–73. Cambridge, UK: Cambridge University Press.

object of the superior man is truth. Food is not his object. … The superior man is anxious lest he should not get truth; he is not anxious lest poverty should come upon him." He is also believed to have said, "The mind of the superior man is conversant with righteousness; the mind of the mean man is conversant with gain."[3] Similarly, in Medieval Europe, Christian doctrine told Christians to not become merchants, because earning money was immoral. However, human nature conditioned most people to consider their own interests. They cannot refrain from seeking interest or "making food their object." The result was a large number of people acted in the name of altruism but benefited themselves at the expense of others. In ancient society, the degree of cooperation was very low. It was basically limited to acquaintances.

Two hundred years ago, humanity underwent a revolution in moral thought. This revolution was started by Scottish economist Adam Smith. Before Adam Smith, pursuing individual interest was considered immoral. Adam Smith overturned this traditional viewpoint. He showed that self-interest itself was not immoral. To the contrary, under the market economy, self-interest is the primary driving force behind activity that benefits others. Smith said[4]:

Man has almost constant occasion for the help of his brethren, and it is in vain for him to expect it from their benevolence only. He will be more likely to prevail if he can interest their self-love in his favour, and shew them that it is for their own advantage to do for him what he requires of them. … It is not from the benevolence of the butcher, the brewer, or the baker, that we expect our dinner, but from their regard to their own interest. We address ourselves, not to their humanity but to their self-love, and never talk to them of our own necessities but of their advantages. (Book I, Chapter II)

He also said:

Every individual is continually exerting himself to find out the most advantageous employment for whatever capital he can command. It is his own advantage, indeed, and not that of the society, which he has in view. (Book IV, Chapter II)

[3] Legge, James (translator). *Tao Te Ching*. Digitized by the Chinese Text Project.

[4] Adam Smith's *An Inquiry into the Nature and Causes of the Wealth of Nations*, as edited by Edwin Cannan in 1904 and digitized by the Library of Economics and Liberty.

Every individual is "led by an invisible hand to promote an end which was no part of his intention. Nor is it always the worse for the society that it was no part of it. By pursuing his own interest he frequently promotes that of the society more effectually than when he really intends to promote it." (Book IV, Chapter II)

The relationship between self-interest and altruism as revealed by Adam Smith is what I call "the logic of the market." The logic of the market is: In a market economy, to make oneself happy, one must first make others happy. If you cannot make others happy, you also will not be happy. For example, in order for an entrepreneur to make money, he or she must first create value for the consumer and satisfy the consumer. If you do not provide products that satisfy consumers, then you will not make money. This logic is not only suitable for entrepreneurs, but also for each individual.

Now, I will provide an analytical framework related to the Confucian "gentleman" according to the logic of the market. Anything someone does can be evaluated from two dimensions. The first is whether it benefits the individual himself (herself). The second is whether it benefits others. In this way, there are four possibilities: First, it benefits oneself and benefits others; second, it benefits oneself and harms others; third, it benefits others and harms oneself; fourth, it harms oneself and harms others.

Utilize this framework to understand the classification of people in ancient Chinese thought. The first type of person is a Confucian "gentleman." The second type of person is a petty man. Note the difference between a gentleman and a petty man is not based on self-interest but is instead based on harm to others. The third type of person is a "sage." The difference between a gentleman and a sage is not based on benefitting others but is instead based on willingness to sacrifice self-interest for others. The last type of person can either be called wicked or a fool.

From this we can see that the logic of the market is the way of virtue. The market does not require us to become "sages" and harm ourselves to benefit others, but the market will punish "petty men" that harm others to benefit themselves. I have summarized five standards of behavior in the market.

First, benefit yourself by first benefiting others. What does the saying "a gentleman makes money in a just way" mean? It means you must create value for others. If you are an entrepreneur, the price you collect from customers should not exceed the value you create for them. If you can accomplish this, and you make more money, it is virtuous. In the market, when every individual pursues self-interest, he or she must ask whether an activity brings benefit to others. If the benefit for others exceeds my gain, then it is virtuous.

Second, keep your word. The market economy is not a one-time game or a one-and-done sale. Instead, it is a repeated game. Everyone knows the most important thing in a repeated game is your reputation, meaning whether people believe you. If other people believe you, then they will be willing to continue doing business, buy your products, or form some other type of cooperative relationship with you. Only then can you make more money. Therefore, it could be said honesty is the best commercial policy in the market economy. If a person cannot establish a good reputation, then he cannot keep making money. Even if swindles succeed in the short term, they always fail in the end. The reason this type of person is a "petty man" is not because he is selfish, but instead because he is a fool. This type of person does not know honesty is the key to long-term interest.

From this perspective, we can re-interpret the saying: "The mind of the superior man is conversant with righteousness; the mind of the mean man is conversant with gain."[5] Here, "righteousness" can be understood as long-term interest. "Gain" refers to immediate, tiny benefit. The gentleman focuses on long-term interest, whereas the petty man focuses on immediate gain. The behavioral norms advocated by ancient Confucians can be unified with the behavioral norms people should respect in the market.

Third, think from other's perspective. In *Yan Yuan*, Confucius said: "What you do not want done to yourself, do not do to others." In *Yong Ye*, Confucius said: "Now the man of perfect virtue, wishing to be established himself, seeks also to establish others; wishing to be enlarged himself, he seeks also to enlarge others." These are the Confucian "principles of benevolence and loyalty." These principles come from humanity's ability to think from someone else's perspective. Without this ability, humanity could not cooperate. The principles of benevolence and loyalty imply the assumption that people are equals, so we should treat each person equally. Therefore, when we do any activity, not only should we consider ourselves, but also others. You want to make money, but so do other people. You want to gain from an exchange, but so do other people. Only by thinking in this way can you truly realize your own interests. This is the meaning of Adam Smith's sentence "never talk to them of our own

[5] Legge, James (translator). *The Confucian Analects.* Digitized by the Chinese Text Project.

necessities but of their advantages." (Book I, Chapter II) If a person only thinks of his own benefit when doing business, but does not think about other's desire for benefit, then an exchange cannot occur. The "principles of benevolence and loyalty" are not only suitable for individuals, but also for dealing with relations between nations. If a person only considers himself, but not others, we could say he is a fool, or extremely selfish. Similarly, if we believe only the interests of our own country are important, but find no need to consider the interests of other countries, is this the way of virtue?

Fourth, respect property rights and the basic rights of every individual. Property rights are the foundation of the logic of the market. Respecting property rights means respecting the desires of others. Any exchange must be built upon the foundation of other people's desires. It is only good when people desire it. We cannot use force to make people exchange. Respect for property rights is the basic requirement of justice, more important than mercifulness. Even if a person donates to charity every day, but he does not respect the property rights or basic rights of others (including the freedom of speech), then this person cannot be called virtuous. This applies to both businesspeople and government officials.

Fifth, have an innovative spirit. Over the long term, all of human society's progress came from innovation. The market economy is an innovation economy, not a circular economy. The things we consume today are very different from 200 years ago. The total number of products consumed by humanity 200 years ago was between 100 and 1000 products. Today, it is between 100 million and 10 billion products.[6] These new products are all the result of innovation. In modern society, each person that wants to be virtuous must have an innovative mind or innovative spirit. At the very least, you should not obstruct other's innovation. A person that does not innovate and always tries to obstruct other's innovation also cannot be called virtuous. Because innovation always faces uncertainty, meaning risk of failure, the virtuous man should also have a spirit of tolerance.

According to the logic of the market, the market economy is certainly dominated by virtue. From the perspective of each individual, gain can only come from contributing to others. The pretense of entrepreneurial

[6] See page 9, Eric D. Beinhocker, 2006, *The Origin of Wealth: Evolution, Complexity and the Radical Remaking of Economics*. Boston MA: Harvard Business School Press.

income is creating value for customers. If employees cannot contribute to the output of the firm, then they cannot maintain their livelihood. The reason entrepreneurs like Bill Gates and Ma Huateng could become billionaires is precisely because they served the mass consumer, and thus are truly virtuous. They are the virtuous men among virtuous men. Everyone has a cell phone in their pocket and can use WeChat. With WeChat, communicating with family and friends became much more convenient. We can also obtain information we otherwise could not. This is the reason Ma Huateng is rich.[7]

In contrast, the traditional society is the petty society, not the virtuous society. Why? Because in that type of society, getting rich depended on the logic of theft, not the logic of the market. The people with the highest social status, greatest wealth, and most admiration often killed the most, plundered the most, and enslaved the most. The more people they killed, the more heroic they were! As the saying goes: "Petty criminals are hanged but big criminals are crowned." According to the standard I just mentioned, most nobles, knights, generals, and politicians from ancient times were far from virtuous men. The story below proves this point.

In the beginning of the last century, British Prime Minister Lloyd George established new peerages and granted them to self-made millionaires. This caused extreme dissatisfaction among hereditary peers. When asked how his ancestor got his peerage, the hereditary peer replied, "with the battle axe, sir, with the battle axe!"[8] This was the origin of the ancient nobility.

Unfortunately, in our society and culture, many people admire the murderous "heroes" of traditional society. They see them as virtuous men but resent entrepreneurs that create wealth.

Of course, "benefiting others first to benefit yourself" is the ideal situation, but "petty men" that harm others to benefit themselves will always exist in the market. Why? The primary reason is our system has loopholes. The legal system and social norms are the most important systems. If property rights are not effectively protected in a society, a commercial environment with fair competition cannot possibly form. At that point, it

[7] Ma Huateng is the founder and CEO of Tencent Corporation, a leading Chinese Internet company.

[8] Cited from Steven Pinker, 2011, *The Better Angels of Our Nature: Why Violence Has Declined*. New York, NY: Viking. Page 82.

will be difficult for virtuous men to out-compete petty men, so the number of virtuous men will decline.

A question that requires discussion is: Can respect for the law differentiate "virtuous men" and "petty men"? Stated simply, the ideal state is that it can, but this is not the current state. In the ideal state, the rational option is the legal option and the legal option is the rational option. At that point, respecting the law benefits others and yourself, whereas violating the law harms others and yourself. This makes it easy to be a virtuous man. Because it is legitimate to follow the law, then people that break the law cannot be virtuous. However, if a society does not acknowledge natural law, then the rational option is not legal, and the legal option is not rational. This makes it difficult to be virtuous, because a lawbreaker might not be a "petty man," but a law-abiding person might not be "virtuous." For example, when the market is excessively regulated, and the entrepreneurial spirit cannot operate normally, then commercial activity that creates value for the consumer is often illegal. Virtuous men might also break the law.

If we discover a society that makes harming others more worthwhile than benefiting others, then virtuous men will not prevail against petty men. That society's petty men will increase, and virtuous men will decrease. This proves that society's system truly has a problem.

At that point, our best option is to change the system. Only after the system is changed can we turn more people into virtuous men, not petty men. A good system can turn petty men into virtuous men and a bad system can turn virtuous men into petty men. Any law or policy that inhibits free competition or suppresses entrepreneurship opens a path for petty men. It helps petty men and inhibits the development of virtuous men.

From China's perspective, only after we become a country with a true market economy can we become a nation of virtuous men. I hope that our common efforts will make our country a more open, free, and fair rule-of-law country. I believe by that time our country will have many more virtuous men. I also believe each one of us can become virtuous.

CHAPTER 5

What Is a Good Market Theory?

Mainstream economics is not a good theory of the market.

A good market theory should include: First, a theory about how the market promotes human cooperation. Second, a theory about how the market works through trust and the reputation mechanism. Third, a theory about how the market brings about development and change, instead of equilibrium and stability. Fourth, the theory of entrepreneurship. Fifth, a correct understanding of economic cycles and fluctuations. Sixth, a market theory based on rights, not utilitarianism.[1]

* * *

In my view, recorded human history can be divided into two stages. The first stage is the period of history dominated by the logic of theft. The second stage is the period of history dominated by the logic of the market. History dominated by the logic of theft is full of war, famine, and looting. Interactions were primarily zero-sum games. Human progress was extremely slow, and standards of living were stagnant for a very long time. When the logic of the market became dominant, people primarily spent energy on production and exchange. Interactions were primarily

[1] The original version of this chapter was written in January 2016.

W. Zhang, *Ideas for China's Future*,
https://doi.org/10.1007/978-981-15-4304-3_5

positive-sum games. Technology advanced and wealth increased. Standards of living continuously increased and humanity achieved tremendous progress.

From the entire world's perspective, the logic of theft was dominant for the largest portion of history. Even if we consider the last 5000 years of human civilization, the logic of theft was dominant in the first 4800 years. The logic of the market was dominant only in the last 200 years.

Economics is the theory of how the market operates. Mainstream economics is the mainstream theories of how the market operates. So-called mainstream economics is the economics we learn from textbooks. It is simply called "neoclassical economics." I believe the mainstream economics we learn from textbooks does not provide good theories about the market economy. Therefore, there is a need to reflect on and criticize it.

Of course, for a long time, there has been no shortage of critics of neoclassical economics. The primary criticism is neoclassical economics embellishes the market. However, in my view, this criticism has not grasped the substantial defect of neoclassical economics. To the contrary, neoclassical economics defiles the market. To prove the market is efficient, neoclassical economics makes a series of assumptions, but none of these assumptions are satisfied in reality. This gives opponents of the market a voice, because none of these assumptions can be satisfied, so the market cannot be as effective as proposed in neoclassical economics. Many people who read economics textbooks are not left with a deep impression about how efficient the market is. Instead, their impression is the market fails and government intervention is necessary. In the real world, the effective and efficient operation of the market does not require those assumptions, as shown by experimental economists.[2] The rationale for government intervention in the market derived from these impractical assumptions also does not stand!

In China, another criticism of mainstream economics is it can only explain Western market economies, but not China. It especially cannot explain China's economic miracle over the last 30 years. I believe this is scientific relativism.

If a theory cannot explain the Chinese economy, then it is certainly not a good theory in general. China is not so special that we require a theory

[2]Vernon Smith, 2008, *Rationality in Economics: Constructivist and Ecological Forms*. New York, NY: Cambridge University Press.

created specifically to suit China. A good market theory is certainly universal, meaning its explanation for the West is the same as for China.

My understanding of a good market theory should include a few aspects. First, it is a theory about how the market promotes human cooperation, instead of a simple theory of how the market allocates resources. Second, it is a theory about how the market makes humanity build trust and how the reputation mechanism plays a role in the market, instead of only a price theory. Third, it is a theory about how the market brings about development and change, instead of how the market realizes equilibrium and stability. Fourth, it not only includes an impersonal price theory, but also should include the theory of the entrepreneur. Fifth, it can provide a correct understanding of economic cycles and fluctuations. Sixth, it should be a market theory based on rights, not utilitarianism.

Advancing Human Cooperation

All of humanity's progress came from cooperation. Human cooperation existed since ancient times, but only in the market economy system did humanity's cooperation reach unprecedented breadth and depth. Stated simply, human cooperation in traditional societies was cooperation among acquaintances. It was cooperation among people that knew each other, and the scope of cooperation was limited. The market can expand interpersonal cooperation into cooperation among strangers. Today, human cooperation is global in scope among a few billion people. We have never heard of 99.99% of the people that provide us with goods and services. We are even less likely to have even seen their face, yet we cooperate. This is the "extended order" of human cooperation conceptualized by F.A. Hayek.[3]

Cooperation is itself a positive-sum game. It benefits everyone involved. However, because humanity's long history was a period of zero-sum games dominated by the logic of theft, from an evolutionary psychology perspective, humanity's current mentality is still a zero-sum game mentality. Therefore, many people still understand the market economy from a zero-sum game perspective. When we see some people make money, we believe some people have certainly been exploited, or someone else lost

[3] F. A. Hayek, 1988. *The Fatal Conceit: The Errors of Socialism*, edited by W. W. Bartley III. Chicago: University of Chicago Press.

wealth. This is a classic zero-sum game way of thinking. It should be said mainstream economics made an important contribution to getting rid of the zero-sum game mentality.

Human cooperation in the market economy is not simply mutual aid in the traditional society or a few people cooperating to move stones. Instead, it is mutual dependence. This mutual dependence comes from cooperation in the market economy being based on the division of labor and specialization. Every person does different things. Because of specialization and division of labor, each person's potential can be maximized and each person's way of doing things can continuously improve. Only then can society's overall wealth grow. However, according to textbook mainstream economics, division of labor and specialization will lead to market failure and efficiency loss. Why is this so? First, the benefits of division of labor and specialization come from economies of scale. However, according to textbook economic theories, economies of scale lead to imperfect competition and a small number of large firms (or even one firm) monopolizing the market. This will lead to inefficient resource allocation. Traditionally, this is known as the "contradiction between the pin factory and the invisible hand."[4] Because this contradiction exists in theory, Adam Smith's theory of division of labor disappeared from neoclassical economics. Only by dropping the division of labor can the efficiency of the "invisible hand" be mathematically proven. The academic ambition of Xiaokai Yang, an outstanding Chinese economist, was to resolve this contradiction.[5] Unfortunately, his contribution has not yet been widely accepted!

Second, specialized division of labor brings about information asymmetry. In other words, the superiority of specialized division of labor precisely comes from asymmetric information (because each person only needs to grasp his or her specialized knowledge). However, according to mainstream economic theories, asymmetric information leads to adverse selection, which brings about market failure. If the theory that asymmetric information leads to market failure is correct, then how could the autarkic traditional economy with perfectly symmetric information possibly evolve into a market economy with asymmetric information? Therefore, traditional economics is not a correct or good market theory.

[4]Allyn Young. 1928. "Increasing Returns and Economic Progress." *Economic Journal*. Vol. XXXVIII. No. 152: 529–542; George Stigler. 1951. "The Division of Labor Is Limited by the Extent of the Market." *The Journal of Political Economy*. Vol. LIX. No.3: 185–193.

[5]Xiaokai Yang, and Y-K Ng. 1993. *Specialization and Economic Organization: A New Classical Microeconomic Framework*. Amsterdam: North-Holland.

Reputation and Behavioral Constraints

As previously mentioned, today's market is cooperation among strangers. How can unacquainted people trust each other? This is the function of the market's reputation mechanism. Traditional economics believes the market is an invisible hand, but the market also has an invisible eye. The market remembers and propagates information. It stores and disseminates the behavior of entities. In a true market economy, any bad actions will be punished (especially through lost reputation). Similarly, good actions will be rewarded. In the market economy, "the millstones of the gods grind late, but they grind fine." Precisely for this reason, honesty is considered the best commercial strategy.

In the reputation mechanism's formation process, a firm is an artificial construct with an extremely important role. It is the bearer of reputation for the entire market economy.[6] Why are we willing to purchase products from strangers or cooperate with them? Because their products are produced and sold to us under the name of some trademark. We remember these trademarks. In addition, these trademarks have owners. If they cheat us, the trademark's reputation will be damaged, which also injures the interests of the trademark owner. Therefore, trademark owners have an incentive to establish a good brand. The better the brand, the more customers favor them. I do not know the people that manufacture vehicles, but I know that the vehicle manufacturer has a set of systems to make someone accountable for workers' mistakes. This is the reason I trust the vehicle manufacturer.

In addition, a vehicle often has many component suppliers. The value added to a vehicle by the factory might not exceed 20% of the final retail price. The thousands of upstream vendors do not deal with me directly, so why should I trust them? Because the vehicle manufacturer supervises them for me. If these suppliers produce inferior components that are assembled into a vehicle, then the vehicle manufacturer must assume joint liability. In the market, a vehicle manufacturer is like a general contractor, because it takes responsibility for any component that has a problem. This is the value of branded firms.

Precisely for this reason, I say profit comes from responsibility. The ability to assume liability determines firms' ability to make money. The

[6] David Kreps. 1986. "Corporate Culture and Economic Theory." in *Technological Innovation and Business Strategy*, edited by M. Tsuchiya. Nippon Keizai Shimbuunsha Press. Also, in *Rational Perspective on Political Science*, edited by J. Alt and K. Shepsle. Cambridge, MA: Harvard University Press, 1999.

reason big firms can make big money is because they must assume joint liability for a large number of employees and suppliers. If a firm does not want to assume this liability, or does not have the ability to assume it, not only will it not become large, but also might go bankrupt.

However, traditional economics believes a firm that becomes large has price-setting power and monopolizes the market. This reduces consumer surplus and brings about efficiency loss. Therefore, opposition to monopolies has become opposition to large firms. However, a market without large firms or firms with a certain degree of scale cannot effectively operate. In an atomized market with "perfect competition," trust cannot be built between customers and producers. Cooperation among suppliers is impossible. Mainstream economists tell us asymmetric information leads to market failure because they ignore the market's reputation mechanism. Government intervention can only lead to reputation mechanism failure. It cannot resolve adverse selection. Worldwide, the countries with more government intervention have more severe adverse selection and a more chaotic market order. Traditional theories tell us the way to resolve adverse selection is to rely on government intervention. The reality we see is precisely the opposite.

Development and Change

Markets have existed since ancient times but as an economic system, the market only has about a 200-year history. Since the Industrial Revolution more than 200 years ago, the market economy has brought about the true benefits of continuous change and development. The things we consume today are much different from 200 years ago. There is also a big difference from 20 years ago. At all times, new products are introduced, new technologies appear, product quality continuously improves, industry structures continuously evolve, and consumption structures continuously change. These are all brought about by the market. Correct economic theories must explain how new products and new technologies appear.

However, textbook mainstream economics is a theory of the circular economy. It assumes product types and production technologies are given. Its focal point is how an unchanging economy realizes "equilibrium" and "stability" through the price mechanism. It treats equilibrium and stability as the standard for measuring whether the market is efficient. Because technology, resources, and people's preferences are assumed to be given, traditional economics cannot explain development and change. So-called "developmental economics" arose in the 1950s. It was a response to defects in mainstream economics. However, developmental economics often became anti-market economics. If we have a good market theory, developmental economics is unnecessary.

The Entrepreneur

Entrepreneurs are the soul of the market economy, but do not make an appearance in mainstream economic theories. The basic assumptions of traditional economics exclude entrepreneurs because it assumes the world is certain. In a world of certainty, every person is similarly intelligent and all-knowing. Every decision can be made with a calculation, so no one needs an imagination to make judgments about the future. Thus entrepreneurship is unnecessary. The real world is not like this. The future is uncertain. We do not know what consumers want. We do not know how technology will change. We need an imagination, and this imagination can only come from entrepreneurship.

Economic development either comes from increased resource allocation efficiency or technological innovation. Traditional resource allocation efficiency and the appearance of new products or new technologies are all the result of entrepreneurship. Without entrepreneurship, we would not even know how much of something should sell, so the market could not possibly trend toward equilibrium. Without entrepreneurship, large-scale innovation and technological progress are impossible.[7]

We know that new technologies occasionally appeared in traditional societies, but they rarely became a means for humanity to create value. For example, the steam engine existed during the Roman Empire, but it did not become a part of Roman life. It did not bring about true economic growth for the Roman Empire.

Emphasis on entrepreneurship is not excessive under any situation. Our greatest mistake in emphasizing demand-side management in the past was ignoring entrepreneurship. We mistakenly believed we could rely on monetary policy and adjustments to aggregate demand, investment, consumption, and foreign trade to bring the economy out of recession or inhibit

[7] Schumpeter correctly identified innovation and growth with entrepreneurship. See J. A. Schumpeter. 1934. *The Theory of Economic Development*. 1980 edition. London, Oxford and New York: Oxford University Press.

overheating. Now, the Chinese government is starting to emphasize supply-side policies, and this is good. However, if the focus points of supply-side policies are not on liberating the entrepreneurial spirit, allowing entrepreneurs to have more freedom to do business and innovate, or giving entrepreneurs more stable expectations about the future, then these supply side policies cannot truly succeed.

Economic Cycles and Fluctuations

The theories about economic cycles and fluctuations we currently learn from textbooks are just the Keynesian theory of aggregate demand. This theory believes all economic fluctuations, both in times of prosperity and depression, come from changes in aggregate demand. Aggregate demand is either excessive or insufficient, so the way to resolve the issue is to adjust aggregate demand through monetary and fiscal policy. Experience has shown this theory has problems. Any country that implements these theories will have many problems.

During the Global Financial Crisis of 2009, China stimulated its economy according to this type of theory. China achieved 9.2% growth in 2009 and exceeded 10% in 2010. However, a careful study will find that many of the economic problems China face today, especially excess capacity, were caused precisely by the aggregate demand stimulus policies implemented at that time.

Within economics, there is a better cycle theory called the Austrian school's theory of the business cycle.[8] This theory was originally developed by Ludwig von Mises and systematically developed by F.A. Hayek. For this theory, F.A. Hayek won the 1974 Nobel Prize in Economics. According to this theory, any artificial prosperity created with monetary policy will certainly lead to a depression. The greater the degree of stimulus, the more serious the ultimate downturn will be. If we understand and acknowledge this theory, I believe we will make fewer mistakes in our economic policies, especially macroeconomic policies.

[8] For a brief introduction to the Austrian business cycle theory, see Richard M. Ebeling, 2015, *Monetary Central Planning and the State*, Chapter 3, published by The Future of Freedom Foundation; or Murray N. Rothbard, 1983 (1963). *America's Great Depression*. 4th edition, Chapter 1. New York: Richardson & Snyder.

Rights Versus Utilitarianism

The market liberates people. It lets people break free from the shackles of theocracy and autocracy to live a free and dignified life. Utilitarianism justifies the legitimacy of the means based on the legitimacy of the ends. If the ends are legitimate, any means can be used. Mainstream economics is utilitarian economics. This utilitarian economics evaluates any policy based on "efficiency" and "growth." However, if we ignore people's basic rights and dignity to obtain "efficiency" and "growth," then more serious problems will arise.

According to utilitarian economics, liberty and human rights are means, not ends. The opponents of liberty often ask, "can you eat freedom?" In other words, their view is anything that "cannot be eaten" is valueless. This is the utilitarian way of thinking.

Each person's basic rights are ends in themselves. Liberty and human rights should have priority over efficiency and growth. A system or policy, even under special circumstances, might be very efficient and bring about high levels of economic growth, but if it violates basic individual rights, then it is anti-market, and should not be implemented.

Over the long term, the consequences of utilitarian policies are extremely severe. China has many utilitarian policies, such as forced demolitions. The reason behind forced demolition is very simple: In order to develop a location's economy, I need to pave roads and build plazas. If people have houses in these areas, my economic development objective is obstructed, and so I have the power to forcefully tear them down. From the short-term perspective, this policy gets roads paved faster and makes urban infrastructure more modern. The long-term consequences are social instability and personal insecurity. Today, many of China's mass incidents are related to forced demolitions.

Another example is family planning. When the One Child Policy was implemented, it was entirely utilitarian. The reason was a larger population was not conducive to economic development. Why are two children allowed now? It is also for utilitarian reasons related to economic development. After 30 years of the One Child Policy, China's labor force shrank, and the population aged. A market without young people will have difficulty being an innovation market, so we should loosen population controls. From the perspective of rights, reproduction is a basic right. The government cannot deprive this right for any other reason.

If we consider issues from the perspective of rights, then we will make fewer policy mistakes. The previously discussed demolitions have caused a series of social contradictions, including destruction of the country's culture and cultural relics. These cannot be remedied. Therefore, I believe we economists have a responsibility to transition market theories from utility to rights.

The above is my reflections on market theories.

CHAPTER 6

The Fallacy of Market Failure Theory

Neoclassical economics takes "perfect competition" as the benchmark and argues that any deviation from it would lead to market failure. If this theory was correct, the market would succeed nowhere, and any government intervention could be justified.

The efficiency of the market of the real world does not depend on economists' unrealistic assumptions. We shall not mistake market theory failure as market failure.[1]

* * *

Professor Steven N. S. Cheung's *Economic Explanations* is a collection of his thoughts on economics over 50–60 years.[2] Xiaokai Yang convinced me to read Professor Cheung's work in the 1980s and I am still reading it. I believe this book needs to be read repeatedly, because he proposes many innovative thoughts on economics. Even though these innovative ideas have been around for decades, they have not been commonly accepted in economics.

[1] The original version of this chapter was written in November 2014.

[2] The Chinese version of the *Economic Explanations (Jingji Jieshi)* was published by CITIC Press in 2014. The English version is not yet available.

W. Zhang, *Ideas for China's Future*,
https://doi.org/10.1007/978-981-15-4304-3_6

Today, the issue I want to discuss is the "fallacy of market failure theories." We know that market failure theory is still an important component of economics, especially neoclassical economics. Neoclassical economics is considered to be theories that prove the market is efficient. However, the conclusion with the deepest influence and the most important influence on economic policy is market failure, not the success of the market. I believe these market failure theories are all incorrect. We must reflect on economics itself, especially the basic paradigm of neoclassical economics, because market failure theory came out of this paradigm. To prove the efficiency of the market, neoclassical economics made many assumptions. Basically, none of these assumptions are valid. The result is people started to use the unrealism of these assumptions to attack the market itself. In my view, the effective operation of the market does not require the assumptions of neoclassical economics. The purpose of these assumptions is to prove the efficiency of the market contained within these theorists' minds, not the efficiency of the real-world market.

Below, I will briefly discuss three issues. The first is about externalities, which is one of Professor Cheung's most important contributions. The second is about monopolies. The third is about information asymmetry.

The Fallacy of Externalities

First, let us discuss externalities. We know when neoclassical economists prove the efficiency of markets, they assume externalities do not exist. To assume externalities do not exist is to assume society does not exist. As long as more than two people exist, so-called "externalities" will exist. For example, a person's appearance will have some sensory and emotional effects on others. A high or low voice will make others feel comfortable or uncomfortable. Every activity has externalities. If we use externalities to prove market failure and from there legitimize government intervention, then there is no single activity that does not require government intervention. As Ronald Coase already proved, externalities are an issue of property rights delineation.[3] Professor Cheung's "The Fable of the Bees" tells us the people involved can resolve mutual externalities.[4]

[3] Ronald Coase. 1960. "The Problem of Social Cost." *Journal of Law and Economics* 3: 1–44.

[4] Steven N. S. Cheung. 1973. "Fable of the Bees: An Economic Investigation." *Journal of Law and Economics*, 16: 11–33.

According to traditional economic theories, when a firm generates environmental pollution, there are externalities. The firm harmed others without compensation, so its choices are not the most efficient. Government intervention is required. However, assume I open a restaurant that services customers much better than the competitor's. When I put another restaurant out of business, is this an externality? Yes. Should I compensate the other restaurant? I believe we economists would not agree I should compensate the other restaurant. Why should compensation occur in the first instance, but not the second? Externality theory has no way of responding to this question. Some economists make a distinction between technological (nonpecuniary) externality and pecuniary externality. They argue that the externality theory only refers to the former, not the latter. But this distinction does not make sense. For the owner of the failed restaurant, it makes no difference whether the failure is caused by my competition or by the pollution discharged from a neighboring factory such that customers are no longer willing to come.[5]

The core issue is property rights delineation, meaning what is my right and what is not. It is my right to do better than a competitor, and my competitor has the right to do the same. However, if for example, I stand at the door of the other restaurant and prohibit customers from entering, then I have violated the restaurant owner's rights, so government intervention is necessary. Stated simply, this issue can only be resolved through defined property rights. In other words, any activity that violates individual property rights is illegitimate and should be restricted. On the other hand, any activity that does not violate individual property rights, regardless how significant the externality is, also does not require compensation. In the early years, Ford Corporation put a lot of coachmen out of work, but Ford Corporation is not required to compensate them. Similarly, today we see many Internet companies putting traditional companies out of business. These externalities also do not require compensation. Therefore, a simple conclusion is we must examine externality issues from the perspective of property rights, otherwise we will be caught in a mistake.

I will again emphasize technological progress. Economists have done a significant amount of research on the externalities of technological progress, known as the spillover effect. According to current economic

[5] For a critical analysis of the distinction between technological and pecuniary externalities, see Brian Simpson. 2005. *Market Don't Fail,* Chapter 4. Lexington Books.

theories, because inventors and innovators cannot enjoy all the benefits brought about by technological progress, technological progress in the market economy must be lower than the optimal level. If we want to have socially optimal technological progress, then government subsidies for innovation are required. This conclusion is absurd. The market economy or the capitalist economy has most effectively promoted technological progress, yet we economists still believe it does not provide enough incentives for technological progress. An important means of understanding technological progress includes the concepts of natural selection and survival competition discussed in Professor Cheung's books, but not traditional cost-benefit analysis. In other words, in the market economy, you innovate because you must be better than others. It is a question of your survival, not whether you can obtain the entire benefit created by the innovation.

This is my first viewpoint. Utilizing externality theory to prove the rationality of government intervention in the market, or proving market failure, is entirely wrong.

Traditional Anti-Monopoly Theories Oppose True Competition

The monopoly issue is second. Traditional economics believes as soon as firms attain monopoly status, efficiency declines. This is market failure. Why? Because monopoly theory's frame of reference is perfect competition. However, it is totally incorrect to set perfect competition as the standard for market efficiency. So-called perfect competition is a lack of competition. For example, how can economics professors implement perfect competition for ourselves? Perfect competition means that we all write the same articles, teach the same content, and charge the same price! We know, however, an economics professor must compete with others by having different viewpoints and different writings. This is true competition. However, according to the traditional explanation in economics, as long as one person does something different from others, there is a monopoly. According to this standard, Professor Steven Cheung has monopolized the market for economics. His share of the market is too large with too many readers. The government should intervene. Obviously, this is wrong.

As argued by Schumpeter long time ago, much of the so-called monopoly behavior discussed in traditional economics is actually competitive conduct in the market.[6] The Anti-Monopoly Law opposes true competitive behavior. According to the theories currently provided by economics, there is no way firms can be competitive. If you set prices higher than others, that is monopolistic pricing. If you set prices lower than others, that is dumping. If you set prices equivalent to others, that is conspiracy. Any type of pricing behavior can be called monopolistic behavior. How can firms compete in the market?

Monopoly theory in economics is totally inconsistent with reality. Monopoly theory says that prices will rise after two firms merge. However, a large amount of research has proven there are no historical examples of prices trending upwards after two large firms merged. Instead, prices declined.[7] Economic theory believes after firms obtain market power, they do not think about progress, so technological progress will slow down. However, where have we seen a large amount of the world's new technology come from? They came from so-called "monopolistic firms," such as the Aluminum Company of America (Alcoa) and International Business Machines (IBM) in the early days or Microsoft, Apple, and Google today. They are the primary drivers of technological progress. According to the definition of monopoly in economics, Tencent and China Mobile are both monopolies. This is ridiculous. China Mobile does not have to work very hard to still make money, whereas even though Tencent controls 80–90% of the market, it will be gone in six months if it does not work hard. Within a few short years, WeChat is already on its sixth version. Therefore, we economists must change the traditional way of thinking. We must correctly recognize how competition occurs in the market and the things market efficiency relies on.

Theories on monopoly in traditional economics are all built upon the assumption that firms are just a production function. Actually, firms are not only a production function, but also an innovation function. Equally important, firms are also a reputation mechanism vector. They establish market trust. Why can the cooperation we see today be global in scope? Because of large firms! If there were no large firms, but instead there were

[6] J. A. Schumpeter. 1942. *Capitalism, Socialism and Democracy,* Chapter 8. Fifth edition, 1976. London: Routledge.

[7] D. T. Armentano. 1972. The Myth of Antitrust Economic Theory and Legal Cases. New York: Arlington House; 1990. Antitrust and Monopoly Anatomy of A Policy Failure. 2nd edition. San Francisco: Independent Institute.

an infinite number of small firms competing, who would trust anyone? No one would trust anyone else! Precisely because there are large firms using their brands and reputations to vouch for upstream firms, we have an efficient, orderly, and trustworthy market. For example, a consumer that buys a BMW does not have to supervise producers of components, steel, or iron ore. We only need to monitor BMW, and BMW takes responsibility for supervising all linked upstream production on our behalf. If there were not 10 or so large firms in the auto industry, but instead there were tens of thousands of small firms without the ability to influence price, could we have an auto industry that is as developed as it is today? Impossible. This is the reason I say this is a major mistake in traditional economics. It only sees firms as a production function but does not see firms simultaneously as an innovation function or as part of the trust-building mechanism.

Without Asymmetric Information, There Is No Market

Asymmetric information is the third issue I want to discuss. Asymmetric information theory is extremely useful, but many of this theory's conclusions will mislead us if we do not deeply consider them. According to the theories of traditional economics, the existence of asymmetric information will lead to adverse selection. Survival of the fittest will not occur, so the government must intervene. Thus, we need to establish a large number of regulatory agencies, such as the Food and Drug Administration, to determine entry qualifications, to inspect product quality, and approve new products. I believe these theories are also entirely incorrect.

Why are they wrong? According to asymmetric information theory, asymmetric information leads to market failure or even disappearance. However, if that was true, the market would never exist at all. The reason is that the market was born with asymmetric information. In other words, it is the market that creates asymmetric information. If everyone is self-sufficient and produces the products he consumes, then there is no asymmetric information.

Furthermore, the efficiency of the market would not exist without asymmetric information. The market is based on specialization and division of labor. In the market economy, everyone is a specialist. Specialization is good exactly because specialists only need limited knowledge of their specialized fields for performing their jobs. Without asymmetric information in the sense everyone has the same knowledge, none of the market's advantages will exist. Of course, certain issues highlighted by asymmetric information theory is helpful for understanding how market institutions operate. Why does the market still work under asymmetric information? Because it can resolve the issues brought about by asymmetric information. Under any circumstances, if the market cannot resolve the issues brought about by asymmetric information, then it will not create asymmetric information and thus does not exist in the first place.

An important point to recognize is the market is not just an "invisible hand," but also an "invisible eye." The market has a very good memory. It rewards your good activity with a better reputation and a bigger market. It punishes your bad behavior. The most successful firms we see on the market are not firms that rely on asymmetric information to cheat people, instead the most successful firms are those which are the most trustworthy. According to George Akerlof's writings, asymmetric information causes the "bad-money-drives-out-good-money" phenomena in the second-hand car market, meaning good cars do not sell, but bad cars do. However, in which markets do good cars not sell and bad cars sell well? In all real markets, good cars sell well, and bad cars may not. The reason "bad money" drives out "good money" as defined by the so-called Gresham's law is because the government distorts the price of different currency, not because of asymmetric information.[8]

According to asymmetric information theory, government intervention is required to solve the adverse selection problem. However, as argued by Vernon Smith, the 2002 Nobel Prize laureate in economics, the contributions of the asymmetric information model provide no theoretical legitimacy for the interventionist policies. It goes too far from the abstract model of the static equilibrium to the practical policy.[9] In the real world, which country has the most severe adverse selection? It is certainly a country with the most government interference in the market. Compare China and the United States, specifically observing the market for talent. In which country does the inferior beat out the superior? In which country does the superior beat out the inferior? Obviously, in China it is not the most outstanding people that succeed in competition. If we truly abide

[8] Murry N. Rothbard, 2005 (1991). *What Has Government Done to Our Money?* Auburn, Alabama: The Mises Institute.

[9] Vernon Smith. 2008. *Rationality in Economics: Constructivist and Ecological Forms.* Chapter Five. New York: Cambridge University Press.

by market rules, then the most talented people will obtain the highest compensation and be the most successful.

To summarize, theories about market failure in traditional economics are wrong. First, externalities are not a legitimate reason for government intervention in the economy. Society cannot exist without externalities. Second, traditional anti-monopoly theories are totally wrong. The Anti-Monopoly Law opposes true competition. Third, without asymmetric information, markets will not exist, will not be efficient, and will not bring about much human progress.

Therefore, we must again reflect on the basic paradigm of economics. These market failure theories are built upon a foundation of economics' basic paradigms. If we do not reflect on these paradigms, then economic theory will provide a sturdy foundation for government intervention. For example, if you ask officials of the National Development and Reform Commission the reasons prices must be regulated, they will say the market's efficiency depends on perfect competition and symmetric information, but many large firms make competition imperfect and information is asymmetric, so the government must intervene to resolve market failure.

We must not mistake the failure of traditional market theories as failures of the market itself.[10]

[10]Weiying Zhang. 2015. "Reflections on Economics: Market Failure or Market Theory Failure?" *China Economic Journal*. Vol. 8, No. 2, 109–121.

CHAPTER 7

What Did China Obtain from Globalization?

What does globalization mean today? It is mutual learning and cooperation between people of different regions and countries by utilizing all of humanity's wisdom. Every region is interconnected, and no region can progress in isolation.

History has shown whenever the logic of the market is dominant, humanity will progress. Whenever the logic of theft is dominant, humanity will regress.

In the Globalization Era, if we cannot act according to the rules of the game common throughout the world, then we cannot enjoy the benefits of human cooperation in its entirety.[1]

* * *

When we talk about the history of globalization, we must understand that long before globalization, humanity globalized. Modern humans ("homo sapiens") likely appeared 200,000 years ago in today's East Africa. Humanity left East Africa 100,000 years ago, first arriving in Southwest Asia (the Middle East). Australia was reached 60,000 years ago and Europe

[1] The original version of this chapter was written in July 2013.

W. Zhang, *Ideas for China's Future*,
https://doi.org/10.1007/978-981-15-4304-3_7

was reached 40,000 years ago. China was reached at the same time (although there are debates about whether or not China was reached 68,000 years ago). The Bering Strait was crossed 13,000 years ago. In this way, overall, humanity had already traveled from one area to every hospitable area 10,000 years ago. After the Ice Age ended, melting glaciers caused sea levels to rise. This separated humanity into three different worlds. Europe, Asia, and Africa was one world. The Americas were another, as well as Australia and Papua New Guinea.[2] People in these three worlds did not interact for over 10,000 years, even though there was interaction within each region, such as the Silk Road that linked Eurasia. However, after being separated for more than 10,000 years, in the last 500 years, these three worlds have again begun to connect. This started what we now call "globalization." The benchmark for the start of this globalization is the arrival of Christopher Columbus in the Americas in 1492. Therefore, the last 500 years could be seen as humanity's process of rejoining after 10,000 years of separation. This process is related to the transformation of humanity's ideas. If Columbus did not believe the world was spherical, he would not have sailed west in search of India and end up discovering the Americas (although Columbus went to the grave believing he found India). At the very least, this process would have been delayed considerably. Therefore, I believe this contains a very important realization: The transformation of ideas is extremely important to human society's development and change.

Globalization brought about common benefits for humanity. We know—at least over the last 10,000 years—all of human progress came from cooperation, and not genetic changes. Additionally, the greater the scope of cooperation, the faster humanity's progress was. This is the significance of globalization. Globalization allowed human cooperation to expand to a global scope. This is the primary reason the pace of human progress accelerated over the last 500 years.

What does globalization mean today? It is mutual learning and cooperation between people of different regions and countries by utilizing all of humanity's wisdom. Every region is interconnected, and no region can progress in isolation. Globalization brings about deeper, more complete human cooperation. From the value chain perspective, today we rarely see

[2] For the history of the geographic spreading of homo sapiens, see Chapter One of *The World History*, by Felipe Fernandez-Armesto, published by Prentice Hall in 2010.

a product that is produced entirely by one country. Even a bottle of water is a global product, because its value chain is spread across the globe.

Human society has operated along two types of logics. One type is the logic of theft, and the other is the logic of the market. The so-called logic of theft means that your happiness is built upon the unhappiness of others. The logic of the market means that you must first make others happy in order to make yourself happy. Over the past 500 years of globalization, the logic of the market, as Adam Smith described it, has continuously expanded on a global scale. Even today, this process is continuing. Over the last 200 years, even though the logic of theft was ever present, the logic of the market succeeded overall. Trade freedom continuously expanded. History has shown that whenever the logic of the market is dominant, humanity will progress. Whenever the logic of theft is dominant, humanity will regress. Before 1914, globalization of the world economy had already reached a corresponding degree. However, with the outbreak of the Great War, the logic of the market was undermined. Afterwards, protectionism flourished. By the end of the Second World War, the level of globalization as measured by international trade had not recovered its pre-Great War level. After the Second World War, humanity re-started globalization through the logic of the market. Here, Japan and Germany are two classic examples. These two countries started the Second World War. They sought to conquer the world using the logic of theft. We know they failed in the end. After the Second World War, they used the logic of the market to conquer the world. They succeeded and became economic superpowers.

What did China obtain from globalization? I used Angus Maddison's economic history data to calculate the change in the correlation coefficient between population and economic scales of different regions. Before 1820, the correlation coefficient was close to 1, meaning standards of living were not significantly different between countries. Later, the number continuously decreased until reaching 0.148 in 1973. This is the so-called "Great Divergence." From that point, the correlation coefficient began to increase. It reached 0.52 in 2003 and is expected to reach 0.73 in 2030.[3] This could be called the "Great Convergence."

Both the divergence and the convergence are highly correlated with China. The continuous divergence between population scale and

[3] See Chapter 17 of *The Logic of the Market* by Weiying Zhang, published by the Cato Institute in 2015.

economic scale was actually primarily due to China's stagnation. Similarly, the increased correlation coefficient between population scale and GDP scale over the last 30 years is also considerably due to China's rapid development. Over 100 years ago, when we encountered the trend of globalization, we were passive. The Westernization Movement was actually forced out. At that time, we did not truly join the world. However, since the start of Reform and Opening, we are active participants. We actively turned towards the world and actively utilized the logic of the market. The world market combined with China's cheap labor became our "late-mover's advantage." Xiaokai Yang warned us that the late-mover's advantage can turn into the late-mover's curse. This is an important warning and should not be ignored. Regardless, over the past 30 years, we utilized this late-mover's advantage. We did not create any new technology or new management methods, but our economy became the world's second largest. Globalization gave this to us.

People often believe that we cannot make assumptions about history. However, if we do not make assumptions, we will have difficulty understanding history. In 1792, King George III of England sent George Macartney to China with the goal of initiating negotiations to expand trade and interactions between Great Britain and China. Of course, Great Britain sought to obtain certain privileges. In China at that time, engaging in commerce was a type of special privilege that could not be done without government permission. From the perspective of today's standards, we cannot say that Great Britain's requests were entirely reasonable, but we also cannot say they were excessive. At the very least, Great Britain's desire to establish an embassy in Beijing and expand trade were not excessive. Imagine the Qing government had treated Great Britain as an equal sovereign nation—not a vassal state—and seriously studied Great Britain's requests to negotiate an equal agreement. If it had agreed to open a British embassy in Beijing and opened a few ports, while at the same time requiring a Chinese embassy in London and encouraging Chinese merchants to do business in Great Britain, then China's history—and even world history—might have been very different.[4]

[4]The reader might be interested in reading *An Embassy to China* by George Macartney, edited by J. L. Crammer-Byng, and published by Longman (London), in 1962 and *Travels in China* by John Barrow, published by A. Strahan (London), in 1806. John Barrow was the assistant to Macartney during his visit.

We often call Western countries at the time "powers." This implies that they were both powerful, but also transgressors. Actually, these "powers" used "cannons" to blow open the gate to China. However, according to my understanding, these powers originally came to China still hoping to engage in commerce according to the logic of the market. If the authorities in China at the time had understood the logic of the market and adapted to globalization trends; and if they had actively opened the gates, reformed the system, and had a suitable foreign relations strategy, then China might not have needed to cede land and pay compensation. It might have been on an equal footing with the powers, like Japan. However, we rejected the logic of the market, and in the end we were conquered by the logic of theft. From there, we had the 200 years of Chinese history as we know it.

Do not mistakenly believe only thieves use the logic of theft to consider issues. It is often the opposite. Some people view international relations in zero-sum terms. Apparently, during negotiations to join the World Trade Organization, representatives reported to the central leadership that China should reach a win-win agreement with the United States. At that point, someone of high level said, "How can there be win-win between China and the United States?" This is the logic of theft way of thinking.

Why did I refer to history first? Because humanity came from the same place. When we refer to Chinese people, we should put emphasis on "people" not "Chinese." Humanity came from the same place, and this fact is important. Today, all of humanity's cultural differences were formed over the last few thousand years. They did not originally exist and are not based on genetics. We also know that this difference might be exaggerated. Two thousand years ago, Axial Age thinkers (I call them "institutional entrepreneurs"), regardless if they were in the Orient or the Occident, set many common rules of the game for humanity, although they had different methods of expression. Even today, there are cultural differences between China and the West, but using Ronald Coase's theories to explain phenomena in China is still convincing. This proves that there is not much difference of human nature between the East and West.

We are always emphasizing Chinese characteristics, but we must acknowledge that China's civilization is also the result of cooperation with the outside world. What belongs to China? If we start from the very beginning, barely anything is entirely Chinese. The wheat that we eat was not originally cultivated in China. It came from the Middle East. The corn that we eat came from the Americas. Besides rice and a few other crops, almost nothing was cultivated or domesticated by the Chinese themselves. We can at least say that bronze is also not Chinese, but instead came from Mesopotamia. That area used bronze one thousand years before China did. Additionally, archeology has discovered that along the Silk Road, excavated bronze artifacts are older on the western portion. This means that a so-called Bronze Road perhaps predated the Silk Road.

We must be especially vigilant towards the trend of nationalist thought in globalization. In the Globalization Era, if we cannot act according to the rules of the game common throughout the world, then we cannot fully enjoy the benefits brought about by human cooperation. At the same time, we must also acknowledge that now there are many rules "with Chinese characteristics" (such as collusion between government and business). As China joins the world, certain Chinese firms like to use these rules to conquer the world, and certain foreign firms are "doing as the Romans do." I think this is very lamentable. After China joins the world, will it make the world's commercial culture better or worse? This is something we must consider.

For humanity's future, and for the future of Chinese, I hope we can act according to common values that conform to human nature, not adverse special values. I believe only in this way can we have a better world.

PART II

Entrepreneurship and the Rule of Law

CHAPTER 8

Entrepreneurs and Capitalists in the Market

The entrepreneur plays a major role in market operation and economic development. However, the entrepreneur is totally absent from mainstream economics. The reason is that the assumptions of the mainstream economics make entrepreneurship useless.

Government can substitute neither for capitalists and nor for entrepreneurs. When a country eliminates private capitalists, it actually also eliminates the mechanism for selecting entrepreneurs. The state-owned enterprise system cannot produce entrepreneurs.[1]

* * *

The relationship between entrepreneurs and capital was the subject of my research over the last 30 years. In 1984, I published a paper about entrepreneurs. Later, I co-authored the book *Entrepreneurs: The Kings of Economic Growth* with Sheng Bin. I have never left the theme set in that paper and that book.[2]

Below, I will discuss six viewpoints.

[1] The original version of this chapter was written in September 2015.

[2] The article is titled "It is time to have innovating entrepreneurs." and was published in *Dushu* (Reading) Magazine, No. 9 in 1984. The book was published by the People's Press in 1989. The book has been reprinted several times since 2003. The current edition is published under the Horizon imprint of the Shanghai People's Press.

W. Zhang, *Ideas for China's Future*,
https://doi.org/10.1007/978-981-15-4304-3_8

Entrepreneurs as the Main Part of the Market

Both resource allocation and technological progress all come from the application of entrepreneurship. Unfortunately, if you study economics, then the conclusion you will obtain from economics textbooks is the market is only a price system. It continuously adjusts through prices until supply and demand reach equilibrium. Why are entrepreneurs absent from mainstream economics? There are two reasons.

The first reason is the assumptions of mainstream economics. Mainstream economics assumes this world is certain, information is perfect, preferences and technology are given, and everyone is equally intelligent. If the world is certain, then each person can see the future. If information is perfect, then everyone has sufficient knowledge and information to make decisions. If everyone is equally intelligent, then everyone is an omnipotent "entrepreneur." Naturally, entrepreneurship is useless. Actually, the world is uncertain. Judging the future is no easy task. When we invest, we do not know whether there will be future benefit. Most information is unknown, so there is no way to make decisions according to a computer program. We can only rely on our own judgment and imagination. In addition, people are different. Some people have better judgement and are more imaginative. Whether or not the market is efficient depends on people with the greatest wisdom, judgment, and imagination making decisions. These people are entrepreneurs.[3]

The second reason is mainstream economics focuses on equilibrium and stability, not development and change. Equilibrium and stability are not the true essence of the market economy. Instead, development and change are. Over the last 200 years, the West was the earliest to implement the market economy. New products and new technologies continuously appeared while industry and consumption structures also continuously changed. Therefore, the products used today are different from 200 years ago, and even 30 years ago. We did not have cell phones 30 years ago, but now everyone has one. WeChat did not exist 10 years ago, but now we all use it. The market economy is the constant change and development economy.

[3] For Austrian criticism of how neoclassical assumptions drive out entrepreneurs from the market, see: Israel Kirzner. 1997. "Entrepreneurial Discovery and the Competitive Market Process: An Austrian Approach." *Journal of Economic Literature* Vol. XXXV, pp. 60–85.

These types of change and development come from innovation. Who are the true mainstay of innovation? Entrepreneurs. However, the assumptions and focus points of economics cause entrepreneurs to be absent from our textbooks. Even certain economists that study growth do not truly focus on entrepreneurs.

For example, the so-called neoclassical growth model is the most well-known growth theory.[4] It focuses on how capital accumulation brings about economic growth, or how economic growth depends on capital accumulation. However, it does not focus on how capital accumulation is implemented, or how capital accumulation drives the appearance of new technologies and new products. It only cares about the quantity of capital, not who is accumulating it or who is investing. The new so-called endogenous growth theory focuses on the importance of knowledge and R&D to economic growth. Nevertheless, it does not focus on how a certain group of people—entrepreneurs—turn knowledge and R&D into a source of economic development. It also mistakes innovation as a production process of knowledge.[5]

In 1986, the first sentence of an article I wrote was: "The commodity economy = price + entrepreneurs." At that point in time, the commodity economy referred to what we now call the market economy. Unfortunately, mainstream economics only focuses on prices, not on entrepreneurs.

Many of China's debates about policy today, such as whether economic development should be guided by the government or the market, or whether industrial policy is effective, depend on how we understand the relationship between entrepreneurs and the market. If we cannot truly understand how entrepreneurs play a role in the market, or how efficient market operations and technological progress depend on entrepreneurship, then all the policy we advocate might have the opposite result. During the era of central planning, we only emphasized the importance of

[4] Technological progress in the neoclassical model is exogenous, although the empirical studies show that nearly 80% of growth during 1900–1950 in the United States came from the increase in the total factor productivity (TFP). Robert Solow. 1956. "A Contribution to the Theory of Economic Growth." *Quarterly Journal of Economics*. Vol. 70: 65–94; Robert Solow. 1957. "Technical Change and the Aggregate Production Function." *Review of Economics and Statistics* 39: 312–320.

[5] Paul Romer is one of pioneering contributors to the endogenous growth model. See Paul Romer. 1990. "Endogenous Technological Change." *Journal of Political Economy*. Vol. 98. No. 5: S71–102.

capital accumulation, but did not understand the importance of entrepreneurs. We mistakenly believed the government could substitute for entrepreneurs in capital accumulation. The result was disastrous. Actually, capital is only a tool entrepreneurs use to shift resources and implement innovation. Relying on capital accumulation by the government cannot bring about true growth.

Entrepreneur Selection as the Role of Capitalists

After I wrote the article about entrepreneurs in 1984 and later the book *Entrepreneurs*, the importance of entrepreneurs to Chinese society gradually became the consensus. In other words, entrepreneurs are important, so entrepreneurs are required for Chinese reform to succeed.

But what kind of ownership system can produce true entrepreneurs? At that time, one viewpoint was entrepreneurs are important, but the ownership system is irrelevant. Entrepreneurs are necessary, but capitalists are not. I disagreed.

In 1986, I wrote another paper titled "Entrepreneurs and the Ownership System."[6] The core viewpoint of this paper is that entrepreneurs are the product of the private property system. Without the private property system, entrepreneurs cannot truly exist. Later, this paper became the subject of my doctoral thesis at Oxford University. I developed a theory called "an entrepreneurial/contractual theory of the firm" attempting to understand why capital hires labor, meaning the reasons the owners of capital have such an important status and their relationship to entrepreneurship in the market economy. My theory had two major conclusions.[7]

First, the incentive problem requires the entrepreneur to be the residual claimant. Among all members of the firm entrepreneurs can slack off most

[6] The full version of the paper was first printed in an internal reference magazine of the Economic Reform Institute of China, and the first part of the paper was published in *Economic Research*, No.1 (1987). The full paper was collected in my book *Prices, Markets and Entrepreneurs*, published by Peking University Press in 2006.

[7] My doctoral thesis is titled "Entrepreneurial Ability, Personal Wealth and the Assignment of the Principalship: An Entrepreneurial/Contractual Theory of the Firm," submitted to Oxford University in Hilary Term 1994. Its Chinese version was published by Shanghai People's Press in 1995. Its English version was published by Springer (Singapore) in 2018, with the title: *The Origin of the Capitalist Firm: An Entrepreneurial/Contractual Theory of the Firm.*

easily. When they make a decision, we lack a certain and hard indicator to supervise and restrain them. The only way to make them accountable for their own behavior is to make them assume risk. This means letting them keep the residual, but not have a fixed contractual income. Common workers have a contractual wage. Regardless how much money the firm makes, as long as common workers get to work on time and are not obviously negligent, then they have a right to a pre-determined wage. Entrepreneurs cannot take a salary. Only after everyone else takes what they should does the residual belong to the entrepreneur. This is the reason an entrepreneur's income is called residual income (profit). Only in this way do entrepreneurs have an incentive to make correct decisions and work hard.

Second, the difficulty in observing entrepreneurial ability entitles the capitalist to select and monitor the entrepreneur. In any society, only a small group of people truly have sufficient entrepreneurial talent. As for who has entrepreneurial talents, we also do not have a firm indicator to determine this, such as a test or a certification of entrepreneurial talents. To guarantee people with true entrepreneurial talents run firms, there must be a system that causes non-entrepreneurial people to not dare say they are entrepreneurial. At the same time, it must cause entrepreneurial people to dare start a business and innovate. I proved this system is capital-hiring-labor.

If any person could start a business with other people's money, meaning that person keeps the profits, but others take the losses, then too many non-entrepreneurial people will imitate entrepreneurs.

If a person must take risks with his or her own capital, then the question will be: Should I run the business, or have someone else do it? If that person's entrepreneurial ability is insufficient, then he or she will not pretend to have a greater ability.

Of course, many entrepreneurial people have insufficient capital. This gives owners of capital the power to select entrepreneurs.

When an entrepreneur has an idea, whether or not it succeeds in the end depends on other people providing capital. Only with capital can entrepreneurs shift resources. Given the world's uncertainty and the difficulty observing entrepreneurial talents, providers of capital must take risks. If they choose the wrong person and give capital to a non-entrepreneurial person that screws up the firm, then the capitalists will lose money. On the contrary, they have an incentive to select entrepreneurial people to manage the firm precisely because capitalists must assume risk. Therefore, the capitalist functions as a type of owner. This function further evolved into joint-stock companies of today.

So-called venture capital is the evaluation and selection of entrepreneurs. Naturally, investors supervise and constrain the entrepreneurs they invest in.

The implication of my theory is: When a country eliminates private capitalists, it actually also eliminates the mechanism for selecting entrepreneurs and the entrepreneurial environment. We see in countries without capitalists there are no rules that can guarantee the most entrepreneurial people run a company and the people that do manage companies cannot possibly be entrepreneurial. This is the circumstance in every country with a centrally planned economy.

The Government Can Substitute Neither for Entrepreneurs Nor for Capitalists

When decisions are made in centrally planned economies, they are made by the government, but that means by officials in the government. What firms produce, how they produce it, and who they produce it for are all determined by government officials. All production materials are owned by the state, and the state determines how to allocate them. The government replaces both the entrepreneur and the capitalist. Stated simply, the essence of the planned economy is an attempt to replace the entrepreneur and capitalist.

Every experiment with central economic planning has failed. Every country that has replaced entrepreneurs and capitalists with the government has failed. This is the cause of the failures of the Soviet Union and was the reason China and India had to reform. Here, I want to point out many people mistakenly believe India has always been a market economy. Actually, after India gained independence, the government followed the planned economy of the Soviet Union, but the degree of planning was not as high as in Eastern Europe or China. Some activity was left to private firms, but state planning was still dominant. By 1990, India already completed eight five-year plans. In the beginning of the 1990s, India started market-oriented reforms.

We will look back to explain the reason the government can replace neither entrepreneurs nor capitalists. The reasons are very simple. First, government officials do not have business talent like entrepreneurs. Entrepreneurs have special talents. They must make independent judgments about the future. The government needs people that can follow orders. Entrepreneurs do not fear making mistakes, whereas the government needs people that do not make mistakes. Entrepreneurs do the right thing, whereas government officials do things the right way. Government officials focus on procedures, not whether the substance is correct or worthwhile.

This point becomes clear upon observing government officials' actual performance. Any person that goes into the government and acts according to the methods set by the government cannot possibly become entrepreneurial.

Second, government officials do not have the type of incentive mechanism as entrepreneurs do. When an entrepreneur makes a mistake, he or she might go bankrupt or even commit suicide. As long as a government official respects procedure, no cost will be personally borne for poor decisions. Government officials are also not accountable for selecting wrong candidates like capitalists are. When a capitalist selects the wrong person, the capitalist assumes the risk. Giving your own money to a non-entrepreneurial person to run your firm or invest your money might leave you with nothing. When a government official gives public money to a non-entrepreneurial person, does the government official have any liability for losses? No! This is the reason nepotism is a serious problem for the selection of state-owned enterprise managers. We still have an incorrect viewpoint the government can be used to imitate the market. It is assumed stock ownership by government departments can imitate capital owners. This will never succeed because there will never be a way to make government officials take the risks for their own decisions like private capital owners do.

The government's inability to replace entrepreneurs and capitalists is related to entrepreneurs' innovation function.

All innovation is unforeseeable. The best technology and new products we use today were not foreseen by anyone 20 or 30 years ago. Looking back, when James Watt invented the steam engine more than 240 years ago, few people predicted the steam engine would be important. It was difficult for Watt to raise money. Only entrepreneurs like John Roebuck and Matthew Boulton were willing to risk bankruptcy to finance him. When George Stephenson invented the steam locomotive, no one thought the locomotive was much of anything. The British government mandated locomotives could not exceed the speed of horse carts. When Karl Benz invented the automobile over 130 years ago, no one thought much of automobiles. A local government in Germany mandated automobiles could not exceed walking pace. These examples are endless.

Innovation being unforeseeable means the government cannot plan for innovation. It can only be left to the trial and error of entrepreneurs in the market. It cannot be funded by the government. Only investors in the market can make judgments, and investors must be diverse. When governments want to play the role of entrepreneurs and investors, they must act according to a unified procedure, but there is no unified standard for innovation.

I will give two examples. The world-famous Cisco is the first example. The company was started by a husband and wife alumni of Stanford University. After they founded the company, they sought out funding. They went to 72 investors, but none of them were willing to invest. The 73rd investor they met with was willing to invest.

Another example is Mr. Ma Huateng of China. When he first started Tencent, it was difficult to find investors. I once met a famous venture capitalist that said he is filled with remorse when he thinks about Ma Huateng. The reason is Ma Huateng once asked him for US$500,000, but the venture capitalist was not optimistic about the technology and turned it down. Eventually, Ma Huateng found a South African venture capital firm called Naspers. Today, Tencent's biggest shareholder is not Ma Huateng, but instead is this South African investor.

These two stories tell us innovation cannot be foreseen and relies on diverse financing institutions. If I have an idea I want to turn into a product, I can keep going to the next person until I find someone to invest. I can do something to change humanity's destiny.

If the government established a committee to manage investments, then projects would be scored, and only the qualified ones would get investment. But who does the scoring? Would government officials do the scoring? Unless they are more entrepreneurial than entrepreneurs, then they would not have the ability to evaluate entrepreneurs' proposals. Would specialists do the scoring? Specialists are also not entrepreneurs, they are only experts in one area, but do not have the ability to judge market prospects. Numerous actual examples prove the way of thinking many specialists believe is unworkable is—in fact—workable, whereas the ideas they believe are workable often fail. Scoring by specialists will also be biased towards their own industry. Many specialists write reports on the prospects of technology in order to obtain research funding.

Can a committee composed of entrepreneurs make investment decisions on the government's behalf? This will also not work. The entrepreneurs recruited for this committee would be successful entrepreneurs, but an entrepreneur successful in the past is not the same as an entrepreneur in the future. In Joseph Schumpeter's words, innovation is creative destruction.[8] New products replace old products and new entrepreneurs replace old entrepreneurs. The appearance of trains had nothing to do with the people that made horse carriages for the postal system. In the end, railroads replaced horse carriages and even canals. Digital cameras were not developed by traditional camera manufacturers. The Internet was not developed by telecommunications companies. Major innovation was accomplished by new entrepreneurs.

Successful entrepreneurs easily think of their success as their starting point. Imagine the American government organized an industrial committee in 1990, chaired by Bill Gates, to decide the direction of government investment. What would the result have been? According to my understanding, Bill Gates was not optimistic about the Internet in 1990. If he was allowed to guide this industrial policy committee, the result would have been massive investment in personal computers, but not the Internet.

If China established an industry investment committee 15 years ago comprised of the then most famous, most respected corporate leaders such as Liu Chuanzhi (the founder of Lenovo) and Zhang Ruimin (CEO of Haier), what would the result be? Most likely, state investment would have primarily focused on televisions and personal computers. No matter how much the government values the opinions of specialists and entrepreneurs, it is impossible to overcome the dilemma of industrial policy.

The lack of innovation in Chinese enterprises is related to the government's attempt to replace entrepreneurs and capitalists. To this day, most investment funds are still controlled by the government and state-owned

[8] J. A. Schumpeter. 1942. *Capitalism, Socialism and Democracy*. Fifth edition, 1976. Chapter 7. London: Routledge.

banks. Among those famous Internet companies, tell me which one the Chinese government invested in? None of them were. China has the highest savings rate and highest reserves of any country, but none of the new technology companies were invested in using China's own capital. Instead, foreign capital invested in companies like Baidu, Alibaba, Tencent, and HC360. The government and state-owned banks cannot truly provide funding for innovation. At best, they can only maintain a circular economy.

The State-Owned Enterprise System Cannot Produce Entrepreneurs

In my 1986 article, I proposed the "impossibility of entrepreneurs under the state ownership system theorem." At that time, many people were under the illusion that if we turned state-owned enterprises into joint-stock companies, established holding companies, and implemented interlocking shareholding, then we could have the same market economy as Western capitalism. If we separated ownership and operation, then we would have entrepreneurs. I said this was impossible. Why is this impossible? I listed five reasons.[9]

The first reason is the impossibility of separating the government and enterprises. If state-owned enterprises exist, do not even think about having true separation of government and enterprises. Early in the 1980s, the direction of state-owned enterprise reform was separation, but even today we have not accomplished the separation of government and enterprises. We have not even accomplished the separation of party and enterprises. Relatively speaking, the separation of party and enterprises should be easier, yet we have still not accomplished it.[10] We do not have a way to cause the leaders of state-owned enterprises to make choices according to market methods.

The second reason is the impossibility of ownership constraints. The reason entrepreneurs in the market economy want to work hard and

[9] Pages 118–129, in Weiying Zhang's *Prices, Markets and Entrepreneurs*, published by Peking University Press, 2006.

[10] More recently, the Central Committee of the Communist Party of China reemphasized the party's absolute control of the SOEs and it even requires that the party secretary be chairman of the board of directors and all "important decisions" be pre-determined by the party committee of the enterprise.

innovate is because there is the ownership right constraint in the background. The state or government officials represent ownership rights, but they cannot truly constrain the operators of enterprises like capitalists can. They have their own incentive problems.

The third reason is the impossibility of resolving the short-term behavior of operators. The problem of short-term behavior exists in all state-owned enterprises. The leaders of state-owned enterprises only consider short-term issues. They cannot consider matters further than three years away. However, we know an entrepreneur without long-term considerations cannot truly create an outstanding or innovative enterprise. Why? Innovation is a sustained process. Three to five years might pass between new product inception and market acceptance. Ten or twenty years might be needed for a major technological breakthrough. If an entrepreneur does not consider the long run, he cannot actually create a truly innovative enterprise in the market economy.

How come leaders of state-owned enterprises cannot consider the long run? Because their positions are political appointments. The standard for appointment cannot be entrepreneurship, nor can it be long-term performance. The people with the power to appoint you will not allow you to continue because of good performance, nor will they remove you for bad performance. Whether or not a position is secure depends more on political factors and personal relationships. This is just the way leaders of state-owned enterprises are.

I have said before if the leaders of state-owned enterprises want job security, they should pursue mediocracy. Why? If they perform too well, someone with better relationships will take over the position. Of course, if they perform too poorly, that is also a problem. I know of a large state-owned conglomerate with five subsidiaries. One very capable leader turned the fifth-ranked subsidiary into the first-ranked subsidiary. In the end, the head of the conglomerate appointed his secretary to replace the very capable person. The former secretary turned the first-ranked subsidiary back into the fifth-ranked subsidiary. This type of example is prevalent. This is the reason I say managers of state-owned enterprises cannot be made to truly consider the long-term.

The fourth reason is the impossibility of hard budget constraints. We know state-owned enterprises have a systematic default, which is Hungarian economist Janos Kornai's concept of the "soft budget constraint."[11] Under the private ownership system, budget constraints are firm. If your earnings cannot offset your costs, then you will go bankrupt. What does a soft budget constraint mean? Even if your earnings are smaller than your costs, you can still survive because the government continues to provide support. Starting in the 1980s, our government attempted to continuously harden state-owned enterprise budgets, but there is still no resolution for this issue. As soon as a state-owned enterprise has a financial problem, the government certainly saves them. Of course, the larger the enterprise, the greater the government help. Currently, our fiscal budget includes subsidies for state-owned enterprise losses. Even certain very profitable state-owned enterprises still receive billions of yuan in "policy subsidies" every year.

The fifth reason is the impossibility of checks and balances between managers and employees. Starting in the 1980s, many managers and employees partnered to continuously increase their wages and bonuses. In today's terms, they partitioned state assets. This problem has yet to be resolved. Therefore, whenever a state-owned enterprise relies on a monopoly to make money, employee wages will always be higher than the market equilibrium wage. Part of that wage should be capital gains or consumer surplus, not labor income.

In addition to the five points from above, I also want to add state-owned enterprises cannot become innovative firms, nor the vectors of innovation. The reason this is impossible is related to both the previously mentioned short-term behavior of state-owned enterprise leaders and the required supervision of state-owned assets.

As was previously mentioned, innovation cannot be foreseen. It might succeed, but it also might fail. Imagine a state-owned enterprise leader that attempts innovation and fails. What should happen? Could we assume the government will forgive the person, because innovation might fail? If this were the case, then many state-owned enterprise leaders would attempt meaningless innovation (including buying patents from individuals), and thus embezzle state-owned assets.

[11] J. Kornai. 1980. *The Economics of Shortage*. North-Holland.

On the other hand, if the innovation fails and people are held personally liable, then will truly innovative people innovate? They will not. If 100 attempts are successful, but one is a failure, he might not just face disciplinary action, but also prison time. There have been examples of this. If this is the way it is, then truly innovative state-owned enterprise leaders will not innovate. Maintaining the status quo, as opposed to innovating, is the rational choice for state-owned enterprise leaders!

Entrepreneurs as the Center of Corporate Governance

In the early 1990s, corporate governance became a hot topic, even in China. The State Securities Regulatory Commission, China Banking Regulatory Commission, and the China Insurance Regulatory Commission put out a huge number of documents and policies to standardize corporate governance structures, especially for listed companies. However, in my view, there were problems with these documents and the theories behind them. Of course, the supporting theories were not developed by Chinese, but they still had problems. What was the problem? The problem is that it is a manager-centric model. This model understood corporate governance as an issue of incentivizing and constraining managers' behavior.[12] This issue is important, but it is not the most important. Going back to my previous statement, entrepreneurs are the core of the market economy. We need an entrepreneur-centric corporate governance model. An effective corporate governance structure must put the most entrepreneurial people in control of the corporation, as well as incentivize them to innovate and create. We do not want to just select a few non-corrupt people and be done with it. A defect in the current corporate governance theory is it puts too much energy, law, and policy on constraining entrepreneurship and making corporations more bureaucratic. If we continue with the current corporate governance model, I believe our corporations might be less corrupt in the future, but at the same time will be less entrepreneurial. At that point, sustainable economic development is impossible.

[12]Weiying Zhang. 2018. "Six understandings of corporate governance structure in the context of China." *The European Journal of Finance*, 24:16, 1375–1387. https://doi.org/10.1080/1351847X.2015.1113194.

Entrepreneur Transformation Depends on System Reform

The five viewpoints I discussed are a summary of the main viewpoints in my four books on enterprise theory.[13] As China is currently facing an economic transformation, I want to mention the transformation Chinese entrepreneurs are undergoing.

China's high levels of growth over the last 40 years depended on arbitrage entrepreneurs. They discovered disequilibrium in the market, so they organized people to provide products the market needs. They personally made money and social resource allocation efficiency improved, so the overall economy developed. Yet, as arbitrage opportunities are shrinking, China's sustainable economic growth in the future needs innovation entrepreneurs.[14] Even if we only grow at 5%, I believe we still need to rely on innovation. Innovation entrepreneurs are different from arbitrage entrepreneurs. Arbitrage entrepreneurs have existed since ancient times, but innovation entrepreneurs only came to be in the modern economy. Why? Because the degree of sensitivity to institutions is different for innovation and arbitrage.

Arbitrage entrepreneurs still exist under the harshest government controls. I will provide an example. There is a Northern Shaanxi folksong called "Gǎn Shēng Líng" composed by Zhang Tian'en. I am from the same county as he. That folksong talks about the people in traditional societies who sold things from one place to another. They were arbitrage entrepreneurs. During the "Cultural Revolution," Mr. Zhang Tian'en spent four years in prison for his speculation activities. Controls at that time were extremely harsh, yet people still sought out arbitrage, because some arbitrage activities could be done covertly. Innovation is different. Innovation requires three to five years, or even longer than a decade. It cannot be done covertly. Arbitrage can be done under cover of night,

[13] My four books on the enterprise theory and reform include: (1) *An Entrepreneurial/Contractual Theory of the Firm*; (2) *The Theory of the Firma and Chinese Enterprise Reform*; (3) *Understanding Corporates: Property Rights, Incentive and Governance*; and (4) *Entrepreneurs: The Kings of Economic Growth* (with Sheng Bin). All the current Chinese editions of the four books are published by Horizon Press under Shanghai People Press.

[14] Weiying Zhang. 2017. "China's Future Growth Depends on Innovation Entrepreneurs." *Journal of Chinese Economic and Business Studies*. Vol. 15, issue 1, 19–40.

unlike innovation. Without stable expectations, without effective protections for private property, and without rule of law mottos becoming actual practice, I believe China cannot transition towards an innovative country, because Chinese firms cannot have a true incentive to innovate.

Therefore, to make our country transition from growth driven by allocation efficiency to growth driven by innovation, we must implement large economic and political system reforms. Deng Xiaoping's economic system reform gave us some freedom and awoke arbitrage entrepreneurs. In the future, only with political and legal system reforms can our country produce true innovation entrepreneurs. This is the only way our country has hope.

CHAPTER 9

Future Economic Growth Depends on Innovation Entrepreneurs

The first thing that entrepreneurs do is discover disequilibrium, or discover opportunities to make money. The second function of entrepreneurs is to break equilibriums or create new potential equilibriums through innovation.

Over the last 30 years, what were Chinese entrepreneurs doing? Primarily, they discovered disequilibrium, which is also called "arbitrage." The key to China's future growth is whether or not Chinese entrepreneurs can transition from arbitrage to true innovation.[1]

* * *

First, I will make a judgment about two aspects of China's future economic growth. One aspect is the trend and the other aspect is the cycle. From the trend perspective, after the Chinese economy experienced more than 30 years of high growth, it must trend downwards. This is unavoidable. How much will it downgrade? People tend to accept that it is about 7% or so. I believe it will be much lower than this. High growth over the past 30 years was to a large degree our late-mover's advantage. This type of

[1] The original version of this chapter was written in August 2015.

W. Zhang, *Ideas for China's Future*,
https://doi.org/10.1007/978-981-15-4304-3_9

late-mover's advantage is disappearing. From the cyclical perspective—especially after 2009, when the Chinese government promoted extremely strong economic stimulus policies while the world's growth was either zero or negative—China maintained a 9.2% growth rate in that year, but we paid a price for this growth rate. We have not yet paid the full price, and the biggest price to pay has yet to come. This is the next issue we face. The problems caused by the stimulus policies appeared back in 2011, but we are still trying to avoid them. I believe they are unavoidable. From both the cyclical and trend perspective, China's economy will face tremendous difficulties within the next few years.

I like to use one of Hayek's metaphors. If a country uses monetary policy to maintain growth, it is like grabbing a tiger by the tail.[2] There are only two outcomes from grabbing a tiger's tail: Either you run with the tiger and exhaust yourself, or you let go and get eaten by the tiger. In June 2013, we might have wanted to let go of the tiger's tail, and were almost eaten in the so-called "money famine." We quickly grabbed tighter to the tiger's tail. However, this is not sustainable. The next problem to explode might be local debt. Local government debt is estimated to be twenty trillion yuan. Many local governments cannot repay the money they owe. This will impact firms. Many firms do projects for the government, but will not get paid. This is a problem from both the trend and cyclical perspective.

What will the economy be like over the long term? I believe the Chinese economy still has significant potential. Market scale, which includes industrialization and urbanization, is its greatest potential. Over 200 years ago, Adam Smith emphasized the importance of market scale. Market scale brings about division of labor. Division of labor brings about technological progress. Technological progress brings about economic growth. However, what do all of these depend on? They depend on the entrepreneurial spirit, not government bureaucrats or monetary policy. Today, the new products we consume and the new technology we utilize all grew out of the entrepreneurial spirit. Unfortunately, many people still pin their hopes of maintaining economic growth on monetary policy, fiscal policy, and government investment. If we cannot truly bring into play the role of the entrepreneurial spirit, then whether or not we can achieve the 7% growth previously mentioned is a problem.

[2] Cited from page 54, *The Essential Hayek* by Donald J. Boudreaux, published by Fraser Institute, 2014. Also see F. A. Hayek. 1978 (1972). *A Tiger by the Tail*. London: Institute of Economic Affairs.

What do entrepreneurs do? I have summarized two functions. First, they discover disequilibrium. Second, they create disequilibrium. In economics, "equilibrium" refers to achieving the most efficient utilization of all resources so that there are no opportunities for profit. However, this is not the case in reality. The first thing that entrepreneurs do is discover disequilibrium, or discover opportunities to make money. They pursue opportunities to make money and as a result resource allocation efficiency improves. As more and more people take advantage of this opportunity, profit gradually disappears, so the market trends towards equilibrium. The second function of entrepreneurs is to break equilibriums or create new potential equilibriums. For example, everyone uses a computer, so the computer market became saturated. There was not much money to be made anymore. After Apple produced the iPad, it broke the original equilibrium, so money could be made. Breaking equilibriums primarily depends on innovation. Of course, these two functions are often combined.[3]

From this perspective, what were Chinese entrepreneurs doing over the last 30 years? Primarily, they discovered disequilibrium, also known as "arbitrage." There are three types of arbitrage. The first is inter-market arbitrage, such as discovering that the price of oranges in Sichuan is low, but high in Beijing, so money is made by transporting oranges from Sichuan to Beijing. Merchants are this type of entrepreneur. The second type is timing arbitrage, such as expecting that some type of product will become expensive next year or the year after, so it is either produced or bought today and sold later. Classic arbitrage is financial market arbitrage. Financial arbitrage behavior is similar to speculation. The third type of arbitrage occurs between the factor market and the product market. When there are a lot of people with nothing to do while at the same time there are shortages, then money can be made by organizing the people with nothing to do to produce the products in short supply.

Over the last 30 years, that was mostly the way it was. Speculation and trade made money. Town and village enterprises (TVEs) made money.

[3] The first function is referred to the Kirznerian entrepreneurship and the second function is referred to the Schumpeterian entrepreneurship. See Israel Kirzner. 1973. *Competition and Entrepreneurship*. Chicago and London: University of Chicago Press; Israel Kirzner. 1992. *The Meaning of Market Process: Essays in the Development of Modern Austrian Economics*. London: Routledge; J. A. Schumpeter. 1934. *The Theory of Economic Development*. 1980 edition. London, Oxford and New York: Oxford University Press. J. A. Schumpeter. 1942. *Capitalism, Socialism and Democracy*. Fifth edition, 1976. London: Routledge.

However, room for this is becoming smaller and smaller. There is already overcapacity in most traditional industries, and many things that are produced are unsellable. Because the market is saturated, room for arbitrage is shrinking. Of course, there was some innovation in the past, but it was only imitative innovation. It was bringing foreign technology into the Chinese market. The room for imitation is also shrinking. The late-mover's advantage is slowly disappearing. Therefore, the key to China's future growth is whether or not Chinese entrepreneurs can transition from arbitrage behavior to true innovation.

What is innovation? It is having an idea that most people do not have. Most people will disagree or not acknowledge the idea, but you are able to turn it into a product or service that the market can accept. At that point, you make a contribution to economic growth and also make money for yourself. Today's economic growth depends on many products that no one thought of 30 years ago. Similarly, people have not yet thought of the primary industries that will grow national economies over the next 30 years. Entrepreneurs must come up with them. One hundred years ago, automobiles existed, but they were products for the wealthy. No one thought the common man should have automobiles. However, Henry Ford thought the common man should have automobiles, so he created the assembly line and produced the Model T. More than forty years ago, Bill Gates wanted to create software. When he believed everyone would use this software in the future, very few people agreed. Most people do not know what the economic growth points will be in 10 years. This is the reason we need entrepreneurs.

How can we develop the entrepreneurial spirit? It relies on institutions. Currently, China's institutions create many economic and political obstacles to entrepreneurship.

In terms of the economic system, the first issue is the state-owned sector is too big and too strong. The state-owned sector's strength is incompatible with the market economy. With a state-owned sector as large as the one in China, creating a so-called fair competition environment is impossible.

Second, the government regulates too much. Which rights belong to the people and which powers belong to the government is still unclear. Our country's system nationalized private rights under the planned economy. Later reforms were just the continuous return of private rights to individuals, but there is still work to do. For example, massive amounts of government regulations harm people's freedom to create and start a business.

Third, the financial market is unfree. Massive investments and a long period of time are required to turn an entrepreneur's idea into a product or to form a market. If finance is unfree, innovation will not receive sufficient resources. Fortunately, we know that over the last twenty years, many foreign funds, such as private equity and venture capital, entered China and did us a big favor. However, we can still see China's massive savings are inefficiently used, such as loans to the American government. State-owned enterprises also control tremendous financial resources. The cost of debt for state-owned enterprises is much lower than for private enterprises. Interest rates for state-owned enterprises are 5% or 6%, but 10% or more for private firms.

Fourth, private property rights are not effectively protected. This is not only a legal issue, but often an issue in the administration of justice. As soon as private entrepreneurs are accused of a crime, many of them are arrested and lose their property. This is illegal. That person's property must be dealt with after the court makes a decision, but the government does not respect this kind of rule. Even when that person is released with no charges, his property is already lost.

In the political system, the first issue is the judiciary is not independent, so power is not contained. In a certain sense, our non-implementation of the judicial independence principle is related to the previous statement that property is not protected. Currently, people with power are unrestrained in their rule over others. This is a serious problem. Second, rent seeking and corruption are an issue. Excessive government power certainly leads to corruption. We must not mistakenly believe entrepreneurs solely rely on innovation or arbitrage to make money. Actually, some people rely on rent seeking, including some high technology companies. Some people rely on a good application for a government program and good relationships to obtain state resources. This situation is extremely serious in policy-supported sectors.

In summary, we say China's future economic growth depends on the entrepreneurial spirit, but how we develop and liberate the entrepreneurial spirit depends on further reform in our economic and political systems.

CHAPTER 10

Entrepreneurship Depends on Culture and the Rule of Law

The process of economic growth for a country or a society is centered on the entrepreneur. Market discovery, industry creation, technological progress, and turning higher incomes into new markets all are inseparable from the role of the entrepreneur.

What is the role of government? It is to provide a good institutional environment for entrepreneurs to discover markets, create industries, and transform technologies. Specifically, this involves effective protections of private property and free competition.[1]

* * *

In 1776, Adam Smith published *The Wealth of Nations.* The core thought related to economic growth was: Socio-economic development and increases in wealth rely on innovation and technological progress. We see that the history of humanity is the history of continuous development through innovation and technological progress. What do innovation and technological progress depend on? They depend on the division of labor. The more cellular division of labor is, the faster technological progress will

[1] The original version of this chapter was written in August 2012.

W. Zhang, *Ideas for China's Future*,
https://doi.org/10.1007/978-981-15-4304-3_10

be. The division of labor spoken of here includes the division of labor along the industry chain, and also includes regional division of labor, where different regions do different things. What determines division of labor? Market scale. The greater the scale of the market, the more cellular division of labor will be. The more cellular division of labor is, the faster technological progress will be. The faster technological progress is, the faster the economy will grow. The faster the economy grows, the higher incomes will be and the greater market scale will be. This type of cycle drives economic growth.

What does this cycle rely on to get started? It relies on entrepreneurs. However, Adam Smith did not touch upon this. In the process of economic growth, from market scale and division of labor to innovation and turning income into markets, everything relies on the entrepreneur.

First, we will look at market scale. The market does not objectively exist. Entrepreneurs discover and create it. The market has many potential elements, including population size, but before the appearance of entrepreneurs, many markets do not exist. For example, apparently the two most important inventions by the Japanese in the last century were instant noodles and karaoke. These were markets discovered by Japanese entrepreneurs. Most people have eaten noodles, but in this era of fast lives, consumers do not think of the type of noodles we need to eat. Entrepreneurs do. The Japanese entrepreneurs turned instant noodles into an industry, but actually they created a market. We see that all of the great entrepreneurs created markets. Google and Facebook each created a market. We could say that the most important work of entrepreneurs is to discover markets and create markets. They turn potential demand in places others do not see into actual demand.

Second, at the same time that markets are discovered and created, new divisions of labor are formed. With this, the major role of entrepreneurs is to create industries. He might turn division of labor within the firm into the activity of an independent firm. If firms currently do something for themselves that I can do better, then I can form an independent part of the value chain. Microsoft is a classic example. The software industry did not exist before Bill Gates, but software existed. IBM did both hardware and software until Bill Gates turned software into an independent industry. After that, his accomplishment was not limited to Microsoft, but also countless software firms. Microsoft built a platform for many new firms to join and turn the software industry into a huge industry. This is also the case for Apple Computers. Steve Jobs created an industry, with many suppliers. The iPhone created many app industries. We could say for certain great entrepreneurs are entrepreneurs that create industries.[2]

Third, what does technological innovation rely on? It also relies on entrepreneurs. The discovery of markets and creation of industries mentioned above are not possible without technological progress and innovation. Using instant noodles as an example, without technological innovation above and beyond the traditional way of preparing noodles, the instant noodle industry could not exist. The instant noodle industry appeared only after there was equipment and technological innovation to produce instant noodles. Therefore, we say that the role of entrepreneurs in the process of technological progress is similarly important.

Fourth, after technological progress brings about economic growth and everyone becomes wealthy, what is an entrepreneur to do? He turns new wealth into new markets. After people's income levels increase, we cannot produce according to the original consumption pattern. If that were the case, society could not possibly progress. Therefore, the major role of entrepreneurs in economic growth is to turn continuously increasing wealth into new markets. We often talk about economic transformations, which is actually the way in which entrepreneurs create new products and new industries along with increases in incomes.

This is the process of economic growth for a country or society as I understand it. Entrepreneurs have a central role. Market discovery, industry creation, technological progress, or turning increased income into new markets are all inseparable from the role of entrepreneurs.

What is the role of government? It is to provide a good institutional environment for entrepreneurs to discover markets, create industries, and transform technology. Specifically, this means private property and effective protections for free competition.

Currently, there is a competitive trend among various regions in China. Local governments often emphasize geographic location when seeking out their competitive advantage. However, I want to emphasize a few points.

[2] Walter Issacson provides an excellent story of how a group of technological entrepreneurs created various information industries. See Walter Issacson, *The Innovations: How a Group of Hackers, Geniuses and Greeks created the Digital Revolution*, published by Simon & Schuster; Reprint edition (October 6, 2015).

First, the importance of geography has changed in different parts of history. From the perspective of history, Western civilization was born between the Tigris and Euphrates Rivers and Chinese civilization was born between the Yellow and Yangtze Rivers. The Renaissance occurred in Italy, the Industrial Revolution began in Great Britain, and even China's Reform and Opening primarily occurred along the coast in the first 30 years. These all prove the importance of geographic location. However, along with technological progress, geographic location became less and less important, especially in the twenty-first century with the development of airplanes, high-speed rail, highways, and information technology. In my many years of economic research, anywhere I go that talks about geographic advantage is basically always a relatively backwards place. If we have good institutions, we do not need to speak of geographic advantages. Entrepreneurs have a clearer view of geographic advantage than anyone. There are many more suitable examples to the contrary. Zhejiang Province's economy is currently very developed, but what geographic or resource advantage does it have? Who would have thought Yiwu City would become world-famous for merchandise distribution? We would not have made this determination based on its resources.

Now, the entrepreneurial spirit is becoming more and more important. The entrepreneurial spirit relies on the rule of law and cultural environment. I want to specifically emphasize that it does not rely on preferential policies. Some localities give preferential treatment to entrepreneurs. When entrepreneurs travel by plane to those areas, they do not have to go through normal airport security. Are you willing to invest in a place like this? On the contrary, I would not, because it does not have any rules to follow. From an entrepreneur's perspective, whether or not he feels safe in the rule of law and cultural environment is most important. In many places, the government often comes knocking on the door, so entrepreneurs do not dare to invest there.

Here, it must be noted that liberty is a premise of security. Security without liberty is meaningless. For example, without considering liberty, people in prison are safest. They are not afraid of their property being stolen, but that type of life is meaningless. Entrepreneurs, like any individual, require safety but premised on freedom. The liberty spoken of here is equal liberty. It is not liberty for one group of people that is deprived from another group. It is a right, not a privilege. It means that as long as we do not harm others, we have the right to do anything we believe will make a contribution to society (or consumer demand).

We also must discuss industrial policy. Industrial policies often benefit specific groups but not everyone. The result is rent seeking and corruption. Certain entrepreneurs are experts at rent seeking. As long as the government implements preferential policies, they think of ways to get this money from the government. They are not thinking of ways to produce a better product for the consumer. Therefore, it is said that industrial policy has had little positive effect in China over the last 30 years. From another perspective, precisely because it did not play a role, was China's economy able to perform well. If industrial policy played a role in the past, the Chinese would still be watching analog televisions.[3]

I must remind everyone a troublesome issue faced by entrepreneurs is government personnel turnover. Entrepreneurs spend considerable effort signing a contract with a mayor or party secretary to invest in an area. As soon as it is ready, the new officers in the government often do not recognize the contract. Or, they might not say they do not recognize the contract, but they put it off for a few years, so nothing happens. This is a big problem for entrepreneurs investing all over China. The reason they lack confidence or are not willing to invest is related to this situation.

What is this thing called modern governance? Modern government is a legal person, it is a non-personalized organization. If the commitments of one government place no constraints on the next government, then this is not modern governance. In ancient times, the power of government belonged to one person. When that person died, it was all over. We must recognize, as a modern country, bureaucrats only occupy a position. Their power comes from this position. Everything they do in this position represents the organization. Any commitment made by one government should constrain the next government.

In summary, the most important role of entrepreneurs is to develop markets. The government's responsibility is to create a good environment for entrepreneurs.

[3] There is the widely reported debate on industrial policy between Weiying Zhang and Justin Y. F. Lin in fall 2016. See "China's Industrial Policy: Plan V Market.", *The Economist*, Nov. 15th, 2016; Weiying Zhang: "Why I oppose Industrial Policy; Debate with Justin Yifu Lin." *Comparative Studies* (*Bijiao*), (2016) No.6:174–2002; Justin Y. F. Lin: "Industrial Policy and Economic Development: Perspectives from New Structural Economics." *Comparative Studies* (*bijiao*), (2016) No.6: 163–173.

CHAPTER 11

Innovation Requires Good Institutions

Innovation is a process full of uncertainty. Whether or not an innovation can succeed cannot ex-ante *be predicted. The cycle of innovation is long. These two features of innovation resolve it to require a type of institution that causes entrepreneurs and investors to have stable expectations over the long term. If a society does not have effective protections for intellectual property or a relatively robust rule of law, then it will be difficult for innovation to occur.*

China's current system is suitable for arbitrage, but not innovation. Apart from property rights protection, the following three other systematic and policy obstacles to innovation also need to be cleared: government regulation, the Anti-Monopoly Law, and industrial policy.[1]

* * *

Entrepreneurship drives economic growth. How do entrepreneurs drive economic growth? First, they discover the market's disequilibrium and engage in arbitrage. This causes resources to be allocated more efficiently. Second, they disrupt existing equilibrium through innovation. This pushes the production possibility frontier outward. These two aspects are

[1] The original version of this chapter was written in September 2016.

W. Zhang, *Ideas for China's Future*,
https://doi.org/10.1007/978-981-15-4304-3_11

extremely important and require certain institutional conditions. The most basic systematic conditions are liberty, private property, and the rule of law. However, I want to emphasize innovation has higher requirements for the institutions. The reason is that innovation has two basic features: A high level of uncertainty and a long cycle.

Innovation is a process full of uncertainty. It is very similar to scientific discovery in that it cannot be predicted. Many people mix uncertainty and risk together, but they are different.

In 1921, American economist Frank Knight differentiated the two.[2] Stated simply, risk follows statistical laws, whereas uncertainty does not. Whether or not an innovation can succeed cannot *ex-ante* be predicted. Not only is innovation itself difficult to predict, but the value of innovation depends on a series of forthcoming innovation. For example, IBM developed the computer in 1945, but it did not have any true commercial value at the time, so IBM did not rapidly take it to the market. At that time, computers worked on vacuum tubes, which were both expensive and slow. Economically, they were inefficient. A few years later, transistors, and especially integrated circuit technology, made computers have true commercial value. For this reason, computers became the driving force of information technology. Uncertainty means having no way to plan beforehand. Many people are innovating, but most fail. A few succeed, and we remember the stories of success. It is easy to forget the stories of failure.

The cycle of innovation is long.[3] James Watt drafted a design of the steam engine in 1764 but applied for a patent five years later. The steam engine was brought to market in 1775, but Matthew Boulton and James Watt's company did not make a profit until 1786. The Wright Brothers invented the airplane in 1903, but the airplane did not enter commercial use until 33 years later. Even a simple innovation like the disposable diaper took Procter & Gamble 10 years to develop and commercialize. Today, some Internet companies can get money from investors more quickly than from customers. Their innovation still has a long way to go for profitability.

[2] Frank Knight. 1921. *Risk, Uncertainty and Profit.* Houghton Mifflin Company. Martino Fine Books (2014).

[3] Nathan Rosenberg. 1994. *Exploring the Black Box: Technology, economics and history.* Chapter 4. Cambridge, UK: Cambridge University Press; Nathan Rosenberg. 1976. *Perspectives on Technology.* Chapter 4. Cambridge, UK: Cambridge University Press.

Why is the innovation cycle so long? Many people misunderstand innovation as obtaining patents. Historically, obtaining the patent is only the first step of innovation. We could say it is the first step in a long journey. Innovating and inventing are different. Obtaining a patent is an invention. Innovation gives commercial value to patents. A series of obstacles must be overcome to give patents commercial value. Features have to be improved, quality has to be increased, and costs must be reduced until the market can accept it. Innovation must also overcome traditional obstacles. Many companies do not die during the invention process, instead they die during the commercialization process. Watt obtained the steam engine patent in 1769, but it did not stop his investor, John Roebuck, from going bankrupt in 1773.

The uncertainty and long cycle of innovation conditions it to lose money in the beginning. Arbitrage makes money from the start, but competition causes profits to decrease. This trends towards what economists call "equilibrium." Innovation loses money in the beginning, but after a certain period, when you are proven successful, you begin to make money. As you make more and more money, imitators appear and reduce the amount of money that can be made. Stated simply, if money can be made from the beginning doing something, then it is not innovation. Losses might be incurred over a very long time. Today, many Internet companies have obtained billions of dollars in investments but have still not made money.

The two features of innovation described above resolve it to require a type of institution that causes entrepreneurs and investors to have stable expectations over the long term. Arbitrage can be done quickly, sometimes even within days. In financial markets, arbitrage can be completed in seconds. Innovation takes years, sometimes decades. It is the pursuit of things that take years to see to fruition. If a society does not have effective protections for intellectual property or a relatively robust rule of law, then it will be difficult for innovation to occur. There is special emphasis on the financial system due to the question of who pays for the early losses incurred. Consumers will not pay the bill, but investors will. Innovation has very high requirements for the financial system. I believe China's current system is suitable for arbitrage, but not innovation.

Research has shown effective legal protections of intellectual property rights not only determine the speed of innovation, but also the direction of innovation.[4] If a country has weak protections for intellectual property, then innovation will primarily be focused on areas with alternative means of protection, such as commercial secrets. Jurists have more to say on this subject, so I will not discuss it much. Below, I will focus on the three other systematic and policy obstacles to innovation: Government regulation, the Anti-Monopoly Law, and industrial policy.

Since the Industrial Revolution began in Great Britain, government regulation has been a major factor inhibiting innovation. According to Joseph Schumpeter, innovation is creative destruction. It means new products replace old products, new firms replace old firms, and new industries replace old industries, so it will upset vested interests. Vested interests often call for government regulation as a way to protect their own interests. Government regulation is done in the name of protecting the interests of consumers and maintaining market order, but in essence it protects vested interests.[5] It is no surprise many regulatory measures from the start of the Industrial Revolution to the present have stifled innovation.

I will provide a few examples from China. In the 1980s, the Ministry of Posts and Telecommunications explicitly prohibited individual use of fax machines in households. Non-compliance led to a large fine. The Ministry of Broadcasting and Television prohibited residential installation and use of satellite dishes. Today, innovation in new media is also restricted in various ways. The Ministry of Transportation sought opinions on taxi reform. Even though it was not implemented, it reflected the severity of the problem. Online ride sharing was resisted by traditional vested interests, especially companies that operate taxis.

Second, I will specifically mention innovation hindered by the Anti-Monopoly Law. The "Anti-Monopoly Law" should actually be called the "Anti-Competition Law" because everything it opposes are means of competing in the market.[6] Why did this occur? Economists are at fault!

[4] Petra Moser. 2005. "How Do Patent Laws Influence Innovation? Evidence from Nineteenth-Century World's Fairs." American Economic Review. Vol. 95, No. 4: 1214–1236.

[5] For historical cases of the vested interest-initiated political resistance, see: Mark Zachary Taylor. 2016. *The Politics of Innovation: Why Some Countries Are Better than others at Science & Technology*. Chapter 7. New York: Oxford University Press; Calstous Juma. 2016. *Innovation and Its Enemies: Why People Resist New Technologies*. Oxford and New York: Oxford University Press.

[6] Weiying Zhang. 2015. *The Logic of the Market: An Insider's View of Chinese Economic Reform*. Chapter 4. Washington, DC: Cato Institute.

Economists got the definitions of monopoly and competition totally wrong. What do economics textbooks describe as the best competition? Perfect competition! So-called perfect competition refers to numerous vendors producing equivalent products with equivalent costs. This type of perfect competition is incompatible with innovation. As long as there is innovation, competition is necessarily "imperfect", and may even lead to so-called "monopoly." When you innovate, you do things differently than others. Market share is the best test of innovation. Successful innovation will attract more customers. However, according to the definition in traditional economics, having more customers limits competition. Historically, many innovative companies have been investigated, or even broken up, by anti-monopoly laws. Some have said if you want to understand which American companies have been the most innovative, just look at which companies have been investigated for anti-trust violations. They have been the most outstanding companies, such as Standard Oil, Alcoa, IBM, Microsoft, Google, and so on. They have all been investigated or punished for anti-trust violations.

After James Watt invented the steam engine, Boulton's company was the sole producer. It was a total monopoly with 100% market share. Watt and Boulton did not charge very much for the steam engine. They only charged the cost of the product plus one-third of the savings from using steam power. This appears very reasonable. However, this made a lot of users dissatisfied. They organized a movement to petition Parliament to cancel Watt's steam engine patent. How did Watt respond? He complained bitterly about it:

> *They charge us with establishing a monopoly, but if a monopoly, it is one by means of which their mines are made more productive than ever they were before … They say it is inconvenient for mining interest to be burden with the payment of engine dues, just as it is inconvenient for the person who wishes to get at my purse that I should keep my beeches-pocket button … We have no power to compel anybody to erect our engine. What, then, will parliament say to any man who comes there to complain of a grievance he can avoid?*[7]

[7]Quoted from Paul Mantoux's *The Industrial Revolution in the Eighteenth Century*, p. 331, published by Routledge (London and New York), 2006.

Watt was an inventor more than an entrepreneur, but his understanding of so-called monopoly accusations was quite deep.

When loss-making Uber sold its China operations to Didi, the Ministry of Commerce undertook an anti-monopoly investigation. Imagine if Uber China went out of business instead of merging with Didi. Should the Ministry of Commerce investigate? Probably not. Nevertheless, the result is the same. Uber China merged with Didi because it could not compete or maintain operations, so it exited the market.

Economists are accustomed to using the number of firms or degree of concentration to determine the degree of monopoly. Historically, there has not been much of a relationship between the degree of competition in a market and how many firms are in the market. Everyone is using WeChat, of which Tencent is the only provider, but it must continuously innovate because there are people waiting to replace them. If Ma Huateng thought of himself as a monopolist that could exploit customers, I believe he would be done for within a year or two. No firm can truly monopolize a market without protection from the government. If the government implements protective measures, even with quite a few firms, there will not be full competition. There are more than 600 firms in China's publishing industry, but can we call it a free market?

Monopolies must be opposed, but what we must oppose is monopolies created by laws and policies, not so-called monopolies formed by market competition. If we oppose so-called monopolies formed on the market, we actually oppose innovation. All innovation forms monopolies according to economists' definition. The greater the innovation, the more commercially valuable the innovation is, the greater the degree of monopoly. If you make a small innovation, it will not have a big role. Subversive innovation will form monopolies, such as railroads and automobiles at the time.

The third issue is industrial policy. I have said before industrial policy is determined to fail because of humanity's limited knowledge and the distorted incentive mechanism. Therefore, the government should not implement industrial policy.[8] Here, I will discuss how industrial policy inhibits innovation. Overall, there are four aspects.

[8]Weiying Zhang. (2016). "Why I oppose Industrial Policy; Debate with Justin Yifu Lin." *Comparative Studies* (*Bijiao*), (2016) No.6:174–2002.

First, industrial policy leads to rent-seeking behavior. If the government has an industrial policy, it will discriminate against different industries and firms. People that excel at rent-seeking will make relationships with the government. People that obtain preferential treatment are often rent-seeking experts, not innovators.

Second, industrial policy makes arbitrage more profitable than innovation. Innovation is risky. Currently, many manufacturers of so-called new energy vehicles are better at obtaining subsidies through policy arbitrage than innovation. The media has already reported on this. This is not a new phenomenon. From ancient times to the present, this problem exists whenever the government gives special treatment.

Third, industrial policy misleads the investment choices of entrepreneurs. Originally, what entrepreneurs invest in or the direction of innovation depends on market prospects and the future profitability of products. Now, they do not look at market prospects, but instead look at which field will obtain government support and funding. This is the same for academic research applications. I once met a professor that was applying for a research topic. I asked him if he was interested in this topic. He said he was not very interested in it. I asked him if he thought it was significant research. He said it was not. I asked him why he applied. He said it was easy to apply for government money. Therefore, a large amount of state scientific funding does not support significant research, instead it allures people to apply for funding. Its contribution is not up to the mark.

Finally, industrial policy easily leads to unfair competition. Firms that obtain government support are at an advantage to those that do not. Even firms with superior products, better quality, and lower costs still cannot compete with firms that obtain government support.

In addition to intellectual property protections and the rule of law, reforming the regulatory system, reforming the Anti-Monopoly Law, and abolishing industrial policy are extremely important for innovation. If we cannot make meaningful reforms, China's innovation potential cannot be brought into full play.

First, industrial policy leads to rent-seeking behavior. If the government has an industrial policy, it will [illegible] industries and firms. People that [illegible] make relationships with the government. Despite [illegible] are often [illegible]

[illegible]

CHAPTER 12

The Law of God and Law of the King

No one should use "the law" as a pretext for unjust action. When the law does not satisfy natural law, when you must choose between conscience and the law, you should choose to stand on the side of natural law.

The rule of law is not equivalent to rule by law. The rule of law is foremost "rule of natural law." If the law does not satisfy natural law and the judiciary does not promote conscience, then true rule of law cannot exist. A society with no laws is not a good society, but a society with laws but no natural law is also not a good society![1]

* * *

[1] The original version of this chapter was written in August 2013.

W. Zhang, *Ideas for China's Future*,
https://doi.org/10.1007/978-981-15-4304-3_12

The Zeng Chengjie Case

The secret execution of Zeng Chengjie for "crowdfunding fraud" sent shockwaves through Chinese society.[2] Among entrepreneurs, there was a sense of mourning. We lived in the same world, under the same judicial system. With the possibility what happened to Mr. Zeng could happen to any of us, how could we not feel a sense of grief?

This type of feeling was described by Mencius 2000 years ago as "a feeling of commiseration." More than two-hundred fifty years ago, Adam Smith described this feeling as "sympathy." Mencius said: "The feeling of commiseration belongs to all men." Adam Smith began *The Theory of Moral Sentiments* by saying:

> *How selfish soever man may be supposed, there are evidently some principles in his nature, which interest him in the fortune of others, and render their happiness necessary to him, though he derives nothing from it except the pleasure of seeing it. Of this kind is pity or compassion, the emotion which we feel for the misery of others, when we either see it, or are made to conceive it in a very lively manner. … this sentiment, like all the other original passions of human nature, is by no means confined to the virtuous and humane, though they perhaps may feel it with the most exquisite sensibility. The greatest ruffian, the most hardened violator of the laws of society, is not altogether without it.* (p. 11)[3]

Commiseration and sympathy are significant for our understanding of social morals and justice. Mencius believed the feeling of commiseration is benevolence. Adam Smith believed sympathy is the psychological source

[2] Zeng Chengjie, born in 1958, was an entrepreneur from Hunan Province and the founder of the San Guan Property Development Company. In 2003, he was invited by the government of Xiangxi Autonomous District to invest in that region and allowed to raise some funds from the public for this investment. His investors included some local officials. Later, when his company fell into financial trouble, he was charged for "crowdfunding fraud" in 2008. He once made an installment repayment deal with investors. But that deal was rejected by the local authority. Zeng was sentenced to death by the Changsha City Court in May 2011 and the death sentence was confirmed by the Hunan Provincial High Court in December 2011. He was secretly executed without notifying his family on July 11, 2013 after final approval from China's Supreme Court.

[3] Adam Smith. 2007 (1759). *The Theory of Moral Sentiment.* edit by Knud hasskonssen. Cambridge UK: Cambridge University Press.

of human morals. It is precisely the resonance of other people's emotions in our hearts that cause humans to have a conscience. It is precisely the respect for fair spectators, great judges, and arbitrators that gives us justice.

The sympathy throughout society for Zeng Chengjie after his sentencing proves that our society's conscience has not yet been totally destroyed.

Is Natural Law Greater Than Positive Law?

Why was Zeng Chengjie sentenced to death? Because he "violated the law," or at least the court believed he did. One question is: When Mr. Zeng raised money on behalf of the local government, did he know he was doing something illegal? I cannot speculate well on this point. Regardless, the court will not waive a person's crimes because of ignorance, although the judge will consider this when determining the sentence. The question I am more concerned about is: Even if he really violated the law on which the court's decision is based, and was aware of it, was his punishment just?

To answer this question, we must understand the relationship between principles and laws. Ten years ago, I proposed such an analytical framework.[4] There are two standards for evaluating a behavior. The first is whether it is legitimate (rational). The second is whether it is legal. Everything we do can be categorized in four ways: legitimate and legal, legitimate and illegal, legal and illegitimate, and illegal and illegitimate. In a normal society, basically everything is in the first or fourth category. This means legitimate activities are legal and illegal activities are also illegitimate. At that point, making decisions is relatively easy, because respecting the law is respecting justice. However, in a society like ours, there are many second- and third-category activities. Sometimes, the proportion exceeds the first and second category. This is a dilemma people that live in our society face and is also the reason we must reform.

What academia calls "positive law" or "legislative law," the Chinese traditionally call "*wáng fǎ*" (law of the king) or "*lǜ fǎ*." Whether or not something is legal or not is relatively clear, or at least government officials and judges believe it is clear.

[4] Also see Chap. 4 in the current book.

What academia calls "natural law," the Chinese call "*tiānlǐ*," "*gōnglǐ*," "*dàolǐ*," or "*tiānjīngdìyì*." In the West, natural law is also referred to as the law of God or the law of reason. They are the basic meaning of conscience, justice, and virtue. So-called natural law is the most common laws or conditions that human beings discovered through reason and emotion for the survival and development of mankind. Examples are the death penalty for murder, repayment of debts, gratitude, sincerity, the right to self-defense, and the right to pursue happiness.

Is natural law greater than positive law? Yes. Natural law is humanity's collective wisdom. It naturally evolved through history. People commonly acknowledge it. It is consistent with human nature and reflected in people's conscience. Positive law is set by government. The government is composed of people that are as selfish, nepotistic, ignorant, arrogant, and emotional as the average person. If positive law is not restrained by natural law, then there will be unjust law, even "legal tyranny."[5]

Natural law is the "meta rule" of positive law, or what Immanuel Kant called a "categorical imperative."[6] Natural law being greater than positive law means only laws consistent with natural law have legitimacy and should be respected. The reason humanity needs laws enacted by government is because natural laws are somewhat vague. It is difficult to operate with only principles and no rules. In other words, positive law should be the specification and operation of natural law, not its negation. For example, even though we all know that we should keep to the right when driving, without stripes down the middle of the road, it would be relatively difficult to determine who was at fault for a traffic violation. If the government painted the line too far to the left or too far to the right so that cars coming from the other direction could not pass, then this type of rule does not conform to natural law and cannot possibly be respected.

[5] Hayek identifies natural law with *nomos* (the law of liberty), which has evolved and was discovered bottom-up, and the legislative law with *thesis,* which is made by the government and top-down imposed. See F. A. Hayek. 2013 (1973, 1976 and 1979). *Law, Legislation and Liberty.* Routledge Classics Edition. London and New York: Routledge.

[6] Kant's categorical imperative consists of the two principles: (1) Act in such a way that you treat humanity, whether in your own person or in the person of any other, never merely as a means to an end, but always at the same time as an end; and (2) Act only according to that maxim whereby you can at the same time will that it should become a universal law. Kant, Immanuel (1993) [1785]. *Grounding for the Metaphysics of Morals.* Translated by Ellington, James W. (3rd ed.). Hackett. p. 30 and p. 36, respectively.

From ancient times to the present, the supremacy of natural law over positive law has been rooted in everyone's basic consciousness. People despise those that are irrational, not those that are law-breakers. This is why we often say, "With reason, you can go anywhere; but cannot take one step without it." We do not say, "With the law, you can go anywhere; but cannot take one step without it."

The Three Basic Principles of Natural Law

Since ancient times, natural law lived in people's hearts. The expression and argumentation of natural law is the work of thinkers. Scottish Enlightenment thinker David Hume summarized the three fundamental laws of nature in the book titled *A Treatise of Human Nature*.[7] The first is the stability of possession. This condition comes from the human need for survival, stability, and peace, as well as the limited resources available to meet this need. It avoids the war of all against all (wealth is often the cause of fatalities). Because it brings about peace, it is the most important law of nature. The second is transference by consent. The original owners of property often are not able to get the most value from it. Voluntary exchange can lead to property value maximization. Cooperative win-win becomes possible. Any behavior that uses violence to force others to transfer property violates natural law, unless this violence is punishment for violating natural law. The third is performance of promises. Most of humanity's cooperation begins with words (promise) and ends with action (performance). If people do not do as they say, then cooperative action is impossible. The progress of humanity is also impossible.

These three laws of nature are the basic meaning of justice as commonly stated. Any violation of one condition is a violation of the principles of justice. As F. A. Hayek pointed out, the main features of all developed legal orders are very similar, so we can say they are only detailed interpretations of these three basic laws of nature.[8]

From this perspective, Mr. Zeng's financing and business activities did not violate the laws of nature. He did not utilize violence or fraud to

[7] David Hume. *Treatise of Human Nature* (Works, vol. 2 p. 293). Dover Publications; New edition (2003). Part. 3, Chapter 2.

[8] F.A. Hayek. 2011 (1960) *The Constitution of Liberty*, p. 226. Chicago: University of Chicago Press. P. 226.

obtain property from others. The financing activity was a voluntary exchange among the people involved. He also did not violate his original commitment. After government policy changed, he still renegotiated a repayment agreement with his lenders.

In contrast, the behavior of the relevant government departments and the judiciary actually violated these three laws of nature. Mr. Zeng was deprived of his property before the court made a decision. Without Mr. Zeng's consent, his property was transferred to the government's own enterprises, which violated the first law of nature. Not allowing him to carry out the repayment agreement with his lenders violated the second law of nature. The initial encouragement and support for Mr. Zeng's private financing, followed by a declaration that he illegally raised money violated the third law of nature.

Natural Law's Universality and Permanence

Natural law is both universal and eternal. The great moral thinkers, whether they lived in the East or West, ancient times or the present, advocated "principles of heaven" that had more in common than differences.

In the book *Leviathan*, Thomas Hobbes summed up nineteen natural laws. Then, he stated:

> *And though this may seem too subtle a deduction of the laws of nature to be taken notice of by all men, whereof the most part are too busy in getting food, and the rest too negligent to understand; yet to leave all men inexcusable, they have been contracted into one easy sum, intelligible even to the meanest capacity; and that is: Do not that to another which thou wouldest not have done to thyself.*[9]

This general principle proves that only one thing must be done to acknowledge natural law: Think from the perspective of others. Adam Smith spoke of an impartial spectator that existed in the hearts of every person.[10] This was the same basic method of reasoning in John Rawls' theory of justice. We could even say it is the method of reasoning in Aristotle's theory of justice.

[9] Thomas Hobbes. 1996. *Leviathan*. Oxford World Classics. Oxford, UK: Oxford University Press. P. 104.

[10] Adam Smith. 2007 (1759). *The Theory of Moral Sentiment*. edit by Knud Hasskonssen. Cambridge UK: Cambridge University Press. P. 182.

Obviously, "What you do not want done to yourself, do not do to others," inherently implies the principle of equality between people. Only equal people will consider issues from each other's perspective. This type of equality is moral equality or equality before "God." The three laws of nature from David Hume can all be inferred from this general principle. You do not want other people to deprive you of life or property, so you should not deprive others of life and property. You do not want other people to force you into a transaction, so you should not force others into a transaction. Alternatively, you hope other people respect your right of voluntary exchange, so you should also respect the same right of others. You do not want to cooperate with unfaithful people, so you should keep your word.

This concept is often called the "Golden Rule." Confucius' proposal of this basic principle for handling interpersonal relationships was a major feat, but many other great thinkers from the Axial Age also proposed it. Some of them even proposed it earlier than Confucius. It could be considered a consensus among Axial Age thinkers. Almost every culture and religion has this type of rule. Pittacus, an ancient Greek philosopher, said: "Do not do to your neighbor what you would take ill from him." Thales, another ancient Greek philosopher that lived at about the same time, said: "Avoid doing what you would blame others for doing." There are similar sayings in Dharma, such as treat others how you would like to be treated, or if you do not want to be harmed by others, then do not harm others. Jesus Christ said: "Do unto others as you would have them do unto you." There are numerous other examples. These maxims can all be translated into the Chinese phrase "*jǐ suǒ bù yù, wù shī yú rén*." Actually, Christianity believes the "Golden Rule" came from Jesus Christ. If we do not strictly interpret the text, many statements in *Mo Tzu* and *Tao Te Ching* have similar meanings.

We could say the "Golden Rule" is universal and eternal. We could also say that it is natural law. Denying the universality of natural law, whether it is for private gain or the public interest, is foolish behavior. The reason Confucian culture can dominate Chinese society for more than 2000 years is because it placed heavenly principles above the king's law. Some Western scholars believe Confucian culture is natural law.[11] Although this is

[11] Joseph Needham perhaps was the first scholar to propose the Confucian natural law idea, See Joseph Needham. 1981. The *Shorter Science and Civilization of China*. Vol. 1. Cambridge, UK: Cambridge University Press.

debatable, it at least proves that Confucians give priority to heavenly principles. Confucian "ritual law" embodies the spirit of natural law. This is the biggest difference between Confucianism and Legalism. A major reason the Qin dynasty only lasted two generations was the First Emperor of Qin recognized the king's law, not heavenly principles.

Conscience Is More Important Than the Law

To conclude, what law did Mr. Zeng violate? Perhaps he violated "man-made law," which was the so-called "illegal financing" law set by the government, as determined by the court. However, he did not violate "natural law" or do anything unconscionable.

The execution of Mr. Zeng might not have violated man-made law. Not informing his relatives before the execution also might not have violated man-made law (as the court claims). However, this violated natural law and violated the conscience of humanity!

Mr. Zeng's misfortune is both the responsibility of the law and the judge. Laws are primarily upheld by judges. Our basic requirement of judges is not kindness, but justice. In the English language, the words justice and judge have the same root. We must acknowledge, from the judge's perspective, conscience is more important than the law. A judge without conscience is more terrifying than a judge that does not understand the law. As long as a judge has a conscience, even without an understanding of the legal text, he will not make un-just judgments. On the contrary, even if a judge understands the law like the back of his hand, but does not have a conscience, then justice will disappear. John Marshall is generally believed to be one of the greatest judges in American history. However, before becoming the Chief Justice of the United States Supreme Court, he did not have any legal background. This is the value of the "trial by jury" system in the West. Jury members are all commoners without professional legal training. Their judgments are based on conscience, not the law.

"Having Laws and Lacking Principles" Is Not a Rule of Law Society

Among Chinese, establishing a rule of law society has become a consensus. However, we must acknowledge the rationality and legitimacy of the law are preconditions for a rule of law society. The laws enacted by government must conform to natural law and conscience. No one should use "the law" as a pretext for unjust things. When the law is incompatible with natural law, or when there is a contest between your conscience and the law, you should choose to stand on the side of natural law. Of course, many people are incapable of this, because human nature is both selfish and weak. Generally speaking, punishment for violating the law of man is immediate, whereas punishment for violating natural law is in the future. However, we should be in awe of those who would rather violate the man-made law than violate natural law. At the least, we should not despise these people.

Of course, it is most important the law enacted by the government is consistent to conscience and natural law. Any legislation that violates natural law cannot be called a real law. It can only be called a "bad law" and is morally improper. Such legislation is contempt for human reason and a violation of human dignity. It provides no benefit to human happiness. Contemporary China does not lack laws, it lacks natural law. In other words, a legal and judicial system that conforms to natural law is lacking. Before Reform and Opening, we had neither natural law, nor laws. The "Cultural Revolution" caused people to acknowledge "no laws" might be a disaster for everyone, so after Reform and Opening, the government enacted a series of laws. However, Mr. Zeng's case, and many others like it, prove the rule of law is not the same as rule by law. The rule of law is at first "rule of natural law." Without law that conforms to natural law and a judiciary with a conscience, true rule of law cannot exist. A society without laws or the rule of law is not a good society, but neither is a society with laws but no rule of law.

CHAPTER 13

Establishing a Market Economy Requires Constitutionalism

If China does not implement true political system reform, such as implementing constitutional law and establishing the rule of law, then economic reform cannot continue. A true market economy will not be established.

If the majority of people actively exercise rights conferred by constitutional law, then society will develop in a good direction.[1]

* * *

My specialty is economics, so what caused me to focus on constitutional law and democracy? It is primarily based on my understanding of the market economy. Liberty, private property, and entrepreneurship are the most important foundations of the market economy. After experiencing decades of reform, I have discovered government departments still arbitrarily interfere with economic liberty and private property is not effectively protected. Entrepreneurship is still suppressed and distorted. I feel if China

[1] The original version of this chapter was written in July 2017.

W. Zhang, *Ideas for China's Future*,
https://doi.org/10.1007/978-981-15-4304-3_13

does not implement true political system reform, such as implementing constitutional law and establishing the rule of law, then economic reform cannot continue. A true market economy will not be established. This is an issue I care about. In regard to constitutional law and the rule of law, I will discuss a few viewpoints.

First, implementing a constitution provides the foundation for legitimacy and authority of political power.

In theory, any regime that has a constitution but does not abide by it has negated its own legitimacy and authority. Currently, there is power, but not legitimacy. People's obedience to government decrees are largely based on fear rather than respect. This is a big problem. A major reason is the constitution has not been truly put into effect. A few years ago, I said few clauses of China's constitution have been put into effect, except the clause of the leadership of the Communist Party. Some clauses are implemented in form, but not in substance. Some constitutional clauses have not even been implemented in form.

The 1982 Constitution (including later amendments) is basically good, but mostly has not been put into effect. This is the background of President Xi's statement "implementation is the life of a constitution."[2] As I understand it, there was not necessarily the intent to implement certain clauses even when they were formulated. Why? The reason is that certain things that represent humanity's mainstream values could not be openly negated. When they became part of the text, no one dared to say they could not be written. This includes the freedom of speech, the freedom of assembly, democratic elections, judicial independence, etc. However, this gives this constitution vitality, because it provides conditions for our steady reform. Change in many other countries requires the constitution to be amended or even a constitution to be established. However, we only need to put the constitution we already have into effect, or at least we can for a very long time.

At this point, to truly implement the constitution, we must return to the basic and common values of human civilization. Otherwise, not only will the constitution lack vitality, the regime will also lack legitimacy and authority. For example, the National People's Congress system is set by the constitution, but if representatives are not truly elected, they will not

[2] President Xi Jinping made this statement in his speech on December 4th 2012, at The 30th Anniversary Conference of the 1982 Constitution. It is another issue whether he really intended to do so.

gain the people's respect. In the past, people respected National People's Congress members because it was a type of status and honor. The party and leadership looked favorably on members, and members were celebrities. That was enough to earn respect. Now, people's views have changed significantly. The degree of respect for National People's Congress members and Chinese People's Political Consultative Conference delegates is much lower today than it was in the past. Why? Because they are not truly elected, so on what basis can they ask for respect? If elections are not truly implemented for the National People's Congress, then it will lose more and more legitimacy in the eyes of the people. The first point, which is the implementation of the constitution, will help to consolidate the legitimacy and authority of our political parties and political power.

Second, implementing a constitution provides a foundation and guarantee for democracy. A broad democratic system includes a constitution and the rule of law. A narrowly defined democratic system is primarily an issue of selecting leaders by public voting. Without a constitution, or without a constitution put into effect, a true democracy cannot exist. Since ancient Greece to the present, most thinkers have worried democracy will become the "tyranny of the majority."[3] This is people's biggest fear about democracy. How can we prevent the tyranny of the majority? We must put the constitution into effect and implement the rule of law. The law must become the supreme ruler, so that everyone is below the law. The tyranny of the majority can only be prevented when democracy is established on a rule of law foundation. This is the theoretical perspective. In practice, what should be done with people that do not recognize the results of future elections? Without a constitution, without a constitution put into effect, without a basic concept of the rule of law among the people, and without independent decisions from the courts, then there is no way to resolve these problems. It might lead to civil strife. We know that election results in America are contested, but people still must obey court decisions. *Bush v. Gore* is an example. Taiwan also has contested results, but the courts have the final say. In the history of Western nations, many of them had the rule of law first and democracy second. In 1688, England implemented constitutional monarchy and established a constitutional government. Of

[3] For example, both Plato and Aristotle were anti-democracy because democracy marginalizes the wise and there can be no proper leadership in a democracy. See David Held. 2006. *Models of Democracy*. Third Edition. Cambridge, UK: Polity Press. PP. 23–27.

course, this is not to say constitutional government did not exist at all before that. England's true democratization began with reforms in 1832 that increased the electorate to 14.5% of the adult male population. The electorate was expanded a few more times until all women received the right to vote in 1928. Close to 100 years of history had passed.[4]

I imagine China's reform over the next 30 years will truly put the constitution into effect and implement the rule of law, then take the road towards healthy democracy. I believe putting the constitution into effect and implementing the rule of law should be the primary duty in the first 15 years. Democracy should be the primary goal in the following 15 years. In terms of putting the constitution into effect, there are many specific measures required. We cannot just talk in generalities. For example, Article 126 and 131 dictate judicial power and procuratorial power are exercised independently. However, if the appointment and dismissal system for judges is not changed, so that judges have a sense of security, it is unlikely that judicial independence will be implemented. American federal judges are appointed by the president for life. But the president cannot remove judges, so there is independence. After appointment, a judge can go completely against the will of the president. If judges are appointed and dismissed like other government officials at any time, then it will be difficult to implement judicial independence.

Third, putting the constitution into effect will benefit everyone. In other words, everyone has an interest in it. Under the current system, people with special privileges face the most risk. As long as the average person does not "make trouble," their basic personal safety is not at risk. The basic safety of people with special privileges are the least guaranteed. In other words, they have special privileges but no human rights. Special privileges allow for the enjoyment of immediate benefits. Without human rights, though, future safety is not guaranteed. Why did Western nations implement constitutional government in the beginning? The commoners did not desire its implementation. Instead, the vested interests wanted constitutional government implemented. Why did they want constitutional government to be implemented? Before constitutional government, they were harming each other. For example, the rights of the nobles in England were constantly injured by the king. Every war was a win-lose contest. In the end, they realized constitutional government means the

[4] D. Acemoglu and J. A. Robinson. 2006. *Economic Origin of Dictatorship and Democracy*. Cambridge and New York: Cambridge University Press. PP. 2–5.

same rules for everyone, which benefitted all nobles.[5] From contemporary China's perspective, even if interests are obtained through special privileges, legal protections are still required. If the constitution is not implemented, vested interests are the most likely to be harmed. In order to avoid mutual harm and deprivation, it is most imperative for them to put the constitution into effect. Of course, many people do not realize this. Ignorance is an important reason for human error.

Fourth, private property rights are the foundation of the market economy. They are also a guarantee of civil liberties. In this regard, there is not much disagreement among people that study the law and study the economy. However, in other fields of study, there are numerous criticisms of property rights. We must recognize if private property is not effectively protected, then people's basic liberties and security are not guaranteed. Democracy will certainly turn into tyranny, and we also could not possibly establish a true market economy. The events in Chongqing over the last few years,[6] Mr. Zeng's death penalty,[7] and other issues did not threaten a small number of entrepreneurs, but instead threatened the life and liberty of everyone. We must put the constitution into effect to protect private property. Protections for private property are already clearly defined in the constitution, but there is still a long road toward implementation. This includes a change in the average person's viewpoints. The most effective method is to correct misjudged cases. For example, there is the issue of auctioning off assets before a judgment is made in economic crime cases or the miscarriage of justice in the Chongqing Gang Trials. These must be corrected through judicial procedures. Certain government officials and judges should bear the corresponding legal responsibilities. The "Tieben Incident" in 2006 is also a classic case.[8] I am saddened to see these types

[5] Doulas C. North, John Joseph Wallace and Barry R. Weingast. 2009. *Violence and Social Orders: A Conceptual Framework for Interpreting Recorded Human History*. New York: Cambridge University Press.

[6] Under Bo Xilai's leadership, Chongqing government launched a campaign of the so-called "swiping yellow (prostitution) and striking black (organized crime)", which was actually a movement against businesspeople who were not close to Bo. Bo was arrested in March 2012 and sentenced for life later.

[7] See Chap. 12 in this book.

[8] Tieben Steel Company was one of largest private iron and steel companies in China, located in Jiangsu Province and owned by Mr. Dai Guofang, a very capable entrepreneur. Dai was arrested in 2004 for "faking invoices of steel scrap." The true reason was he expanded aggressively his steel business when the central government was implementing tightening policies to cool down the over-heating economy.

of problems in the twenty-first century. However, if trials are re-examined and mistakes are corrected, it will be an impetus to establish a property rights system. The issue of implementing property rights must be done on a case by case basis, including the use of administrative litigation law. If government departments do not approve activities that are allowed under the law, then injured parties should sue in court. Our society requires this type of "earnest" people. In that situation, not only is suing the government the right of individuals and enterprises, but also their social responsibility. In other words, establishing the property rights system is the responsibility of each citizen. The property rights system relates to the interests of every citizen. If the majority of people can actively exercise the rights established by the constitution and the law, then this society has hope to develop in a good direction.

CHAPTER 14

Implementation Is the Life of the Constitution

I believe over the next 10 years, as long as we truly implement the constitution, China will take a giant leap towards democratic liberty and the rule of law society. China's enterprises will have a better environment for survival. The power of the market can play a better role. Every individual will have a more dignified life.[1]

* * *

After the 18th National Congress of the Communist Party of China, two sentences had the greatest impact on me. First, General Secretary Xi Jinping, in a speech marking the 30th anniversary of the 1982 Constitution, said: "Implementation is the life of the constitution." Second, Premier Li Keqiang said: "Reform pays the biggest dividend." I believe if these two sentences truly become the guiding thought of our future reforms, then China's enterprises will have a better growth environment, China's society will become more democratic and free, and the power of the market can play a better role.

I believe there are five important aspects related to implementing the constitution.

[1] The original version of this chapter was written in December 2012.

W. Zhang, *Ideas for China's Future*,
https://doi.org/10.1007/978-981-15-4304-3_14

First, we should truly achieve judicial independence. Judicial independence is the foundation of the rule of law society. If a nation does not have an independent judiciary, then it cannot have a rule of law society. Only when judicial independence has legal authority, the public has trust in the law, and the people feel safe, can judges have a professional spirit and corruption be truly contained. Judicial independence is also the foundation of political stability. We see that the countries with judicial independence rarely have political turmoil. In countries without judicial independence, political turmoil is frequent. As soon as turmoil begins, it is difficult to bring the situation under control.

In our constitution, judicial independence is clearly stated. Article 126 states: “The people’s courts exercise judicial power independently, in accordance with the provisions of law, and not subject to interference by any administrative organ, public organization or individual.” Article 131 states: “The people’s procuratorates exercise procuratorial power independently, in accordance with the provisions of law, and not subject to interference by any administrative organ, public organization or individual.” However, we know this is not the case in reality.

To realize true judicial independence and implement Article 126 and Article 131, I believe an important point will be a significant adjustment to the Central Political and Legal Affairs Commission’s functions. The Political and Legal Affairs Commission should be the supervisory organization that maintains judicial independence. It should not interfere with the judiciary or even interfere in specific judgments.

Second, the National People’s Congress should be democratically elected. Article 2 states: “All power in the People’s Republic of China belongs to the people. The National People’s Congress and the local people’s congresses at various levels are the organs through which the people exercise state power.” Article 3 states: “The National People’s Congress and the local people’s congresses at various levels are constituted through democratic elections. They are responsible to the people and subject to their supervision.” Currently, elections in our country are largely formalities. In true elections, candidates compete with each other to present their ideas to voters. In addition, candidates can independently participate in the election. Article 97 states: “Deputies to the people’s congresses of provinces, municipalities directly under the Central Government and cities divided into districts are elected by the people’s congresses at the next lower level; deputies to the people’s congresses of counties, cities not divided into districts, municipal districts, townships, nationality townships, and towns are elected directly by their constituencies." I believe if people's congresses at the county level or below can be the product of competitive elections, and higher-level people's congresses are elected from the lower level people's congresses, then the National People's Congress can fulfill its role as the organization with the highest power.

Third, effectively guarantee the freedoms enumerated in the constitution. Article 35 states: "Citizens of the People's Republic of China enjoy freedom of speech, of the press, of assembly, of association, of procession and of demonstration." We now have Weibo, WeChat, and other new technologies that have broken through many traditional controls. They have allowed each person to have some degree of opportunity to express personal opinions. However, these types of expressions lack political system guarantees. Freedom of speech demands we have true liberty to express ourselves. Each person can defend their rights and express their own souls. We know Chinese writer Mo Yan won the Nobel Prize. I think every Chinese person feels very proud. However, according to media reports, when interviewed, he said censorship is as necessary as security checks at the airport. If he really said this, I believe it is problematic. We must acknowledge we can only test the truth through competition in the market for ideas. We cannot rely on one group of people to be more correct than others.

Fourth, private property rights must be effectively protected. Article 13 states: "The state protects the right of citizens to own lawfully earned income, savings, houses and other lawful property." However, many rights of citizens, including property rights, are not guaranteed. We can see this from numerous cases. We must especially guard against the government's violation of people's legal rights through legislative and judicial procedures. The situation in China currently is as soon as a person is arrested, even before a guilty verdict is made, the court can auction off that person's property. We saw this in the Wu Ying case.[2] This is a serious violation of individual property rights.

[2] Wu Ying, born 1981, was a female entrepreneur from Zhejiang Province. She did various businesses before founding Zhejiang Ben Se Holding Ltd. in 2006 by raising funds from 11 relatives and acquaintances. She was arrested in 2008 for illegal fundraising and sentenced to death on October 19th 2009 by the Jinhua City Court. The death penalty was confirmed after the second trial by the Zhejiang High Court on January 18th 2012. Upon China's Supreme Court's request for retrial, Zhejiang High Court changed the death sentence with immediate execution to the death sentence with two-year probation on July 11th 2014. On March 23rd 2018, Zhejiang High Court changed the decision again to a 25-year prison sentence.

Fifth, China must start a true constitutional review. Most rule of law countries undertake constitutional reviews. Our constitution is written very clearly. Laws, administrative regulations, and local regulations cannot contravene the constitution. No organization or individual is above the constitution or the law. This is stated in Article 5. However, we have not done this in practice. China joined the World Trade Organization more than 10 years ago. We reviewed the government's regulatory system and laws to determine whether they conflicted with the rules of the WTO or our commitments. Today, we should do something similar. We should examine our laws and the government's regulations to determine whether they conflict with the constitution. We do not have a constitutional court. However, according to the current constitution, we can establish a constitutional review committee in the National People's Congress, then undertake a constitutional review of all laws.

I believe in the next 10 years, as long as we truly implement the constitution, then China will make a giant leap towards democratic liberty and a rule of law society. Chinese enterprises will have a better environment. The power of the market can play a better role. Each person will also live a more dignified life.

PART III

Ideas and Leadership in Reform

CHAPTER 15

The Evolutionary Nature of China's Reform

Two aspects of China's reform were unexpected. First, the process of reform has been much longer than anticipated; and second, the results of reform have far surpassed the original expectation.

The process of China's economic reform shows that the "invisible hand" is not just the most effective method of resource allocation in the market, but is also the primary force for driving systemic innovation.[1]

* * *

China's economic reforms already have a 25-year history.[2] Looking back, two significant phenomena have been completely different from people's expectations at the beginning of reform (or even a relatively long period of time after the start of reform). First, the process of reform has been much longer than anticipated. At the beginning, reformers imagined reform would be complete in about five years. Even in the middle of the 1980s, many reformers still optimistically predicted the end of reform by

[1] The original version of this chapter was written in 2003 and was delivered as a keynote speech at the 25th Anniversary Conference of Chinese Economic Reform.

[2] While this article was written in 2003, my arguments are perfectly applicable even 40 years after reform started.

W. Zhang, *Ideas for China's Future*,
https://doi.org/10.1007/978-981-15-4304-3_15

1990 or 1995 at the latest. Nonetheless, 25 years have passed and China is still in the process of reform. We still do not know when reform will finally end.[3]

Second, the results of reform have far surpassed the original expectation. The goal of the original reforms was to "improve the planned economy based on public ownership." Even though we have not reached a complete market economy, the planned economy no longer exists. Even though state-owned enterprises are still an important pillar of the national economy, in many industries, non-state-owned enterprises have already become or are becoming dominant. Southern Jiangsu was considered the model region of the new publicly-owned economy in the 1980s, but today 100% of village enterprises, 95% of township enterprises, 90% of county enterprises, and 85% of city enterprises are privately operated.

Why is there such a gap between reform in practice and the original idea? Because institutional transformation can only be a process of spontaneous evolution. It cannot be the result of design. Institutions are society's rules of the game. Designing these rules of the game require a huge amount of information about technology and individual behavior. This information is always distributed among numerous individual participants. No planner can obtain sufficient (or even complete) information required to design the system. This is precisely the reason the planned economy failed. F.A. Hayek's explanation for the reasons the planned economy fails is key to my understanding of China's reform process.[4] Of course, this is not to negate the important role reform planners played in the first driving force of reform. Instead, this is to say no designed reform proposal can transcend reform's evolutionary logic.

[3] In 1988, Zhao Ziyang, the then Party General Secretary asked the Economic Reform Commission and a group of economists to design three reform plans: a three-year plan, a five-year plan and an eight-year plan. Mr. Peng Sen recently told the following interesting story. He once asked his direct boss Mr. Li Tieying for the reason to make these three plans. Li replied that Zhao said while the reform was not completed by 1988 as originally thought, he hoped it would be completed by 1995 (that is, in another eight years) and these three plans would be the short period one, the middle period one and the long period one, respectively. At that time, Li was a vice premier and minister of the Economic Reform Commission and Peng was his secretary. Peng later became a vice minister of the National Development and Reform Commission before he retired in 2011.

[4] F.A. Hayek. (1945). "The Use of Knowledge in Society." In *Individualism and Economic Order*, 77–91. London and Henley: Routledge and Kegan Paul, 1976; F.A. Hayek. 1988. *The Fatal Conceit: The Errors of Socialism.* Edited by W.W. Bartley III. Chicago: Chicago University Press.

China's reform is believed to be gradual, but this gradual reform is absolutely not the result of artificial design. China's reforms lacked a consistent goal, and even less so had a blueprint for careful planning. The process of reform was often "from easiest to hardest," step by step, and stop and go. It had a trial and error nature. Many major reform measures were often initiated by local governments, or even grassroot levels of government. They were not implemented from the top down.[5]

China's process of reform was like a random walk. In Deng Xiaoping's words, it was "crossing the river by feeling the stones." The reason we "crossed the river by feeling the stones" was we did not know where the other side was. No one at the beginning of reform in the late 1970s was clear which direction reform should take. Even if China knew in which direction to reform, it still faced the issue of how to change. Designing a transformation from a planned economy to a market economy is not easy. National leaders and economists were not clear how the market mechanism operated. Economists could only learn a few market economic theories from textbooks, but they did not have practical experience. Older economists were fascinated by Marxist economics. They knew the reasons China needed to reform but were unable to respond to how reform should proceed. Young economists had much fewer ideological frameworks and pursued practical things, but many were idealistic.

The reason no one knew how to reform partially was because reform is a "learning by doing" process. The interdependency of different parts of reform can only be revealed one after another. When we were debating "planning dominance" versus "market dominance," we did not understand any introduction of market competition would cause the system of planning to collapse. When we were discussing whether price reform or enterprise reform should go first, we did not understand implementing either aspect would lead to a "domino effect" driving other aspects of reform.

Even if economists and reform leaders had the ability to design a good reform proposal, implementing this type of massive proposal also requires

[5] Weiying Zhang, and Gang Yi. (1997). "China's Gradual Reform: A Historical Perspective." In *China's Economic Growth and Transformation*, edited by Clement A. Tisdell and Joseph G. W. Chai. Nova Science Publisher, Inc., 1997. This paper was also collected in Weiying Zhang. 2015. *The Logic of the Market: An Insider's View of Chinese Economic Reform.* Washington, DC: Cato Institute.

a strong power structure. The implied assumption of the advocates of a constructivist reform program is such a power structure already exists. This assumption is not practical. A lack of powerful support for full reform ideas was the primary reason various types of comprehensive reform plans failed in the 1980s. China's power structure is segmented. Not only is power segmented between upper-level leaders, but also at different levels of government. Under this type of situation, policy setting not only requires alignment at the top, but also requires interdependent government departments to have a positive attitude towards cooperation. They might manipulate the implementation of policies that are not in their interest. In the words of modern economic theory, only when reform proposals satisfy the participation constraint and incentive compatibility constraints of relevant government departments can they be implemented. Because government bureaucrats' interests are diverse, one proposal cannot satisfy them all. Government bureaucrats always use their power to manipulate reform according to their own interests. This often turns reforms that were bold originally into cautious and perfunctory reforms. The end result is similar to the explanation given by Chen (1992): "All the proposed reforms that were tried and failed or successfully implemented were the result of complex political forces under the central planning system, rather than the simple application of abstract economic models."[6]

Economic reform not only changes the system, but also changes people. It changes their customs, value judgements, and behaviors. Under the planned economy, almost everything was determined. People lived an uneventful life. Decisions were concentrated in the hands of a few. The vast majority of people did not need to make their own choices. Even for the decision makers, because of the fixed environment, most of their work was routine, they did not need initiative, creativity, or innovation. From the perspective of the people that lived under this type of system for a long time, it is not easy to adapt to making personal decisions in the unstable environment of the market economy. A certain amount of time had to be spent letting them learn how to face price fluctuations, uncertainty, choice, and competition. If we know that increasing the price of a box of matches from two cents to three cents in the 1980s was a political issue and

[6] Chen, Kang, 1992, "*Crossing the River while Groping for Planned Stones: A Public-Choice Analysis of China's Economic Reform*," mimeo.

discussed several times at the Political Bureau of the Central Committee, then we can understand how hard it was for the public to adapt to the market economy. Many of the delays in reform were caused by the hesitation of ordinary people in such uncertain environments and the inability of managers to adapt to the market. The appearance of the entrepreneurial class was critical to the efficiency of the market economy, but the appearance of this class also took a certain amount of time. A major goal of state-owned enterprise reform was expanding enterprise autonomy, but in the beginning, many managers of SOEs did not like autonomy. They were accustomed to implementing decisions set by higher-ups, not making decisions themselves.

In a sense, China's economic reforms were a process of "lucky shots." Many of the measures that pushed reform forward were precisely the policies that were severely criticized by many reform-minded economists and even some so-called "conservatives." Here, I will use the "fiscal contract system" and the "dual track system" as examples to explain this point.

The fiscal contract system was first introduced in 1980, adjusted in 1984, and fully institutionalized in 1988. According to this system, lower-level governments hand over a fixed percent (or nominal amount) of local revenues and kept the rest. The fiscal surpluses of different levels of government and departments of the same level of government could not be arbitrarily transferred by the central government. This system was fiercely attacked by many of China's reform-oriented economists. They believed this system "strengthened local protectionism, segmented the market, and increased local government interference with enterprises." Actually, in the beginning, this system was not introduced as a market-oriented reform. Instead, the purpose was to stabilize central government revenues. Yet, in the 1980s, this policy played a major role in the marketization of China's economy.

First, this system separated the entire Chinese economy into many small publicly owned economies.[7] It was similar to separating the assets of different levels of government. Each locality became a "giant company." Each level of local government turned into the actual owners of the

[7]Weiying Zhang. (1998). "A Principal-Agent Theory of the Public Economy and Its Applications to China." *Economics of Planning*, Vol 31: 231–251.

surplus portion of the public economy. The incentive for local governments and enterprises to supervise and work increased with separation. Because local governments were closer to "principals" (the public), enterprises faced greater pressure to turn over profits. Further, because local governments cannot print money to provide fiscal support, their budget constraints are harder than for the central government. This fiscal management system stimulated the development of China's township and village enterprises. Now, privately operated "township and village enterprises" have become a major component of the non-state-owned economy, particularly after privatization in the later 1990s.

Second, the fiscal contract system also forced local governments to compete with each other. This benefitted the market-oriented transformation of the overall economy. Even though local governments might use administrative means to control local enterprises, they can only bargain with other governments. Local government bargaining increased the difficulty of centrally planned control. This forced the planned economy towards the "dual-track system." Local protectionism might play a role in the short term, but anti-protectionist forces might be stronger. Enterprises and regions that were economically more efficient wanted to break through obstacles and enter other regions' markets. Local protectionism to a certain degree also contributed to the marketization of the overall economy. The reason I say this is because it forced the enterprises and regions protected by low-priced raw materials from the central government to go into the market.

Third, an empirical study by my research partners and I proved the local decentralization policy led to competition between regions, and competition between regions triggered the privatization wave of the 1990s.[8] The reason was competition between regions in the product market was extremely fierce, so each region had to decrease production costs to the greatest extent possible and maintain the minimum market share required for survival. Without market share, there is no fiscal income. To encourage managers to reduce production costs, local governments had to transfer part or all of their shares to management. The fiercer the competition in the product market, the more local governments transferred, thus

[8] Shaomin Li, Shuhe Li and Weiying Zhang. (2000). "The Road to Capitalism: Competition and Institutional Change in China." *Journal of Comparative Economics*, Vol. 28 (No.2):269–292.

the degree of privatization increased. This is the reason Southern Jiangsu enterprises were privatized, and similarly for other areas in the 1990s.

In 1994, fiscal contracting was replaced by a new tiered tax system. We could say this was to keep pace with the times. Nevertheless, this system should not be underestimated for its tremendous driving force in China's reform.

The "dual-track system" was another major initiative driving China's reform. Although I was the first to propose and systematically demonstrate this way of thinking in April of 1984, the dual-track system occurred spontaneously along with the structural economic reforms and local government decentralization in the early 1980s.[9] In 1980, the government decided to suspend reform within a two-year adjustment period. Yet, from the perspective of results, reform was not actually suspended due to adjustments. To the contrary, the first big market expansion of industrial products of the 1980s was the consequence of the adjustment policy. When the government refocused planned resource allocation from heavy industry to light industry, both heavy industry and light industry produced excess supply. In heavy industry, raw materials like steel products were in excess supply. Due to cancellation of planned orders, the machinery manufacturing sector suffered a setback. In light industry, after experiencing long periods of shortages, traditional consumer goods like watches and sewing machines also experienced excess capacity. Excess supply caused lower product prices and greater competitive pressures. In the beginning, the government attempted to utilize planning measures like price adjustments and limited production to control the situation. However, the severity of the issue gave the government no choice but to give up. From the perspective of enterprises, selling products on the market was the only route to survival. Therefore, the adjustment policy led to the appearance of the first market for industrial products. The watch industry is a good example. According to the records of Byrd and Tidrick (1984), between 1980 and 1983, the government reduced the official price of watches three times for

[9] My original paper was written in April 1984, titled "Taking Price Reform as the Center of Systemic Economic Reform" and printed in an internal reference magazine of the State Council's Center for Technology Research (later merged into the State Council's Development Research Center). For the English translation of the original paper, see. Pp.265–282, in Weiying Zhang. 2015. *The Logic of the Market*. Washington, DC: Cato Institute.

a total reduction of nearly 20%.[10] As it was, enterprises produced much more than the production quota set by the planning department. The retailers only wanted watches that could be easily sold according to the planned price. Watch manufacturers had no choice but to let workers peddle watches at market prices on the streets. Thus, the planned price for watches gradually disappeared. It is worth noting the adjustment policy not only led to the appearance of the market for consumer goods, but also the appearance of the market for production materials. In fact, a subsidiary of the First Ministry of Machine Industry directly sold 46% of its total sales revenue outside of the plan and accounted for 33% of the machine manufacturing market in 1980.[11] By 1983, although the planned price had not been eliminated, most machine and industrial products were already sold according to market prices. In 1985, the government formally made the "dual-track system" the way of thinking for price reform.

The dual-track system was later also utilized in most other reform areas, including the foreign exchange market, the labor market, the housing market, social insurance, and the ownership system. The result by the end of the 1980s was the entire Chinese economy became a dual-track economy.

The dual-track system was the most important characteristic of China's gradual reforms. The key point of the dual-track system was not the coexistence of the market mechanism and the system of planning, but the evolutionary process of the market track over-taking the plan track. Market exchange did not start by reducing planned quotas, but instead intruded the economy from extra supply and demand. Privatization was not accomplished through privatization of state-owned enterprises or removal of state-owned control, but instead by reducing barriers to entry for non-state enterprises.

The dual-track system was widely criticized because of the government corruption it fostered. However, looking back, this might be the price to pay for systemic reform. If we believe reform is necessary, then the new system must at least be a "Kaldor-Hicks improvement," meaning an increase in overall social wealth. Nevertheless, if we cannot turn a

[10] William A. Byrd, and Gene Tidrick. 1984. "Adjustment and Reform in the Chongqing Clock and Watch Industry." *World Bank Staffing Working Paper*, no. 652.

[11] William A. Byrd. 1987. "Impact of the two-tier plan/market system in Chinese Industry." *Journal of Comparative Economics*, 11(3): 295–308.

"Kaldor-Hicks improvement" into a "nearly Pareto improvement," then reform might not progress. Reform is different from revolution because it respects vested interests, otherwise it cannot be a "Pareto improvement." The primary characteristic of the dual-track system is respect for the various interest groups formed under the old system. This is the reason it was not fiercely resisted at the starting point. Many economists believe reform cannot be a Pareto improvement process because some people's situations worsen during economic reform. Government bureaucrats are seen as reform's primary losers. Most of their special privileges and rent-seeking was reduced or eliminated during reform. If that is the case, then successful reform must focus on reducing resistance from the bureaucracy. The dual-track system resolves this problem. Under certain situations, the dual-track system actually makes bureaucrats' circumstances better, not worse. They have more opportunities and more effective methods to obtain economic interests (rent-seeking). This point can explain the reason more and more government departments supported this type of reform. During the start of rural reform, many village cadres opposed reform because they lost privileges. Not before long, they realized they could utilize their personal relationships and understanding of the outside world to get rich quicker than the average peasant. Many of the wealthiest people in the countryside were previously village cadres. Urban reform was a similar phenomenon. Of course, government officials attempted to control reform according to their own interests.

Entrepreneurs are the main players of the market economy. Without entrepreneurs, a market economy does not exist. The dual-track system maintained stability in the economic system while nurturing generations of Chinese entrepreneurs. They were the driving force for China's rapid economic development of the past and will be again in the future.

After 25 years of reform, we could say the dual-track system has died a natural death. However, this is due to the success of the dual-track system, not failure.

The process of China's economic reform shows the "invisible hand" is not just the most effective method of resource allocation in the market, but is also the primary force for driving systemic innovation. Economists can learn distinct lessons from China's experiences. The planned economy's marketization process was a process all interest groups mutually played a role in. Even though the elites of society have the ability to organize a planned economy (although inefficiently), no one can plan for a market economy. The reason is the market economy is a process of all participants (including politicians) pursuing self-interest under the control of the invisible hand. When China's leaders began reform, they had no intention of establishing a market economy. To the contrary, their objective was to stimulate people's incentive to improve the existing planned economy based on public ownership. Reform later paved its own road to the market economy. Policy encouragement and tolerance for self-interested behavior also incentivized and tacitly approved spontaneous institutional innovation. When peasants, workers, and cadres were allowed to pursue self-interest, the defects of the original system were exposed. This creates a need for further reform, and a new system will be produced sooner or later.

Deng Xiaoping's greatness was he understood better than many economists and scholars that systemic reform certainly is a process of spontaneous evolution. No one can plan for it. He knocked down the first "domino" of the old system. We have reason to believe the reforms he started will continue according to their own logic.

CHAPTER 16

Deng Xiaoping Knew What He Did Not Know

Deng Xiaoping did not read Hayek's works, but he comprehended the conclusion Hayek proved from an epistemology perspective: the market is superior to planning and decentralization is better than centralization. In this sense, he is a follower of Hayek.

Deng Xiaoping's acknowledgement of humanity's and his own knowledge limitations not only influenced the selection of goals for China's economic system reforms, but also influenced the selection of reform paths. He understood economic and social reforms are different from building construction. It cannot be constructed according to pre-designed blueprints. Instead, a "cross the river by feeling the stones" approach must be taken.[1]

* * *

Deng Xiaoping was a steadfast market-oriented reformer. He was able to be such a reformer because he was very wise. His greatest wisdom came from knowing his own "ignorance" and acknowledging his own "ignorance." Precisely because he knew neither he nor anyone else was

[1] The original version of this chapter was written in December 2018.

W. Zhang, *Ideas for China's Future*,
https://doi.org/10.1007/978-981-15-4304-3_16

all-knowing, he believed only the market economy could realize a rich population and a strong nation. He also chose the gradual "cross the river by feeling the stones" path to reform.

The Wise Know What They Do Not Know

People are accustomed to using knowledge to distinguish between intelligence and stupidity. People full of knowledge are considered smart, whereas stupid people do not know anything.

Actually, in terms of wisdom, the greatest difference between people is not having specific knowledge, but instead is acknowledging the insufficiency of their own knowledge.

A wise person knows his own ignorance, and bravely acknowledges it. A fool does not know his own ignorance, or even if he does, he also does not acknowledge it.

Laocius said: "To know and yet (think) we do not know is the highest (attainment); not to know (and yet think) we do know is a disease."[2]

Confucius said: "When you know a thing, to hold that you know it; and when you do not know a thing, to allow that you do not know it—this is knowledge."[3] He added: "Am I indeed possessed of knowledge? I am not knowing. But if a mean person, who appears quite empty-like, ask anything of me, I set it forth from one end to the other, and exhaust it."

Socrates supposedly said: "I know that I know nothing." An Athenian who considered himself wiser, wanted to debate Socrates. After the debate, Socrates told his students: "I am wiser than this man; for neither of us really knows anything fine and good, but this man thinks he knows something when he does not, whereas I, as I do not know anything, do not think I do either. I seem, then, in just this little thing to be wiser than this man at any rate, that what I do not know I do not think I know either."

William Shakespeare wrote the line: "The fool doth think he is wise, but the wise man knows himself to be a fool."

[2] Legge, James (translator). *Tao Te Ching*. Digitized by the Chinese Text Project.

[3] Legge, James (translator). *Wei Zheng*. Digitized by the Chinese Text Project. An alternative translation is: "Real knowledge is to know the extent of one's ignorance."

Bertrand Russell wrote: "One of the painful things about our time is that those who feel certainty are stupid, and those with any imagination and understanding are filled with doubt and indecision."

All scientific discoveries started from acknowledging ignorance.

The Ignorant Are Fearless

Why do intelligent people know their own ignorance, but fools do not?

A person's ability to produce and grasp some type of knowledge is also precisely the skill necessary to evaluate the knowledge itself. Lacking this skill not only means a person cannot obtain this type of knowledge, but also means he does not have the ability to recognize he does not have this knowledge. For example, a person that does not understand grammar cannot possibly know whether he or she made a grammatical error. On the other hand, a person that understands grammar knows whether the sentence he or she wrote is grammatically correct.

In psychology, this is called the "Dunning-Kruger effect." Based on four psychological tests assessing humor, logical reasoning, and English grammar, Justin Kruger and David Dunning published an article in the *Journal of Personality and Social Psychology* in 1999.[4] They concluded "that those with limited knowledge in a domain suffer a dual burden: Not only do they reach mistaken conclusions and make regrettable errors, but their incompetence robs them of the ability to realize it." This cognitive bias comes from their inability to recognize their own lack of ability. Because they lack self-awareness of metacognition, they tend to overestimate their actual ability and performance. The degree of overestimation is inversely proportional to actual ability. For example, the experiment's lowest scoring group of participants ranked in the 12th percentile, but ranked themselves in the 62nd percentile. Not only was this estimation much higher than the actual ranking, it exceeded the average ranking (the 50th percentile).

The Dunning-Kruger effect can be found everywhere in real life. For example, when I took the National Higher Education Entrance Examination (Gao Kao) in 1977, several fellow test-takers felt quite good

[4] Justin Kruger and David Dunning. 1999. "Unskilled and Unaware of It: How Difficulties in Recognizing One's Own Incompetence Lead to Inflated Self-Assessments". *Journal of Personality and Social Psychology* 77(6): 1121–1134.

about themselves after each subject, but none of them got into university. The more a person does not know incorrect answers, the less likely he or she knows how low the score will be.

One manifestation of the Dunning-Kruger effect is the saying "the ignorant are fearless." At the start of their article, the authors used an example of a criminal. One day in 1995, a man named McArthur Wheeler robbed two banks in broad daylight without any disguise. At 11:00 pm, the news channel broadcast surveillance footage from the bank, and Wheeler was quickly arrested. When the police showed him the surveillance footage, he had a blank look on his face and mumbled "but I wore the juice!" He mistakenly believed putting lemon juice on his face would make it hard for the surveillance camera to identify his face. This kind of erroneous knowledge led to his misfortune.

The Dunning-Kruger effect deserves our attention not only because it brings about personal tragedy to the incompetent, but more so because it likely leads to disasters for society as a whole. More than one philosopher has said many bad things in human history were done by good people. The reason good people do bad things is because they do not know their own ignorance. The tragedy of the planned economy was a bad thing done by good people.

A Disciple of F. A. Hayek

Why did F. A. Hayek transition from economics to philosophy, especially epistemology, while he was young and had a strong academic reputation? He was almost forgotten by mainstream economics when he won the Nobel Prize in Economics in 1974. The reason for his award was his contribution to business cycle theory in the early 1930s, which is still not appreciated by mainstream economists.

For a long time, my belief was Hayek "changed careers" because he realized he could not out-compete John Maynard Keynes in the field of economics. After all, many of his original followers turned into Keynesian economists and became very well known. This had to have disheartened him.

Now, I recognize this conjecture is too superficial. The real reason Hayek transitioned to philosophy and epistemology is the Great Socialist Calculation Debate made him realize a solid theoretical foundation for the market economy cannot be provided without understanding the market from an epistemological perspective. Without this, it is also impossible to undermine people's belief in the planned economy. He knew the market and central planning were difficult to discriminate within the paradigm of neoclassical economics. This is the reason many economists declared Oskar Lange won the great debate. Lange used strict neoclassical economics to prove the feasibility of the planned economy. Even today, the specter of the planned economy (such as industrial policy) still occasionally makes an appearance. Its amulet is the "Market Failure" theory of neoclassical economics.

Hayek provided an epistemological foundation for the market economy. This is mainly contained in five works he wrote over half a century, including: "Economics and Knowledge" (1937), "The Use of Knowledge in Society" (1945), "Competition as a Discovery Procedure" (1968), "The Pretense of Knowledge" (1974), and "The Fatal Conceit" (1988).[5] Among them, *The Fatal Conceit* was the last work published by Hayek during his lifetime. It can be said it is the essence of his academic thought.

Hayek's basic thought was the planned economy is unfeasible and the market is superior because humanity is ignorant, and the resultant difficulty transferring knowledge. In a division of labor society composed of many people, relevant knowledge for economic decision making is distributed among each person. Information about resources, technology, and preferences is private information. No one person can grasp it entirely and it is not given for any person. That is, every person has partial knowledge, and each person is ignorant. Therefore, the essence of social economic issues is how to use resources in the most optimal way to realize goals with relative importance known only to individuals. In short, economic issues are an issue of how to apply decentralized knowledge.

In Hayek's view, the market is fundamentally a cognitive system; a process of producing and transmitting information. Through prices and entrepreneurship, the market transmits dispersed knowledge to many separate decision makers. They can coordinate actions and achieve efficient resource allocation, while continuously producing new knowledge, new

[5] "Economics and Knowledge" and "The Use of Knowledge in Society" are collected in F. A. Hayek. 1980 (1948). *Individualism and Economic Order*. Chicago and London: The University of Chicago Press. "Competition as A Discovery Procedure" was originally written in German and it was translated into English by Marcellus S. Snow and published in *The Quarterly Journal of Austrian Economic* Vol. 5, No. 2 (Fall 2002): 9–23. "The Pretense of Knowledge" was Hayke's Nobel lecture and published in *The American Economic Review* 79 (6): 3–7. *The Fatal Conceit* was published by Chicago: The University of Chicago Press. 1988.

resources, and new technologies to drive social progress. The reason the planned economy is unfeasible is because dispersed knowledge cannot be concentrated in a central planning organ. Any attempt at this will lead to the dissipation of information. The reason is not only does information about resources and the environment continuously change, but more so because most information related to economic decision-making is subjective and practical. This is what Michael Polanyi spoke of as "tacit knowledge."[6] Tacit knowledge can be known by persons involved but not transmitted. It cannot be coded like scientific knowledge, so there is no way to transmit it through non-price channels.

In Western academic circles, the most common explanation for the failure of the planned economy is its inability to provide suitable incentives. That is, the reason the planned economy failed is people's selfishness. This explanation is not wrong. Nevertheless, Hayek proved even if we leave aside people's selfishness, people's ignorance is sufficient to cause central planning to fail. Altruism cannot save the planned economy.

Defenders of the planned economy have neither acknowledged their own ignorance nor have they acknowledged the essence of human knowledge. They mistakenly believe some powerful organ composed of experts selected through suitable means and granted sufficient authority will have a way to collect the necessary information required to establish economic plans and make rational economic decisions. They understand "scientific knowledge" and statistical information to be the only necessary knowledge for planning. They do not recognize tacit knowledge, which is another type of knowledge that is important but cannot be systematically organized. In this aspect, each individual has a certain advantage over all others. Only when a decision based on this knowledge is made by each individual or through active cooperation, can this knowledge be used. Hayek criticized the naivety of economic planning advocates as "the fatal conceit." This conceit caused them to be unable to see the true function of the price mechanism and entrepreneurship manifested in dispersed decisions. Ambitious attempts to replace individual decisions with central planning led to human disasters.

Humanity's ignorance also means coordination failures might occur in the market and entrepreneurs might make mistakes.

[6] Michael Polany. 1951. *The Logic of Liberty*. Chicago: The University of Chicago Press.

However, when considering the desirability of economic systems, we should not compare some type of system in reality to a perfect Utopia in the minds of economists. Instead, we should compare different systems as they may exist. The reason the market economy is superior to the planned economy is not because the market always efficiently allocates resources. Instead, in the market economy, due to profit-seeking motives and competitive pressures, people always have an incentive to discover and correct mistakes, regardless of who made the mistake. One firm's mistake is another firm's opportunity to make money. Correcting other people's mistakes is profitable. Correcting one's own mistakes can reduce losses. For this reason, the market is a system of continuous mistake correction. In contrast, under the planned economy, decision makers wielding tremendous power not only lack competitive pressure to correct mistakes, but also lack a profit motive for correcting mistakes. Actually, their biggest incentive is to conceal mistakes with more mistakes. The result is a series of small mistakes accumulating into a huge mistake until the economy reaches the edge of collapse.

Deng Xiaoping did not read Hayek's work, and might not have even known who he was. Nevertheless, from the experience China and the outside world had with the planned economy, he comprehended the conclusion Hayek proved from an epistemology perspective: The market is superior to planning. Deng Xiaoping recognized the limits of human knowledge and his own ignorance. Thus, he believed peasants will plant their fields better than when under the guidance of commune cadres. The man illegally peddling sunflower seeds was worthier of respect than the people that wanted to arrest him. Entrepreneurial decision-making was more efficient than bureaucratic decision-making. Decentralization was more suitable than centralized power to adapt to local conditions and drive comparative advantage. This is the epistemological foundation from which Deng Xiaoping started marketization and decentralization reforms. In this sense, he is a follower of Hayek.

Regrettably, due to not understanding Hayek's epistemology, even today, some economists and government bureaucrats still cannot free themselves from the "fatal conceit." Either they do not know their own ignorance or pretend to be all-knowing. Their recommendations for industrial policy and addiction to Keynesian aggregate demand stimulus not only distorted China's economic structure, but also harmed China's market-oriented reforms.

Reform Is Learning by Doing

Deng Xiaoping's acknowledgement of humanity's and his own knowledge limitations not only influenced the selection of goals for China's economic system reforms, but also influenced the selection of reform paths.

Like Hayek, Deng Xiaoping believed a system that can stand the test of time is certainly the result of sustained evolution, not the product of human design. No person has enough information and ability to design a perfect system once and for all. Any designed system will not stand the test of time. This is the reason the planned economy system is unsustainable.

Deng Xiaoping is called the "architect" of Chinese economic reform. However, Deng Xiaoping understood economic and social reforms are different from building construction. It cannot be built according to pre-designed blueprints. Instead, a "cross the river by feeling the stones" approach must be taken.

"Crossing the river by feeling the stones" is the most intuitive, simple, and visual expression of Deng Xiaoping's gradualist reform mindset. Its epistemological foundation is all the knowledge necessary for reform is dispersed, localized, and practical, like all the knowledge required to operate the economic system. No individual or group of leaders can grasp all the necessary information to manipulate the process of reform. Deng Xiaoping himself was no exception.

Since the mid-1980s, the "cross the river by feeling the stones" reform mindset has been continuously criticized. No matter how well their critiques of its faults are, they are still beholden to the "fatal conceit." They think they know the things they do not. To my knowledge, from the date the National Commission for Economic Reform was created to take responsibility for the overall reform plan, a few dozen overall reform proposals were made, but at most they were principled recommendations. None of them could be called a blueprint. This is not because the people making the proposals were not hard working or unintelligent, but instead was because they could not possibly have sufficient knowledge to set a reform blueprint.[7]

Deng Xiaoping understood practical knowledge was the vast amount of knowledge required for reform. Reform is a "learning by doing" process.

[7]Weiying Zhang, and Gang Yi. (1997). "China's Gradual Reform: A Historical Perspective." In *China's Economic Growth and Transformation*, edited by Clement A. Tisdell and Joseph G. W. Chai. Nova Science Publisher, Inc., 1997.

The interdependence between different reforms can only be revealed in the process of reform. For this reason, he advocated starting from the easiest parts and moving step by step forward, not trying to accomplish everything in one stroke. Deng Xiaoping was not interested in "package reform proposals."

For similar reasons, Deng Xiaoping advocated reforming through experiments. Once an experiment is successful, it should be boldly expanded. The establishment of four special economic zones in 1980 was the experiment that received the most praise. They could be called the comprehensive test area for market-oriented reforms and took on the mission of exploring a path for China's future.

In Deng Xiaoping's era, there was not a single major reform measure that did not start with experimentation. Price reform, distribution channel reform, wage and employment reform, fiscal and taxation reform, financial system reform, and foreign exchange and foreign trade reform were no exception. Even for major reforms like establishing stock market exchanges in Shanghai and Shenzhen, he said they could be tried, then improved based on performance of continuous experiments. If it did not work out, they could be closed.

Deng Xiaoping knew scientific projections of events that might occur was impossible due to the limits of human knowledge. Mistakes cannot be avoided in the process of reform, but reform is the only way out. On major issues, he was often willing to boldly push forward before grasping all the facts, while at the same time leaving room for adjustments that might need to occur. He always encouraged bureaucrats and various levels to boldly and bravely experiment, instead of walking like they had bounded feet, afraid of making a mistake. He told the opponents of reform to resign. Under his leadership, "being willing to reform and make mistakes is better than not reforming," became the cultural atmosphere in officialdom. Many successful reform measures came out of risks taken by bureaucrats at various levels.

Deng Xiaoping knew much of the knowledge and viewpoints required for China's reforms and development existed in other countries, especially advanced capitalist countries. His determination to open to the outside world never wavered. He never thought about closing the door out of fear a few flies might get in. When he visited Japan in 1982, he said he went to search for hints to China's modernization. He supported "borrowing," and sent bureaucrats on overseas inspections, encouraged young scholars to study abroad, and invited foreign scholars to give advice. For him, attracting foreign capital was a strategic measure to introduce advanced technology and ideas. He refused to accept the accusation "imperialism was back with its wallet." He made friends internationally and listened to their opinions humbly. He knew the information they provided could reduce the mistakes made by ignorance.

Deng Xiaoping was self-aware. He was decisive, but not obstinate. Even if he did not start an experiment, he gave his support as long as it was effective. If the decisions he made turned out to be mistaken, he would adjust at a suitable time. For the new things he did not have the knowledge or information to make judgments, he had a "wait and see" attitude. Once he had enough information, he would decide. He believed "practice is the only test of truth." He understood he was not an expert in economic affairs, so he delegated economic decisions to people more familiar with economic affairs. Even in the area of diplomacy, which he knew well, he was not eager to solve difficult but not urgent problems. He believed tomorrow's people will be more intelligent and wiser than today's people to resolve these issues.

Deng Xiaoping knew what he did not know!

CHAPTER 17

Can Vested Interests Become Reformers?

Many successful reforms, or even revolutions, are initiated, or even led, by vested interests. If vested interests cannot become reformers, then reform is hopeless.

In a great historical transformation, rulers should share the ideas of George Washington. If they do not share the ideas of George Washington, they should at least share the sense of crisis that his wife had. If they share neither the ideas of George Washington nor Martha Washington's sense of crisis, then there will be trouble.[1]

* * *

Can vested interests become reformers? My response to this question is affirmative. People commonly believe that vested interests are the greatest obstacle to reform. This point is correct. However, if we examine world history, many successful reforms—and even revolutions—were initiated—or even led—by vested interests. If vested interests cannot become

[1] The original version of this chapter was written in February 2013.

W. Zhang, *Ideas for China's Future*,
https://doi.org/10.1007/978-981-15-4304-3_17

reformers, then reform is hopeless. Only when vested interests become reformers can we have hope.

Why can vested interests become reformers? I have summarized three reasons.

First, the power of ideas. Our human behavior is not entirely determined by so-called material interests. The reason humans are humans is because we can think, have values, and be rational. A person's values and thoughts will of course influence his behavior. Scottish Enlightenment thinker David Hume said, more than two hundred and seventy years ago, even though people are swayed by interests, interest itself and all of humanity's affairs, are swayed by ideas. Hume observed:

> *Now, there has been a sudden and sensible change in the opinions of men within these last fifty years, by the progress of learning and of liberty. Most people, in this island, have divested themselves of all superstitious reverence to names and authority: The clergy have much lost their credit: Their pretensions and doctrines have been ridiculed; and even religion can scarcely support itself in the world. The mere name of a king commands little respect; and to talk of a king as GOD's vicegerent on earth, or to give him any of those magnificent titles, which formerly dazzled mankind, would but excite laughter in every one. … the royal power, being no longer supported by the settled principles and opinions of men, will immediately dissolve.*[2]

Throughout history, many great transformations began with a change in ideas.

Solon and Pericles were the primary promoters of ancient Athenian democracy. Both of them were aristocrats, but they expanded the electorate. Why? Because of ideas. After the American War for Independence, George Washington did not become a king. After serving as president for two terms, he returned home to farm. This was based on his ideas, not his interests. After the "Cultural Revolution," Deng Xiaoping initiated a series of reforms, including the elimination of lifetime tenure for leaders of the country. This was based on his ideas, not his interests. Gorbachev's reforms in the Soviet Union were also the result of ideas.

[2] Hume, D. ([1742] 1987) "Whether the British Government Inclines More to Absolute Monarchy, or to a Republic." In E. F. Miller (ed.) *Essays, Moral, Political and Literary*, Part I, Essay VII. P. 51. Indianapolis: Liberty Press.

When we discuss the French Revolution, we always say that it was a class revolution. Actually, the most important driving force of the French Revolution was the Ancien Régime's nobility. The Enlightenment was characteristically aristocratic.[3] Much of the intellectual class came from the nobility. A significant portion of the contributors to the *Encyclopédie* came from the old nobility. Almost all Enlightenment Era salons were held in the homes of the nobility. Rousseau received 30% of his correspondence and Voltaire received 50% of his correspondence from the aristocracy. The revolution that eliminated the nobility was the result of the nobility's own efforts. In their predicament, the threatened elites produced some new ideas that inspired the revolution. The Count of Mirabeau, a French noble, was himself a leader of the revolution.

Let us examine China's recent revolution. We call the Chinese Communist Party the "party of the working class." In fact, the founders and early leaders of the Communist Party of China were basically "vested interests" or their descendants under the old system. These vested interests included landlords, wealthy farmers, capitalists, warlords, government officials, intellectuals, etc. Working families could not possibly have the money to send their children to school, especially not in other countries. They sought revolution, not because the working class desired it, but instead because they accepted a new type of idea. This idea was Marxist-Leninism. Neither Karl Marx nor Vladimir Lenin came from the working class. Marx's father was a very wealthy lawyer, and his father-in-law was a Prussian nobleman. Friedrich Engels, his collaborator and sponsor, was a capitalist that owned many factories. Marx himself did not live the proletarian lifestyle. When he wrote *Das Kapital*, his annual allowance was 400 British pounds. At that time, the average annual income of the top ten percent of people in England was only 72 pounds.[4] According to Marx's own theories, this money came from "surplus value" created by the workers. In the early years of the Chinese Communist Party, only one top leader came from the working class, but we know he later betrayed the party.

[3] Liah Greenfeld. 1992. *Nationalism: Five Roads to Modernity*. Boston: Harvard University Press. P. 149–154

[4] Murray Rothbard. 2006 (1995). *Classical Economics: An Austrian Perspective on the History of Economic Thought*, Volume II. Auburn, Alabama: Ludwig Mises Institute. P. 340

Let us examine the history of the movement to abolish African slavery.[5] The movement to abolish slavery was initiated primarily by white people. The earliest opposition to African slavery was the Catholic Church. According to the Christian spirit, everyone is equal in the eyes of God. In 1775, the first abolitionist society was founded in Philadelphia. Benjamin Franklin served as the president of the organization that came to be known as the Pennsylvania Abolition Society. Great Britain was a major force opposed to African slavery. Starting in the eighteenth century, Quakers and evangelicals within the Church of England pushed to abolish the system of slavery. In 1783, the Quakers petitioned Parliament to abolish slavery, and were later joined by industrial workers. In 1807, the Parliament of the United Kingdom prohibited the slave trade in the British Empire. In 1833, the slave trade was prohibited in British colonies. The West African Squadron of the Royal Navy intercepted slave ships at sea. In 1838, the British government abolished the system of forced apprenticeship. In the end, Great Britain freed 700,000 slaves and spent £20 million.

Similarly, the movement to end foot binding in early twentieth century China was not the result of efforts by women. Instead, it was the result of efforts by men. People like Kang Youwei and Liang Qichao played a significant role at the time. From their perspective, foot binding was a type of national shame that undermined the international image of the Republic of China.[6]

This is the power of ideas!

Second, a game exists between vested interests. When we speak of vested interests, there is a mistaken assumption they are a united group with common goals and will consistently work to defend their own interests. This is not the case. Vested interests are composed of different groupings. Sometimes the conflicts between different groupings are much larger than the conflict between them and the class of people they rule over. The struggles between the groupings might be a question of life or death. Struggles among vested interests often become major forces for systemic change. I will provide a few examples.

Let us first examine the history of the separation of church and state in the West. The separation of church and state is a major foundation of the

[5] For the detailed history, see Kwamr Anthony Appiah. 2010. *The Honor Code: How Moral Revolutions Happen*. New York: W. W. Norton & Company. Chapter Three.

[6] Kwame Anthony Appiah. 2010. *The Honor Code: How Moral Revolutions Happen*. New York: W. W. Norton & Company. Chapter Two.

modern democratic system in the West. In the Early Middle Ages, the state and church were combined. The bishop was appointed by the king, and the church was not truly independent. The separation of church and state was the result of struggles between the church and the rulers. After the enthronement of Pope Gregory VII (serving 1073 until 1085 A.D.), the new pope decided to implement a series of reforms to resolve the issue of corruption in the church but was resisted. To eliminate the obstacles to reform, Gregory VII took the power to depose bishops away from the king. When Henry IV, the Holy Roman Emperor, opposed the action, Gregory VII had him excommunicated. The struggle between the pope and the emperor continued into the next century. Henry V, son of Henry IV, was also excommunicated by a successor of Gregory VII. Finally, in 1122, the Concordat of Worms was reached. The Holy Roman Emperor renounced his power to appoint spiritual leaders, and the Papacy acknowledged the emperor's secular rule.[7]

The French Revolution was the product of struggles between the French nobility. Before the revolution, France's greatest conflict was the conflict between the king and the nobility. The king constantly deprived the nobility of privileges, causing trepidation and dissatisfaction. There were also conflicts among the nobility, such as between hereditary nobles and position nobility, or the old nobility and the new nobility, or the rural nobility and the urban nobility, or the military nobility and the nobles of the robe. Even though the royalists and republicans were both elites and vested interests in French society in the late nineteenth century, it was precisely the struggles between them that drove the establishment of the democratic system in France.[8]

The constitutional reforms and establishment of the rule of law in pre-nineteenth century England was primarily the result of struggles between the nobility and the king, the king and the church, and within the nobility. The so-called "Glorious Revolution" was the victory of the nobility over the king.

The development of the corporate system is a specific example I want to mention. Before the middle of the nineteenth century, starting a

[7] Francis Fukuyama. 2011. *The Origin of Political Order: From Prehuman Times to the French Revolution*. Farrar, Straus and Giroux. P. 264–267.

[8] Liah Greenfeld. 1992. *Nationalism: Five Roads to Modernity*. Boston: Harvard University Press. P. 134–153.

corporation was a privilege in the West. In other words, only with special permission from the king or parliament, could a corporation be formed. Only a small number of influential people could obtain this special privilege. Commoners did not have the means to establish a corporation. Therefore, corporations were themselves monopolies. The East India Company monopolized eastern trade. At that point, imbalance formed among the elites, causing dissatisfaction among other vested interests. The final result of the struggle between elites was corporate formation changed from a permission system to a registration system. Everyone had the right to establish a corporation. This change happened in 1844 in England, 1867 in France, and gradually in the second half of the nineteenth century in America (where corporate registration is determined by state law).[9]

More generally, according to the research of Douglass North and his co-authors, the rule of law and democracy in Western nations was first implemented within the nobility. In other words, the nobility first had the rule of law and democracy, then it was gradually spread to all of society.[10]

Why did the nobility want to implement the rule of law and democracy? Because under an autocratic system, although vested interests have privileges, they do not have human rights. Their internal struggles are actually mutual devastation. The common people feel unsafe under an autocratic system, but they are not the least safe people. The people with special privileges are the least safe. Sometimes they are the upper class, but can quickly become prisoners, or even lose their heads. After considerable time passes, they acknowledge this type of system is not good for anyone. Rights should be used to guarantee the interests and safety of each person. After the rule of law is implemented, the regime can change, but they still feel a sense of security. They still have a sense of personal liberty, and can even live a good life, or at least feel their lives are not at risk. Under the old system, vested interests rarely have a good end. Even if you land safely, you still do not have the freedom of movement. This is a major reason vested interests want to implement the rule of law and democracy in the end.

[9] Doulas C. North, John Joseph Wallace and Barry R. Weingast. 2009. *Violence and Social Orders: A Conceptual Framework for Interpreting Recorded Human History.* New York: Cambridge University Press. Chapter 6.

[10] Doulas C. North, John Joseph Wallace and Barry R. Weingast. 2009. *Violence and Social Orders: A Conceptual Framework for Interpreting Recorded Human History.* New York: Cambridge University Press.

Third, reform is the best way to avoid revolution. Economists Daron Acemoglu and James Robinson researched this systematically.[11]

England is an example. England's true democratization began in 1832 with the passage of the First Reform Act. This act expanded the electorate to the middle class. Before 1832, England experienced sustained riots and mob incidents, including the Luddites that we all know of. The consensus among historians is the motivation for the 1832 Reform Act was to avoid social unrest or even revolution. Apparently, economist James Mill played an important role in persuading the government to acknowledge the crisis.[12]

However, the 1832 reform could not satisfy the demands of the masses for democracy. After 1838, the British working class launched the Chartist Movement to reform Parliament. They proposed universal male suffrage, elimination of the property qualification, payment for Members of Parliament (the lack of salary meant people of modest means could not serve), and other demands. The Chartist Movement lasted until 1848. Although it did not succeed, it had a major influence on later reforms.

As the pressure for reform grew, the British Parliament finally passed the Second Reform Act in 1867. It increased the electorate from 1.36 million people to 2.48 million people, and thus made the working masses the mainstay of urban constituencies. This reform was the result of various factors. The most important were the serious economic depression that increased the threat of riots, as well as the establishment of the National Reform Union in 1864 and the Reform League in 1865. These all made the government recognize not reforming was a dead end.

The British Parliament passed the Third Reform Act in 1884. It expanded the voting rules originally only suitable for urban constituencies to rural constituencies. This caused the electorate to double. From that point on, 60% of adult males had the right to vote. The factors that led to the introduction of this act was also the threat of social unrest.

During World War I, Great Britain passed the Representation of the People Act in 1918. This act extended the right to vote to men over

[11] D. Acemoglu and J. A. Robinson. 2006. *Economic Origin of Dictatorship and Democracy*. Cambridge and New York: Cambridge University Press.

[12] Murray Rothbard said, "Mill was the behind-the-scenes 'Lenin' and master manipulator of the drive for the Reform Bill." See Murray Rothbard. 2006 (1995). *Classical Economics: An Austrian Perspective on the History of Economic Thought*. Volume II. Auburn, Alabama: Ludwig Mises Institute. P. 73–74.

21 years old and women over 30 years old with property qualifications. It was negotiated during wartime, to a certain degree reflecting the government's need to mobilize workers to participate in the war and generate enthusiasm, but to a large degree was influenced by the October Revolution in Russia. After Russia experienced the October Revolution, the British government also feared a revolution would occur, so it proactively implemented democratic reforms. In 1928, British women obtained equal voting rights as men.

Even though certain other factors played a role in the process of democratization in Britain, the main driving force behind the establishment of Britain's democratic system was the threat of social unrest and social revolution. Precisely because of this, Britain's democratization was a gradual process. Every concession only met the demands of the "menace" or "trouble" at that time. For example, in 1832, buying off the middle class could bring about peace, so the electorate was only expanded to the middle class. After a new threat appeared, further concessions were made. This continued until universal suffrage was established in 1928.

In summary, of the three factors I mentioned, the first pertains to ideas, the rest pertain to interests.

Of course, vested interests becoming reformers is only a possibility, and possibility does not equate to necessity. Whether or not vested interests really become reformers is determined by whether or not there are sufficiently intelligent and wise people among them, whether or not these people have sufficient courage and leadership, and whether or not they can make wise choices. Some governments of non-democratic countries are accustomed to suppressing the people's demands for democratization. Or, they muddle along and only make a perfunctory effort in the beginning, then begin reforms when they have no other choice. When it is already too late (such as it was for the Qing government a century ago), revolution awaits.

When George Washington passed away in 1799, his will required all of his slaves to be freed after his wife died. However, his wife, Martha Washington, freed all the slaves the year after his death. When asked the reason, she said she did not want to live among people that hoped she would die.[13]

[13] See Eric Foner. 2008. *Give Me Liberty: An American History*. New York: W. W. Norton & Company. P. 273.

George Washington's manumission was based on ideas. He recognized freedom is a basic right. Martha Washington's manumission was due to interests. She believed she was threatened and had a sense of crisis. History has proven, in large historical transformations, it is best for rulers to have the ideas of George Washington. If they do not have the ideas of George Washington, they should at least have Martha Washington's sense of crisis. If they have neither the ideas of George Washington nor Martha Washington's sense of crisis, there will be trouble.

CHAPTER 18

Reform Stagnation Is the Source of Intensified Social Conflicts

The reform dividends accumulated over the first 25 years made the last decade the best decade in terms of economic growth. The stagnation and even regression of reform over the last 10 years is the primary contributor to our society becoming less and less harmonious. Reform stagnated because the ideas regressed and leadership was weak.[1]

* * *

The Lost Decade

To understand the future, I think we must understand the past, or at least understand the course of reform over the last 35 years. These past 35 years can be divided many ways, but my simplest division is to separate the last 10 years from the previous 25 years.

I will start with the period between 2003 and 2012. Over these ten years, I have made three judgments. The first judgment is the last ten years

[1] The original version of this chapter was written in December 2012.

W. Zhang, *Ideas for China's Future*,
https://doi.org/10.1007/978-981-15-4304-3_18

were the best decade in terms of economic growth. My second judgement is social conflicts and social issues are more severe in the last decade of this 35-year period. My third judgment is it was a lost decade from the perspective of systemic reform. This is my basic evaluation of the last decade.

We will first examine economic growth. Stated simply, our gross domestic product over the last decade grew at an average rate of 10% without much variation.[2] Standards of living have improved significantly. Our exports grew at an average of 20% per year. Our foreign exchange reserves increased from US$200 billion in 2001 to US$3.4 trillion in 2012. Our international status improved significantly. The scale of our economy increased from fifth in the world ten years ago to second in the world three years ago. Therefore, Chinese feel amazing. Some people project China will overtake America in another 20 years.

However, social conflicts are much more intense than in the prior 10 years. I feel it is difficult to find a satisfied social group. Everyone is complaining and there is discontent everywhere. No group is satisfied overall. Businesspeople are full of anxiety and insecurity, so many of them have begun to emigrate. It is easy to understand poor people are dissatisfied, but it is difficult to understand rich people are also dissatisfied. It is easy to understand the citizenry is dissatisfied, but you will find government officials are also dissatisfied. As mass disturbances constantly occur, the distance between bureaucrats, the government, and the citizenry grows. The distance between the government and intellectuals is growing. I feel over the last 35 years, there was never this type of common dissatisfaction. When the government now has a problem, many people see it as a joke. They almost do not see this country as their own. They do not feel any connection to the country, but instead see themselves only as bystanders.

Why is it a "lost decade" from the perspective of systemic reform? Over the last 10 years, there were no major, breakthrough reforms. Instead, some aspects regressed. For example, private enterprises developed rapidly in the first 25 years. By the 1990s, the public sector began to retreat and the private sector advanced. However, over the last 10 years, this trend reversed. State-owned enterprises got stronger and private enterprises got

[2] Per capita real GDP of China increased annually by 8.2% between 1978 and 2001, and by 9.8% between 2001 and 2012.

weaker. The evaluation of the review and approval system originally started 10 years ago, but now the number of review and approval procedures has increased. There is also the rule of law issue. Ten years ago, we emphasized the establishment of a rule of law country. However, over the last 10 years, we stopped stressing it. I do not need to list more examples. Perhaps everybody has personal experiences. There has been no major change in reform over the past decade.

Reform Dividends of the First 25 Years

Naturally, everyone will ask: If economic growth depends on systematic reform, how could there have been such high growth rates, even though as I have said there was no big progress in the aspect of reform over the last 10 years? My answer is the last 10 years of economic growth primarily came from reform dividends accumulated over the prior 25 years. I will give three examples. The first is the development of private enterprises. In the past 10 years, even though private enterprises were stifled, 90% of new employment is resolved by private enterprises. Without the development of private enterprises in the prior 25 years, from when they were surviving in the cracks in the 1980s to when they obtained legal status in the 1990s, how could we have had the high growth rates over the last 10 years? I will give a short review. In the 1980s, individuals doing business could only be sole proprietors. Private enterprises were illegal. Only after 1988, people could register private enterprises at the Industry and Commerce Bureau. Before that, private enterprises took shape as town and village enterprises or collective enterprises, meaning they were "wearing a red hat." In the 1990s, there was a movement to turn informal private enterprises into formally registered private enterprises. A lot of conflicts occurred during this process, such as extortion. However, overall, the proportion of private enterprises continuously increased. More than 10 years ago, Internet enterprises appeared. The Internet industry is basically entirely private, relying on foreign investment and private capital to develop. Of course, a major reason for this is the government did not understand it at the time.

The second example is state-owned enterprise reform. In the beginning, state-owned enterprise reform sought to maintain the system of state ownership while improving the efficiency of state-owned enterprises through "decentralization of power and transfer of profits." However, after the 1990s, most state-owned enterprises lost money. Local governments were forced to sell some state-owned enterprises they controlled.[3] Some local governments sold their state-owned enterprises as a package, whereas others sold them individually.

State-owned enterprise reform was an arduous task a decade or so ago. At that time, a large number of state-owned enterprises were losing money and insolvent. This caused many banks to be in a state of technical default. Starting in 1994, how to resolve state-owned enterprise debt was a big issue, leading to many policy opinions and papers discussing this issue. Finally, Premier Zhu Rongji ruthlessly resolved the bad debt problem. It is amazing that we now say the Industrial and Commercial Bank of China is the world's largest bank by market capitalization. However, imagine if we had not resolved these issues at that time. How could we have gotten through the financial crisis? We would not have needed to wait for America's financial crisis because we would have already been in a crisis. In 1998, close to 20 million state-owned enterprise employees were laid off. Quite a few of them were absorbed by non-state-owned enterprises. If this was not the case, China's social conflicts would have been extremely intense at that time. Of course, there were also a lot of problems related to the state-owned enterprise layoffs, and some of those legacy issues have not been entirely resolved. However, if Zhu Rongji had not ruthlessly resolved the state-owned enterprise issue in the 1990s, without state-owned enterprise restructuring and reorganization at that time, without the strategic retreat of state-owned enterprises in certain competitive areas, then growth would not have been as good as it was over the last 10 years.

The third example is the World Trade Organization. As I just mentioned, in 2001, China's foreign exchange reserves were a little over US$200 billion. When we joined the WTO, many people worried that China was finished. Actually, after we joined the WTO, international trade became a major driving force of China's economic growth. On average, the annual growth of exports has been between 1.5 and 2 times the growth rate of gross domestic product. This resolved the massive employment issue and greatly increased foreign exchange reserves. Joining the WTO allowed China to gain access to the international market, even though

[3] Shaomin Li, Shuhe Li and Weiying Zhang. (2000). "The Road to Capitalism: Competition and Institutional Change in China." *Journal of Comparative Economics*, Vol. 28 (No. 2): 269–292.

foreigners also gained access to our market. Overall, this was a win-win game. Mutual advantage was the source of human progress over the last 500 years. It was the result of market integration and globalization. Globalization is not today's issue, it started a few hundred years ago. In 1792, King George III sent George Macartney to China. The goal was to establish an embassy in Beijing and widen exchange between Great Britain and China. The Qianlong Emperor replied: "Our Celestial Empire has everything in abundance and lacks no product within our lands. There is no need to import the products of foreign barbarians in exchange for our own products." If Britain had been allowed to establish an embassy in Beijing, and China had established an embassy in London, then I believe the events that followed would have been completely different. Perhaps events like the Opium War would not have occurred. Our ignorance and our retreat caused certain issues later. When we discuss history, we should not be too emotional and think we were bullied by imperialism no matter what we did. If we were a little bit smarter, perhaps we would not have been bullied as much. Actually, at that time, our gross domestic product accounted for one third of gross world product, so no country could have easily bullied us. Of course, this is only a number. It cannot prove that we were powerful at that time. In reality, China at that time was like a sick old man, but the West was thriving. The West underwent the Enlightenment and the Industrial Revolution, but we did not.

I used these three examples in order to prove the institutional assets accumulated in the previous 25 years was the primary reason we attained high economic growth rates over the last 10 years.

Reform Stagnation as the Source of Social Conflict Intensification

However, why did social conflicts intensify over the last 10 years? My reasoning is very simple: Because our reform stagnated, and in some cases regressed, over the last 10 years. Even though Hu Jintao's regime proposed establishing a harmonious society more than 10 years ago, everyone discovered this society has become more and more unharmonious. This is the consequence of not reforming.

Corruption is one of the primary causes of the tremendous social conflicts today. In 1992, when I was in Great Britain, I discussed China's corruption problem with a British scholar. He was relatively pessimistic, but I said I was relatively optimistic. He asked me the reason I was optimistic. I said as long as a country's gross domestic product growth rate is higher than the growth in corruption, there will not be too big of a problem. Although the common person is dissatisfied with corruption, with rapid growth in income, everyone can tolerate it overall. However, in the opposite case, there might be big problems. My judgment is in the 1980s and 1990s, overall corruption was growing, but not as quickly as gross domestic product. However, over the last decade, I feel corruption has grown faster than gross domestic product. If government corruption is this serious, how can the common person feel satisfied? How can entrepreneurs feel satisfied?

Why is corruption getting more and more serious? An important point is government officials are getting more powerful. Why are peasants not corrupt? It is not because they are moral, but because they do not have power. I will not disparage the importance of morality. Some powerful officials are corrupt, but some are not. There is a difference in morality among them. However, the allure of power exists for everyone. With our government officials as powerful as they are, can we rely on anti-corruption measures to resolve the corruption issue? I am afraid not. This relates to my earlier discussion about the reasons the West established constitutional government a few hundred years ago, then established democratic systems. Constitutional government and democracy are institutional measures to constrain abuses of power. The freedom of speech is also an important restraint on government. Of course, we have made some progress in this aspect with the Internet and self-media. People can conveniently express their opinions, but overall our speech is not free enough. This is the reason I say the intensification of social conflicts is the consequence of stagnant reform.

Until 10 years ago, reform was justified. Over the last 10 years, it seems the justification for reform has become dubious. In 2011, I said in an interview with the *Economic Observer* the temperament of the country has changed.[4] I have also gotten this feeling from my own personal experience. Starting in 1999, I was involved in reform at the Guanghua School of Management. In 2003, I also initiated the Faculty System reform at

[4] See Webpage: http://www.eeo.com.cn/industry/hr_trends/2011/02/12/193115.shtml.

Peking University.[5] I felt a sense of justice and thought it was my calling. In the first few years, the strength of reform displeased a lot of people, but still went forward. There was an atmosphere of reform, and opposing reform was not legitimate. Even though there were people that opposed reform, they could only complain privately. However, after 2003, I felt the school's reforms became less and less legitimate. People opposed to reform could openly say so in the name of "keeping harmony." The overall atmosphere changed.

This reminds me of a story. In the 1990s, I heard there was a group of young people in Guangzhou that wore vests with the words "don't blame society." They meant you can only blame yourself for not living well, because society gave you opportunities and you had the freedom to make money, even as a street peddler. If you felt poor working in the government or at a school, then you could get into business. Stop complaining about your poor life. Now, this has changed completely. Everyone blames society. As the government becomes more and more involved in everything, who is there to blame besides the government? When people do not have real freedom, resentment builds up and erupts when given the chance. This is also related to the issues with donations to government-run charities. In what type of society are people the most charitable and willing to act in the public interest? It necessarily is free societies and just societies. America is a classic example. America is the freest country among the great powers. Americans give the most to charity, both in terms of average donations and volunteer hours, among all developed countries.[6] If the government is involved in too much, people will believe the government is responsible for everything, not individuals. Under the private property rights system, each person has a sense of responsibility. When the government is involved in too much, no one has a sense of responsibility. People that originally had a sense of responsibility are slowly losing it.

The atmosphere throughout the country changed precisely because our reform stagnated over the last 10 years, or even regressed in some aspects. More and more conflicts are accumulating, and everyone is less and less satisfied. Many people commit crimes, including vicious

[5] For my story of the faculty system reform at Guanghua School of Management as well as Peking University, see Jianying Cha. 2011. *The Players: The Movers and Shakers of a Rising China*. New York: New Press. Chapter 3: Beida, Beida!

[6] Arthur C. Brooks. 2012. *The Road to Freedom: How to Win the Fight for Free Enterprise*. New York: Basic Books.

bombings, because they believe society has treated them unfairly. We must clearly analyze the reasons behind these social issues. Of course, individual beliefs about injustice is not necessarily true injustice. Society will always have some strange people that will believe they are mistreated no matter how well they are treated. However, from the perspective of most people, we will have a commonly acknowledged standard of justice. If most people believe that society is fair, there will not be much resentment. An example is money earned from legal, hard work. I have not discovered much resentment towards Robin Li, Jack Ma, Pony Ma Huateng, or people like them.[7] Most people basically believe they relied on their own effort and wisdom to make it. However, why does everyone resent real estate developers? Clearly, some people make money only because they can obtain cheap land through connections. Of course people will resent them.

Do not mistakenly believe that people making money from business are not resentful. If you always have to be subservient to government officials, even if you make money, you will be angry. If I originally could make money with my ability and effort, but now I cannot, of course I will feel uncomfortable. People that make money are angry, but people that do not make money are even angrier. People can understand why poor people are dissatisfied, yet rich people are also dissatisfied. We have already lost basic, equitable rules. If the rules are equitable, I can be rich or poor and still think society is fair, so I will not be too angry. For example, although there are shortcomings from admitting students to university based on test scores, it is basically a fair system. People that get in and do not get in still feel that it is fair. Therefore, even if I do not get in, I will not kill teachers or the students that got in.

Overall, I want to say the reform dividends accumulated over the prior 25 years made the last 10 years the best 10 years of economic growth. The reform stagnation and regression over the last 10 years was the primary cause of our society becoming more and more unharmonious. It will also make future growth more difficult.

[7] They are respectively the founders of Baidu, Alibaba, and Tencent, the three giant Internet companies in China.

CHAPTER 19

Ideas and Leadership Determines China's Future

What determines China's future? The two most important things are ideas and leadership. The best is strong leaders with right ideas, and the worst is strong leadership with wrong ideas.

Looking back, in the first 25 years of reform, overall China had strong leaders with right ideas. This made great progress in both economic reform and economic performance. However, during the Hu-Wen regime from 2003 to 2012, China's leadership became weak and ideas regressed. As a result, economic reform stagnated, government became more powerful, state sectors regained force, and the rule-of-law building process stopped.

The future of China will depend upon whether it can regain strong leadership with right ideas.[1]

* * *

What determines China's future? I believe the two most important things are ideas and leadership. So-called ideas mean what we believe in, what we do not believe in, and what systems or institutions we believe benefit the development of our country and the people's happiness. So-called

[1] The original version of this chapter was written in May 2013.

W. Zhang, *Ideas for China's Future*,
https://doi.org/10.1007/978-981-15-4304-3_19

leadership refers to the kind of person that leads us, their undertakings, wisdom, courage, and responsibility. Of course, leadership also involves relatively good political means and operational abilities to realize the goals we would like to achieve. A reflection on the past 35 years of reform would benefit our understanding of this point.

Stated simply, during the first 25 years of reform, ideals were basically correct and leadership was strong. Now, as soon as anyone mentions reform, the first reaction is to focus on the difficulty of changing powerful special interests. My view is that from the very beginning there were obstacles to reform by special interests. Special interest objections to reform did not start today.

Special interests exist under any system. To change any system, special interests will always be in opposition. During the rural reforms, who were the special interests? They were the Secretaries of the Production Teams and Directors of the Revolutionary Committees. At that time, certain young people were also vested interests, because they did not work in the fields, instead they preferred to sing and dance, but they received the same rations as the people that worked in the fields. After the Household Responsibility System, everyone had to work in the fields to take care of themselves, so life was not as easy as before. Of course, there were also numerous ideological obstacles. How could we implement the Household Responsibility System on the road to socialism? How could we not take the road to socialism? These were viewpoints that became obstacles. However, we still went through with rural reform. Why? Because we had new ideas and strong leaders. A very important character in the Household Responsibility System Reform was Wan Li. As the party secretary of Anhui Province, Wan Li undertook rural reform in Anhui. At that time, Chen Yonggui was Vice Premier of the State Council in charge of China's agriculture. He began his career as the Chinese Communist Party Branch Committee Secretary of Dazhai Village in Xiyang County, Shanxi Province. Dazhai was established as the role model of collective agriculture, so his authority increased until he became the Vice Premier of the State Council responsible for agriculture. The Household Responsibility System negated collectivization and Vice Premier Chen's political legacy, so how could he support the Household Responsibility System? Wan Li faced many challenges and denouncements for taking the capitalist road and undermining socialism. How did Wan Li respond? He stated that if he was given the choice between peasants having food to eat and the socialist road, he would rather peasants have food to eat. Once, during a meeting at the Ministry of Agriculture held to specifically criticize the Household Responsibility System, a Vice Minister accused Wan Li of taking the capitalist road and thought that is "a new phenomenon of class struggle." Wan Li pounded on the table in anger as he questioned the intentions of the potbellied Vice Minister's opposition to fixing the problem of starvation among peasants. This was a type of ideal. Wan believed only by implementing the Household Responsibility System and the Production Responsibility System would Chinese peasants have the incentive to work and therefore have food to eat. Later, the constitution was revised to dismember the People's Communes. At first, we did not have grain to eat, but by 1984 China had more grain than it could eat, so the price of grain dropped significantly. Before, urban residents could only eat stale grain because the state granaries took in fresh grain but distributed stale grain. Now, urban residents can also buy fresh grain. With the appearance of free markets, anything was available, so debate over the Household Responsibility System ended.[2]

Another example is the reform and opening of Guangdong. At that time, Guangdong and Fujian provinces were front lines, called "the first line" (ready for war). The state did not invest much in these areas. Most money went into "the third line" in the interior of the country. Guangdong is next to Hong Kong, and at that time many Guangdongese were fleeing to Hong Kong, but many of them got caught and died in the barbed wire that was placed between Guangdong and Hong Kong. After being rehabilitated in 1978, Xi Zhongxun was assigned Second Secretary of Guangzhou, under First Secretary Wei Guoqing. After taking the position, Xi organized a meeting to discuss the issue of people fleeing to Hong Kong. During the meeting, one cadre stood up and stated that the reason people were fleeing was because peasants on one side worked all day and all night but had nothing to show for it, whereas on the other side people

[2] E. F. Vogel (2011). *Deng Xiaoping and the Transformation of China*. Cambridge, MA: Harvard University Press. Chapter 15; Weiying Zhang. 2015. "The Power of Ideas and Leadership in China's Transition toward to a Liberal Society." *Cato Journal*, Vol. 35, No. 1: 1–40. P. 13–14.

could have whatever they wanted after working a year. Xi replied that the cadre's way of thinking was problematic, and Xi fired him. The cadre thanked Xi because he hated his job. After the meeting, Xi did his own research and asked around. In the end he realized that the cadre spoke the truth, so the next day Xi called upon the cadre to apologize and persuade him to stay. Then, Xi deliberated on how to allow Guangdongese a way to benefit from the hard work that they did. From there he initiated a series of reform and opening measures, but of course had support from the central government.

Who made the greatest contribution to Guangdong's Reform and Opening? Ren Zhongyi. In November 1980, Ren Zhongyi succeeded Xi Zhongxun as Party Secretary of the Guangdong Provincial Committee. As soon as foreign capital was allowed in, Hong Kong businessmen came over, and corruption appeared. A person from Hong Kong could bring over an electronic watch as a gift for a government official, and then the government would happily accommodate his requests. Without a gift, no accommodations were made. This applied to some people, not all of them. At that time some cadres had ideals, unlike today.

Along with opening up came smuggling. Because prices in each area were so different, many people got rich from smuggling. Corruption and smuggling quickly became a handle for people in both the central and local governments to oppose liberalization policies. There were frequent reports written to superiors that Ren Zhongyi was taking Guangdong on the road to capitalism. Ren was often summoned to Beijing for self-criticism. One meeting was even held by the Central Commission for Discipline Inspection to discuss the Guangdong issue, and Ren was fiercely criticized. In accordance with the rules, if you are criticized, you must reflect, examine your own thought in order to self-criticize. Ren Zhongyi examined his thought, but he wondered: "What should I do when I go back to Guangdong? How can I communicate the spirit of this conference to cadres in Guangdong? If I tell the truth, the cadres in Guangdong will say that the central government's policy changed, and the government will not let Guangdong be open. However, if I do not tell the truth, it seems that it violates our party's principles." He had a dilemma. In order to solve this problem, before returning to Guangzhou, he went to General Secretary Hu Yaobang and asked Hu: "How should I convey the spirit of the conference?" Hu said with a smile, do what you want. Ren Zhongyi took the hint. This is a kind of leadership, and also an ideal. Hu Yaobang wanted to protect those who work and give them some freedom. So Ren Zhongyi later went back to Guangdong to keep working on the province's reform.[3] Of course, both anti-corruption and anti-smuggling efforts needed to be addressed. As long as you engage in openness, you will surely encounter some problems. However, you cannot abandon reform because of the potential problems.

The appearance of sole proprietorships and private enterprises is another example. In the beginning, sole proprietorships appeared as a pragmatic response to 20 million educated youth that returned to the cities after the Down to the Countryside Movement. The government could not arrange work for them, so the only option left was to allow them to be issued sole proprietor licenses. However, the way a business starts is that in the beginning one person does the work, and if he is successful, he hires others to do the work. According to Marxist theories, as soon as someone is hired to do work, the arrangement becomes exploitative. This was not compatible with socialism as we understood it at the time. This was a tremendous obstacle. To overcome this obstacle, a smart economist analyzed Marx's *Das Kapital* to find that "employing less than eight people was not exploitative." With this amulet, small-scale employers became legal. The problem was that as these sole proprietors became successful, they exceeded the eight-person limit, soon finding that they needed to employ dozens or hundreds of people. At that point, the Ministry of Public Security began to contemplate arrests.

A typical example is Nian Guangjiu, who was based in Wuhu City, Anhui Province and known for "Fool's Sunflower Seeds." Nian roasted sunflower seeds and did a great job. The scale of operations continued to expand, employing hundreds of people. According to the Marxist theory, of course, this is exploitation. Local officials wanted to arrest him but did not dare to act rashly. This matter was reported to Deng Xiaoping. Deng Xiaoping said: "Do not arrest him. How could one person destroy socialism?" Deng Xiaoping was very clever. He did not say why we should make great efforts to develop any private enterprise. However, he answered the

[3] E. F. Vogel (2011). *Deng Xiaoping and the Transformation of China.* Cambridge, MA: Harvard University Press. Chapter 14; Weiying Zhang. 2015. "The Power of Ideas and Leadership in China's Transition toward to a Liberal Society." *Cato Journal*, Vol. 35, No. 1: 1–40. P. 14–16.

question in a negative way and sent out an important message: Where should the country go? What kind of system do we need? This is a kind of ideal.

Of course, we know that many sole proprietors were arrested. Even in a place like Wenzhou, which at the time was considerably open and liberal, people were frequently arrested. In 1982, there were the so-called "Eight Big Kings" who were the leading players of respective businesses. The government arrested them in the name of fighting economic crimes. One fled and seven were sent to prison. In 1984, they were politically rehabilitated and labeled a force for progress.

That was how our country was at the time. There were big obstacles to reform, but reform ideas and leadership were also strong. In some years, reformers had the upper hand and reform moved forward. Other years, conservatives had the upper hand and reform was obstructed. Without courageous and idealistic leaders like Deng Xiaoping, Hu Yaobang, and Zhao Ziyang, reform would not have succeeded.

In 1992, 88-year-old Deng Xiaoping made his famous "Southern Tour." Why? After 1989, he saw that reform had stagnated or retrogressed. If he could not turn things around, the reform and opening he had started would have been a waste. He had not been listened to in Shanghai for two years and his voice did not carry in Beijing. The *People's Daily* printed articles to criticize his viewpoints, although his name was not specifically mentioned. He could not take it anymore, so he toured Wuhan and said "whoever does not reform should step down." Then, he went to Shenzhen and Zhuhai. His speech was broadcast by Hong Kong media, then was transmitted to the central authority. The Third Plenary Session of the Fourteenth Central Committee of the Communist Party of China eventually set "establishing a socialist market economy" as a goal. Deng Xiaoping's Southern Tour was a landmark event in the success reform obtained in the 1990s.

Another example is the resumption of the National Higher Education Entrance Examination . I was in the Class of 1977, so I was a direct beneficiary of this policy. After Deng Xiaoping was rehabilitated, he served as the Vice Premier of the State Council. He put himself in charge of education and technology, because he believed they were the core of the Four Modernizations. During the "Cultural Revolution" period, universities were closed. Later, Mao Zedong decided universities should be opened, but only science and technology universities. Admissions were based on political considerations, not aptitude. Students were recommended among the "workers, peasants, and soldiers," and became so-called "worker-peasant-soldier scholars." Of course, when the system of recommendations started, the people recommended were relatively suitable. Many bad systems are not very outrageous in the beginning, but within two years everyone knows the loopholes and it becomes worse. Deng Xiaoping questioned how someone could attend university through recommendation despite only graduating from elementary school. He decided to resume the National Higher Education Examination System to select university students through a process of examination, then let the Ministry of Education deal with it. However, at that point, the people that worked in the Ministry of Education were not in agreement. How could anything decided by Chairman Mao be revised? The "Two Whatevers" had not been overturned. They tried to delay. They reported to Deng Xiaoping resuming the National Higher Education Examination System would be extremely complex and require long-term, serious planning, so it could not be done in 1977. They recommended the current system be continued for that year. Deng Xiaoping told them if they can do it, then do it; but, if they cannot do it, then he knows people that can do it. This sentence resolved the issue.

This is leadership! Convictions must be acted upon with no excuses. Deng Xiaoping could have said "I understand. I hope you will look into it, get opinions from experts, and implement a mature plan." However, Deng Xiaoping was not this type of leader. Therefore, the 1977 National Higher Education Entrance Examination was held in November, although the different provinces did not take the test at the same time. Each province organized its own tests, with some of them earlier than others. Additionally, there was a shortage of paper for testing materials. Deng Xiaoping ordered the work being done on the fifth volume of the *Selected Work of Mao Zedong* to be ended in order to print more tests. This is truly amazing. He dared to use the paper that was going to be used in the fifth volume of the *Selected Works of Mao Zedong* for test materials. Deng Xiaoping had ideas. Great people certainly have ideas.

Joining the World Trade Organization was also a major decision over the previous 25 years of reform, made by Jiang Zemin and Zhu Rongji. I discussed previously the contribution joining the World Trade Organization made to our economic growth. Actually, one point I did not discuss is that joining the World Trade Organization inhibited our economic system from regressing. In other words, had China not joined the World Trade Organization in 2001, the regression in our system over the last 10 years would have been even greater. With the World Trade Organization, we had an international restraint. However, when we joined the World Trade Organization, opposition came from both ideology and vested interests. For example, many state-owned enterprises relied on tariffs and quotas to survive. Protection through tariffs harmed the interests of the common person, but it benefitted some people (including the government officials that allocated quotas). This is also a type of vested interest. Of course, certain people opposed joining the World Trade Organization because of their viewpoints. Regardless of the reason, the resistance was sizable. Zhu Rongji and Long Yongtu were both labeled traitors.[4] However, Jiang Zemin and Zhu Rongji were determined, because they believed that joining the World Trade Organization had more advantages for China than disadvantages. In other words, leaders like Jiang Zemin and Zhu Rongji believed that joining the World Trade Organization and further opening up would benefit China. Therefore, a few concessions when needed was nothing. Reportedly, when the discussions were intense, Li Peng said "Who cares? Join first and then revisit the issue." That was amazing.

Overall, ideas and leadership are extremely important to a country's reform. Without the ideas and leadership of people like Deng Xiaoping and Hu Yaobang, how could reforms have been possible? There was a saying in the 1980s: "It is okay to make mistakes in reform, but it is not okay if you do not reform." In the 1990s, leaders like Jiang Zemin and Zhu Rongji also had ideas, and relatively good leadership.

Unfortunately, over the last ten years, our ideas have not made much progress, and in some areas have even regressed. In the first 25 years of reform, we believed in the market. Of course, our belief in the market underwent a process of gradual deepening. In the beginning, we did not completely believe in it, but after Deng Xiaoping's Southern Tour, we truly believed in the market. Sometimes, we could not imagine the true power of the market. Who could have believed that a few years after the Household Contract Responsibility System was implemented, China would experience a grain surplus? Who could have imagined that after Deng Xiaoping's Southern Tour in 1992, Chinese incomes would have

[4] Long Yongtu was China's chief representative to the negotiation for joining the WTO.

[5] For the detailed discussion of ideas regression during the period from 2003 to 2012, see Weiying Zhang. 2015. "The Power of Ideas and Leadership in China's Transition toward to a Liberal Society." *Cato Journal*, Vol. 35, No. 1: 1–40. P. 23–29.

doubled in just few years? When China joined the WTO at the end of 2001, it had about $200 billion in foreign exchange reserves. Who could foresee that China's foreign exchange reserves would exceed $3.2 trillion within 10 years? This is the power of the market.

However, over the last 10 years, we believed in the market less and less.[5] We have set many policies that strengthen the role of government, one of which is the so-called "industrial policy." In the name of industrial policy, the government has maintained many of the powers from the planned economy era. During the planned economy era, the most important government department was the State Planning Commission. Originally, during the process of reform, the powers of the State Planning Commission decreased. However, over the last ten years, its powers have increased. Of course, it has changed names, and is now called the National Development and Reform Commission. It is almost like a secondary State Council with tremendous power. Almost all economic activities must be approved by it. Some examination and approval processes have been given the title "recording and filing," but are really just examinations and approvals. What is the outcome? Many industries have excess capacity and wasteful investment. In 2009, the government proposed the Ten-Industry Revitalization Plan. After four or five years pass, we know that any industry the government tries to revitalize becomes a disaster. Solar power is a classic example. As soon as the government got involved, problems appeared. Originally, certain private entrepreneurs had developed quite well according to market needs, but as soon as various subsidies and supports were provided, excess capacity and insolvency became common.

During the first 25 years of reform, we believed more and more in private enterprises. The proportion of state-owned enterprise activity in most industries continuously declined. State-owned enterprises completely exited certain competitive industries. However, over the last ten years, the situation has changed. We have transitioned from "state decline and private progress" to "state progress and private decline." Now, state-owned enterprises are involved in everything and expanding. They have re-entered industries they had previously exited from and are forcefully acquiring private enterprises. The State-Owned Asset Supervision and Administration Commission was established to reform state-owned enterprises, but now makes state-owned enterprises larger and stronger. How does it do this? It creates monopolies while reorganizing and bullying private enterprises.

During the first 25 years of reform, we believed "development is the hard principle." It meant that China's economic and social problems could be resolved only through reform, or the process of continuously making the pie bigger and bigger. However, over the last ten years, we have not considered development as a hard principle, but instead focus more on wealth distribution. Originally, fair and just rules of the game were more important than equal distribution of wealth. Equality of opportunity was more important. If your rules of the game are unfair, then a fair allocation is impossible. A mainstream explanation now is that the market is the initial allocation which will certainly lead to unfairness, so the government is required to implement secondary and tertiary allocations to make income distribution fairer in the end. This explanation is incorrect. Why is initial allocation unfair? Because there is too much imposition of government power. People with special privileges can do business and make money easily, but others cannot. The issue with China's income distribution is not a problem with the market itself, but instead is a problem caused by government departments harming the market. Special privileges are the most unfair. Now, the State Council has said it will introduce an income distribution proposal. The motives are good, but if the thought process is built upon the assumption that "the market has problems that only the government can fix," then this income distribution proposal will fail. As long as a country focuses on establishing fair rules of the game, then everything else is a small problem. If the rules of the game are fair, then the market itself has many redistributive mechanisms, including private charities. These redistributive mechanisms are often more effective than the government's. If the rules of the game are not fair, then relying on the government's redistributive policies cannot resolve the root problem. It is like constructing a large building. If the support structure is not done correctly, no matter how thick the cement is, it will still collapse. This is an issue we must clearly acknowledge now when we consider income distribution. Do not believe those theories that say the market leads to inequality. The market will create an income gap, but if this income gap forms under equality of opportunity conditions, then it is desirable, and we cannot say that it is unfair. Without interference from government power, the market will continuously reshuffle income distribution. Under free competition, today's rich people might become tomorrow's poor people, and *vice versa*. In traditional societies, there was no reshuffling, so the nobles were always nobles and commoners were always commoners. The market is reshuffling every day, especially after the invention of the Internet. Reshuffling happens 24 hours a day, because people buy things online.

Over the last ten years, another idea has regressed. The belief in the rule of law has regressed. Ten years ago, we emphasized establishing a rule of law country, but now social stability comes before everything else. For stability, we do not talk about the rule of law, but the outcome is that society is more and more unstable. What type of society is most stable? A rule of law society is most stable. In a rule of law society, the citizenry can resolve problems through judicial means, not political means. However, in a society without the rule of law, legal issues become political issues. Political issues are resolved by the loudest voice, so people agitate to turn small issues into big issues. Violence and mass disturbances frequently occur because that is the only way to get the leadership's attention. If you do not take that step, no one will pay attention to you.

An example of rule of law regression is the "Chongqing Model" over the last few years. In the name of "fighting organized crime," Bo Xilai arrested people at will. The police, prosecutors, and the courts worked together in a way that brought back the "Cultural Revolution." If we had not had a regression in our overall idea about the rule of law, would this phenomenon have happened? Bo Xilai's methods were illegal, so they would have been inhibited. In the "Li Zhuang Case,"[6] not even the rights of lawyers were protected, so how will the rights of ordinary people be protected? We Chinese have a strange viewpoint that people who defend criminals are bad people. Why do we need lawyers? We need lawyers to protect the rights of every person, not to create jobs for lawyers. As individuals, we are weak. We might be harmed at any time, and will need the help of others, so there is a need for lawyers. Once, a provincial Political and Legal Affairs Committee Secretary was arrested. He called his friend that worked in the lawyer's association and asked to have a good lawyer arranged. Friends will help each other, but privately this person told me that he wanted to ask this person how he treated lawyers when he was in a position of power. Bo Xilai might have also had this idea. He wanted a good lawyer to defend him, but he probably did not think of this issue when he was in power. Because rule of law principles have been destroyed, there can be no true stability.

[6] Li Zhuang was a lawyer on the defendant side in the case *Chongqing government v. Gong Ganmo*. Li was arrested for "faking evidences and guide-leading the defendant." All the charges against him were fabricated. Li was sentenced to one and a half years in prison.

The stagnation and regression of reform over the last ten years is related to two incorrect ideological trends. The first trend occurred in 2004 and 2005 with the so-called Market-Oriented Reform Failure Theory. Some people said that the numerous issues facing Chinese society, such as the income gap, poor access to medical care, poor access to education, environmental pollution, regional disparities, etc. are all the outcome of neoliberal and market-oriented reforms. What can be done? We can increase government interference and strengthen the powers of state-owned enterprises. Under the influence of this trend, starting in the second half of 2004, state-owned enterprise reform basically stopped. Some other reforms also stopped, and the government increased its control over the economy. Market-oriented reform measures lost legitimacy. However, after the 2008 and 2009 Global Financial Crisis, China was the only country doing well, so our self-confidence exploded. Why did we previously say that reform had failed, but now everything was good? This brought about the so-called "China Model." It said that the reason we were successful is because China did not accept the so-called "Washington Consensus." We did not take the free market or privatization road. The core of the "China Model" is powerful government interference and state-owned enterprise dominance of the economy. These two trends appear to be different, because one says that our reforms failed while the other says that our reforms succeeded, but they are the same in conclusion. The Reform Failure Theory rejects the market-oriented reforms over the first 25 years, whereas the China Model Theory rejects future market-oriented reforms, although reforms up to this point are considered good enough. If we say that the Reform Failure Theory provided legitimacy for anti-market-oriented reforms after 2004, then the China Model Theory provided legitimacy for the large-scale government investment and advancement of the public sector while the private sector declined since 2009.

We can see how incorrect ideological trends and incorrect ideas inhibited the progress of reform. As was described previously, China's economic miracle came from market-oriented reforms. The future of China will depend upon whether it can regain strong leadership with right ideas, like Deng Xiaoping. Otherwise reform will go astray.

CHAPTER 20

Economic and Political Reforms in the Next Thirty Years of Reform

The grand objective of China's next 30 years of reform should be to establish "a society with liberty, justice, the rule of law, and democracy." This should be the mission of the Chinese Communist Party in its role as the party in power.

In the short term, during a period of transformation, the ideas of leaders are very important, but in the long term, the ideas of the common people determine our future. If the common person's ideas change, society will certainly change. The issue is only the method in which we change. If the ideas of leaders are ahead of the masses, reform takes place; if the ideas of leaders are behind the masses, revolution will take place.[1]

* * *

The Overall Goal of Future Reform

To understand what we must do for future reform, we must have a grand, long-term goal. Without a long-term goal, we will only think of what must be done today but will go astray tomorrow. The most annoying question I am asked is: "What do you think will happen in the next six

[1] The original version of this chapter was written in October 2012.

W. Zhang, *Ideas for China's Future*,
https://doi.org/10.1007/978-981-15-4304-3_20

months?" I do not care about anything that happens in the next three years but am willing to discuss anything that may happen three years or more from now. Unfortunately, many of us only care about how investments will do over the next six months, what consumption levels will be, how much the consumer price index will rise, etc. I am not saying that it is improper to care about the short term, but without big ideas and long-term vision, reactive policy may lead to problems.

I think the grand objective of China's next thirty years of reform should be to establish "a society with liberty, justice, the rule of law, and democracy." This should be the mission of the Chinese Communist Party in its role as the party in power. With this as our mission, if we look at the steps we must take, we should not worry about making some mistakes, because there has never been a historical transition that did not have problems. The first 25 years of reform were astounding. Some say that reform has entered the deep end, so we cannot cross the river by feeling the stones. I believe that it is not actually a problem of being in deep water, instead the problem is that some people do not want to cross the river. Reform is a type of idea, and after we grasp it, the rest is easy. In my view, many of the so-called "rivers" that we must cross are in our heads. If there are rivers to cross everywhere, we do not dare take one step forward. This is why I say that first we must establish a grand objective. We cannot expect that from a grand objective we can design a complete proposal and then implement it. That is not called social transformation; that is called engineering. We currently have a large number of people with backgrounds in the natural sciences and engineering that manage society, so we have a "project" for everything. What part of society is a project? Each person in society is a living, breathing, thinking individual, how can anyone know what each person is thinking every day? If a person is given freedom, results will naturally appear out of the hustle and bustle. If a system could be designed by a central authority, what do we need the market for? If that was the case, our planned economy would have succeeded early on, so what leeway would have been left for the market to exist? Of course, I am not negating the significance of an overall plan, but I believe that ideas are more important than any plan could be. Deng Xiaoping reformed because he had an idea. During the process of reform, he adjusted policy according to actual conditions. "Crossing the river by feeling the stones" was greater and more workable than any plan could have been. Neither the Household Contract Responsibility System, state-owned enterprise reform, sole proprietorships, nor private enterprises were ever part of a plan. If we believe in a person's human nature and give him freedom, he will create.

The two most important aspects of future reform are economic reform and political reform. The two things that must be done for economic reform are further market liberalization and state-owned enterprise privatization. We must have free market ideas and abolish most government examination and approval regulations. These examination and approval regulations not only lead to losses in efficiency, they also lead to corruption and social injustice. The privatization of state-owned enterprises started ten years ago. If we had continued on, we would have been done with it by now. Instead, we stopped midway. Now we must resume.

State-Owned Enterprise Reform

On the aspect of economic reform, I will focus here on state-owned enterprise reform.

State-owned enterprises are currently too strong. I believe that if any country's state-owned enterprises exceed ten percent of GDP, then that country cannot be called a market economy. I am not saying that there should not be any state-owned enterprises, but they must be limited to a tiny number of industries. Great Britain's state-owned enterprises accounted for ten percent of GDP before Lady Thatcher's reforms. Even though it was only ten percent, the British economy could no longer operate effectively, so Lady Thatcher began privatization reforms. We currently are between 35–40%, and the most important sectors are all state-owned monopolies with no entry allowed for private enterprises.

As for the role of state-owned enterprises, there are many misunderstandings. The impression is that without state-owned enterprises, this or that industry could not exist, so the whole country would be doomed, and the people's livelihood destroyed. We think this way because we have never wanted to change. Under the planned economy, every sewing kit was produced by state-owned enterprises, but now state-owned enterprises do not make them. Are we going without? Not only can we still buy sewing kits, but the quality and quantity have both increased. When we hear about the "contributions" of state-owned enterprises, such as how much they contributed to tax revenue, output, and employment, these are all serious misunderstandings because they only examine one aspect. They only look at output without considering input. For example, in 2011, state-owned enterprises accounted for 42% of industrial enterprise assets, but only created 26% of industrial output.[2] Let us use a metaphor. The Qianlong Emperor of the Qing Dynasty had 17 sons and 10 daughters, meaning he had 27 children in total. Now, each family can only have one child. Should we consider the Qianlong Emperor 27 times more productive than today's families? No! His output was high because he had more resources and held special privileges. He had excessive resources because he harmed other people's productivity, which is called "crowding out" in economics. There were 3000 women in the imperial harem, so there were 3000 men that could not find partners, so these 3000 men became eunuchs, causing all of society's output to decline. Similarly, state-owned enterprise's monopoly status and resource advantage not only restricts the growth of private enterprises, it also reduces society's productivity and damages social morality. Employment within state-owned enterprises is a case of nepotism. It is very hard for those without relationships to get in. As it is, how can we make common people be moral? We have not recognized the extent that state-owned enterprises harm social fairness and social morality. We only view them as simple production units, but they are more than that.

State-owned enterprise reform is not as hard as many people think. As long as we are decisive, as we were in the 1980s and 1990s, it is much simpler. Today, most large state-owned enterprises have already listed on the stock market, so the only question the government has to deal with is how to transfer shares to the public and sell off assets. The state-owned enterprise shares owned by the government could be given to the public, or sold to private enterprises. It does not have to be done all at once, it could be done in stages. For example, the government currently owns between 70–80% of state-owned banks. First it should be reduced to 50%, meaning the state still controls them. Later, it can be reduced to 30%, then 10%, and then zero. During this process of step-by-step reduction, corporate governance would improve until in the end they became true private enterprises.

Political System Reform

Political system reform means establishing the rule of law and democracy. We must acknowledge the basic values that apply to all of humanity. The West's natural law and China's *tiānlǐ* or *tiānjǐngdìyì* are basic values that

[2] Calculated from *China Statistical Yearbook*-2012, Table 14.1 and Table 14.4.

are based on the needs of human nature, human survival, and human happiness.[3] How can we not acknowledge being in line with heaven and earth? What does it mean to not acknowledge this value? It means we offend the Heavens and reason. No system can violate *tiānlǐ* or natural law. The laws in our daily lives are set by Man, but there is one law that is higher than laws set by Man, and that is natural law. Without that higher law, any ruler could set any law, so there would be no rule of law to speak of.

The first step of political reform is to implement the constitution and establish the rule of law. The 1982 Constitution is basically good, but it was never truly implemented. Many of the articles set out in the constitution, such as various types of liberties, judicial independence, and People's Congress elections, etc. have not been implemented.

The second step of political reform is democracy. Democratization should come after the rule of law is established. Without the rule of law, democracy often turns into mob rule. Democratization is a slow process. We have lessons to learn from Hong Kong's functional constituencies and Taiwan's experience with democratization.

In the history of the West, constitutional government and democracy came in two stages. Monarchy can be constitutional governance if the king accepts limits of the law. Monarchy unlimited by the law is tyranny. Actually, during the Enlightenment, many people, including Montesquieu, believed that constitutional monarchy was the best system, not democracy.

I believe China should follow this path over the next thirty years, and I believe we can do it. I know that some people are relatively pessimistic and do not think it is possible, but I am relatively optimistic. Thirty years from now, society will be led by people born after 1990 and 2000. Perhaps they will not be willing to live under the current system. Some things are irreversible. The Internet, for example, has already become a way of life for young people, as normal as eating or wearing clothes. It cannot be turned off. No government should try to resist new technology. Resisting it will only breed more discontent. If today one thing is shut down, and tomorrow another thing is shut down, how can people not be dissatisfied? Google is no longer just a tool for the communication of information, it is a vital tool for scientific research. Checking materials, data, and indexes can all be done on Google. We currently cannot enjoy this creation of human progress. As time passes, how can researchers not feel resentful?

[3] See Chapter 12 "The Law of God and the Law of the King" in the current book.

Some historical transitions seem long, whereas others seem short. As was discussed above, close to two hundred years passed between America's independence and black Americans obtaining the right to vote, but only 43 years passed between black Americans obtaining the right to vote and the first black president.

The next twenty years are our only window period for reform. The issues that we face cannot be put off later and later into the future. If we do not accomplish them in the first decade, the second decade will be completely different. The more we delay, the harder it will become.

In the short term, during a period of transformation, the ideas of leaders are very important, but in the long term, the ideas of the common people determine our future. If the common person's ideas change, society will certainly change. The issue is only the method in which we change. If the ideas of leaders are ahead of the masses, reform takes place; if the ideas of leaders are behind the masses, revolution will take place.

CHAPTER 21

China Needs Institutional Entrepreneurs

The problems we face today are the same problems that were faced more than one hundred years ago. We need a new era of enlightenment.

Enlightenment requires idea entrepreneurs. These idea entrepreneurs must use new viewpoints, new theories, and new values in order to convince society to bring about change.

China also requires political entrepreneurs. They are statesmen and politicians that can bring about transformation. Two basic characteristics are the hallmark of a good statesman: right ideas and strong leadership.[1]

* * *

Institutional Entrepreneur: Innovation and Risk

We often speak of entrepreneurs as business entrepreneurs or entrepreneurs within business circles. They deal with technological innovation, business model innovation, and other aspects of innovation such as organizational management. Here I would like to discuss a different kind of

[1] The original version of this chapter was written in October 2012.

W. Zhang, *Ideas for China's Future*,
https://doi.org/10.1007/978-981-15-4304-3_21

entrepreneur: The institutional entrepreneur.[2] The so-called institutional entrepreneur is a person that changes the rules of the game. They deal with institutional innovation.

Institutional entrepreneurs can be separated into two categories. The first category is the idea entrepreneur. They provide us with ideas, change our views, and shape our culture. Examples of this in the ancient world are Aristotle, Confucius, Shakyamuni, and Jesus Christ. Examples from the modern world would be Adam Smith, Ludwig von Mises, F. A. Hayek, Ronald Coase, and so on. These people could all be considered thought institutional entrepreneurs. The second category could be called political entrepreneurs. They serve as statesmen and politicians to change society. Examples of these types of people are Solon and Pericles in Ancient Greece, Lord Shang in Ancient China, and President Washington, the founder of America's system. Mr. Deng Xiaoping, President Reagan, and Lady Thatcher are also all outstanding political entrepreneurs. Political entrepreneurs can be also called implementation institutional entrepreneurs.

What is the essence of entrepreneurship? In Schumpeter's words, it is innovation and creative destruction. In the commercial sphere, each major technological advance eliminates the previous technology. Today's iPhone and iPod have completely replaced the tape recorder, Walkman, and the camcorder. The function of institutional entrepreneurs is also to innovate. Innovation for them means replacing old values with new values; replacing old behaviors with new behaviors; replacing old principles and virtues with new principles and virtues; and replacing old rules of the game with new rules of the game. They lead us to acknowledge things we originally did

[2] S. N. Eisenstadt introduced the word "institutional entrepreneur" in an article published in 1980. See S. N. Eisenstadt. 1980, "Cultural Orientations, Institutional Entrepreneurs and Social Change: Comparative Analyses of Traditional Civilizations." *American Journal of Sociology*, 85: 840–869. P. J. DiMaggio (1988) was a systematic analysis of the role institutional entrepreneur plays in system transformation. See P.J. DiMaggio. 1988. "Interest and Agency in Institutional Theory." in L. Zucker (Ed.), *Institutional Patterns and Organizations*. Cambridge, MA: Ballinger. In the last thirty years, there have been more than one hundred English-language articles about institutional entrepreneurs. For a general summary of this literature, see J. Batttilana, B. Leca and E. Boxenhaum. "Agency and Institution: A Review of Institutional Entrepreneurship." Harvard Business School Working Paper, No. 08–096. May 2008. Cambridge, MA. Cass Sunstein introduced the norm entrepreneur concept. See C. Sunstein. 1996. "Social Norms and Social Roles." *Columbia Law Review*, 96(4): 903–968.

not acknowledge, or no longer acknowledge the things we originally acknowledged. Female foot binding started in the Song dynasty. It was believed that the smaller feet were, the more beautiful they were and the easier it was to get married. In those times, the face was less important than feet. After the Republican Era, foot binding was slowly abolished. We know that putting an end to foot binding was not advocated by women, it was advocated by men.[3] These men, such as Kang Youwei and Liang Qichao, were institutional entrepreneurs. Mr. Deng Xiaoping led our implementation of marketization reforms. In the past, we did not acknowledge the market, but now we do. In the past we acknowledged the planned economy, but now we do not. This change in beliefs was brought about by Deng and other institutional entrepreneurs in the 1980s and 1990s. Many of China's future reforms are related to this type of transformation in our beliefs.

For entrepreneurs in the business world, every innovation must undergo the test of the market. It is the same for institutional entrepreneurs. Whether or not an innovation is successful, such as new rules of the game becoming accepted as common norms of behavior, depends on its ability to satisfy society's needs. A very important part of satisfying the market is a deep understanding of human nature. Entrepreneurs in the commercial sphere cannot succeed if they do not understand human nature. People like Apple's products because these products are designed with human nature as the starting point.

There are also differences between business entrepreneurs and institutional entrepreneurs. For business entrepreneurs, the same industry normally has differentiated products that serve the needs of different people. Institutional entrepreneurs normally face a mass market, but there are no niche markets, only a winner-takes-all market. The mass market must undergo a long period of experimentation. In order for a proposed behavior rule to become accepted by all, it must become what Game Theory calls an "evolutionary stable strategy." This means that as more people respect this behavior rule, the more beneficial it is for everyone to follow it until it is a common behavior rule. Because of this point, institutional entrepreneurs must have a more thorough understanding of human nature

[3] Kwamr Anthony Appiah. 2010. *The Honor Code: How Moral Revolutions Happen*. New York: W. W. Norton & Company. Chapter Three.

than do business entrepreneurs, so great thinkers must all start by discussing human nature.

Similar to business entrepreneurs, institutional entrepreneurs' innovation also face tremendous risk. There are three reasons for this risk. The first is that market demand is uncertain, and their judgments may be incorrect. When many people feel the need to change, but they do not know how to change, institutional entrepreneurs can only make judgments about general trends. The second reason is the risk brought about by the "second-order Prisoner's Dilemma." Simply put, the first-order Prisoner's Dilemma is when it is beneficial to all people to cooperate, but everyone chooses rationally not to cooperate. The second-order Prisoner's Dilemma is when maintaining cooperation requires rules, and violating these rules should carry a punishment, but the enforcer of these rules fears retribution or losing opportunities on the side, so there is no incentive to enforce the rules. In the end, no one respects the rules.[4] We see lots of uncivilized behavior, such as spitting and littering, and many of us would like to say something, but do not dare to. This is a "second-order Prisoner's Dilemma." Changing old rules must also overcome the "second-order Prisoner's Dilemma" because a rule already exists and people are accustomed to following it. Even if changing the old rule is good for everyone, as each person comes forward to change this rule, the first rule-breakers will be punished by others. Face is in our nature, so before we do anything, we must consider other people's possible reaction. A person may desire free love, but do not dare to follow through because others will gossip, so he will accept a bride arranged by his parents, even if he does not like her. The risk brought about by the second-order Prisoner's Dilemma is also considerable. The third reason is that competition between institutional entrepreneurs is intense, much more so than for commercial competition.

Because of the three reasons mentioned above, an institutional entrepreneur's success is very uncertain. During their lifetimes, many great institutional entrepreneurs generally have very bad luck. Today these people's names are renowned, but they did not have an easy life. Confucius

[4] R. Ellickson, 1991, *Order without Law: How Neighbors Settles Disputes*, page 237 (Cambridge MA: Harvard University Press); R. Ellickson, 1999, "The Evolution of Social Norms: A Perspective from the Legal Academy. (*Working Paper No.* 230, Yale Law School, Program for Studies in Law, Economics and Public Policy); R. McAdam, 1997, "The Origin, Development of Regulation of Norms."*Michigan Law Review*, 96(2): 238–433; Weiying Zhang, (2018), *Game Theory and Society*. London and New York: Routledge. Chapter 6.

had a tragic life. As he led his followers around to spread the word, they often had nothing to eat or drink, no one listened to them, and were often driven off. Socrates was put to death by the Athens government. Jesus Christ was crucified by the local Roman governor. When Master Zhu Xi was alive, his ideas were called "false knowledge," he was called a "fake master," and even his students were called "fake students." There is similar risk for political entrepreneurs. An old Chinese saying is "there is no good fate for reformers."

I want to especially emphasize the special characteristics of competition between institutional entrepreneurs. The first characteristic is that it is winner-takes-all. For institutional innovation, winner-takes-all is the rule, but in the commodity market, winner-takes-all is the exception. Even Microsoft is not a winner-takes-all competitor, because there are other platforms and products with smaller network effects. The market for Sichuan, Northeast, and Shaanxi cuisine in Beijing is large enough so that all of them can make money. Competition between institutional entrepreneurs is like competition between different standards of 3G or 5G, even more than between Windows and Linux.

The second characteristic of the market for rules is that competition is long-term competition. The customers of institutional entrepreneurs are different than customers of business entrepreneurs. Customers of business entrepreneurs are mostly in the present, or possibly a little bit later, but almost all are people alive today. Institutional entrepreneurs' customers often come after their lifetimes, even hundreds of years in the future. When Confucius died, his influence was limited. His real customers came more than three hundred years after he died, especially after the Emperor Wu of Han, and even today we are still customers of his. This brings about a problem. Even if business entrepreneurs only want to make money, they can still become great entrepreneurs. Institutional entrepreneurs are different. They cannot possibly have making money as an objective. Even if their customers accept their principles in the end, they have no way to pay them money. Institutions are a public good. Each person can utilize them without paying any money, so an institutional entrepreneur cannot seek profit. Missions are most important.

Why do these people take such big risks to create new rules of the game for humanity? I suppose it is because of their love for humanity and desire to improve the lot of mankind with their lofty ideas and sacred mission. Perhaps this love for humanity is congenial instead of consciously determined. We call these people sages (*shèngrén*). They are different from us common people, so it is difficult for us to understand them. A person may write an article that the authorities oppose, so that person's family and friends will urge him or her not to publish it. For most people, our standard for judging our every action is our immediate interests. However, for sages, immediate interests are not important. We can imagine that if Socrates had pled guilty, he would not have lost his life. If Christ had backed down, he would not have been crucified. If Confucius had submitted to the sovereigns of feudal states, he could have found a good position and lived a prosperous life. I believe that many people would have told them to not be so earnest, but their refusal to do so was not because they did not understand the consequences, but because they were unwilling to give up their principles. These sages are different from us common people, so their sense of mission and love for humanity cannot be understood using our own way of thinking.

Even if they are not sages, they are different from the average person. They care more about their reputation after death than their fame while still alive; otherwise they would not suffer the consequences of upholding their ideas. On the contrary, they do not consider it to be suffering, because in their mind violating their principles would be insufferable. There is a poem by Petofi Sandor that goes "Life is dear, love is dearer. Both can be given up for freedom." If you have a sacred view of freedom, you will not stand for anyone inhibiting on your freedom because you value freedom more than you value life. From this perspective, we can understand the reason that so many outstanding people throughout the history of humanity, no matter whether they are called sages or not, deserve our respect. They are certainly different from the rest of us.

Idea Entrepreneurs in the Two Great Ages

Over the last few thousand years of the history of human civilization, the appearance of ideas entrepreneurs has been concentrated in two periods. The ideas created in these two five-hundred-year periods determined our lives, way of thinking, and rules of the game today.

The first 500-year period was the 500 years before the Common Era, the so-called Axial Age. Overall, it was the 500 years between Confucius and Christ. During this 500-year period, in both the Occident and Orient, many great thinkers appeared, including Confucius, Laocius, Socrates, Aristotle, Plato, Shakyamuni, and Christ. The ideas they created are the cornerstone of all human civilization that came after. They are still influencing our lives.

The second five-hundred-year period started with the Renaissance in fourteenth century Italy and ended with the Enlightenment in eighteenth century Europe. France is generally considered to be the center of the Enlightenment, represented by Montesquieu, Voltaire, Rousseau, etc., but Scotland's David Hume and Adam Smith and Germany's Kant also made huge contributions to the Enlightenment.

What did thinkers in the first 500 years ponder? At that time there was chaos under the heavens, so the issue faced by humanity was how to turn an immoral world into a moral world. They focused on changing people's hearts (minds). Whether they created religions or moral philosophies like Confucianism, their goal was to establish morality under the heavens.

In the 500 years of the millennia before the Common Era, both the West (primarily Southwest Asia) and the East (primarily China and India) were undergoing a transition period between low-end societies and high-end societies. The low-end society mixed religion and state, had God-like kings, used "witchcraft" as a means of ruling, lacked a professional bureaucracy, lacked a professional military, and had no need to collect taxes. In the high-end society, rulers became chief executives separate from the church, leading professional bureaucracies and militaries that relied on tax revenue. During the process of transition from the low-end society and the high-end society, both the East and West experienced constant wars and conquests. The whole world was in a degenerate state. Without a new social order, humanity's suffering would only worsen. Within this environment, we saw the appearance of many great institutional entrepreneurs. These great institutional entrepreneurs thought of how to change moral chaos into morality under the heavens. They wanted to establish morality for humanity.[5] Of course there were disagreements between schools of thought on what constituted morality. China's Hundred Schools of Thought were different types of moral systems, such as Taoism, Confucianism, Legalism, Mohism, and others. These different moral systems served the same type of purpose, but some succeeded and others failed. Confucianism succeeded, whereas Mohism failed. Taoism did not fail, but it has not been as successful as Confucianism.

[5] Morris, I., 2010, *Why the West Rules for Now: The Patterns of History and What They Reveal about the Future*. Profile Books. P. 254–263.

In the past, we always spoke of the differences between the East and West, but in the case of morality, many of the rules proposed by great institutional entrepreneurs in both the East and West were very similar. The difference between Plato's Republic and the Confucian Ideal State are not as significant as the differences between Confucianism and Taoism.

I have summarized them into five commonalities, and I believe these are the most important rules for human cooperation: People first ("*yǐrénwéiběn*"), do unto others as you would have them do unto others ("*tuījǐjírén*"), help and love each other ("*hùzhùyǒu'ài*"), be honest and keep your word ("*chéngshíshǒuxìn*"), and reward good and punish evil ("*jiǎngshànchéng'è*").[6]

I will use Game Theory to re-explain each of these five principles. Humans have the right to pursue their own happiness, but if each person only considers short-term interests, it will lead to the Prisoner's Dilemma and mutual harm. In order to resolve the Prisoner's Dilemma, people must accept basic norms of behavior, such as restraining their selfish desires as well as adhering to the principles listed above. To ensure that these norms of behavior are effectively enforced, people must not only be good at heart, but there must also be an institution that rewards good and punishes evil. If this institution is effectively and justly implemented, then people will understand their long-term interests. Interpersonal relationships will not be mutually harmful. Humanity can escape the Prisoner's Dilemma. People will be able to enjoy a harmonious and happy life.

The second 500-year great age was different from the first. During the second 500-year period, thinkers focused on human rights and human freedom. Most of them no longer believed humanity was created by God or that they must accept theocratic rule. Instead, they believed that everyone had natural rights, with liberty and equality being inherent. With this as our foundation, we must also mutually cooperate for common development. Enlightenment thinkers believed that it is impossible to change people's hearts, but possible to regulate their actions. The "invisible hand" market mechanism that Adam Smith spoke of, as well as the rule of law and democratic principles we use to restrict governments, are all ways in which we allow people to pursue happiness through mutual competition instead of mutual harm. This not only does not bring harm to others, it

[6]Weiying Zhang. 2018. *Game Theory and Society*. London and New York: Routledge. P. 354–262.

creates value for others. For example, in the market, if a person wants to make money, he or she must first create value for others, otherwise they cannot make money. This was Adam Smith's theory. Enlightenment thinkers understood that humanity's harmony and progress required government, but the power of government must be restrained by a constitution and democracy. What is the source of rulers' power? Before it was said that it was granted by God, the so-called Divine Right of Kings or what we Chinese call "the Son of Heaven." Today we do not believe in this. All authority is granted by the consent of the governed. In addition, the rulers are the same as common people in that they have good and bad sides. How do we restrict their bad sides? We use a system of checks and balances on their power. All power must be restricted by law and monitored by the people. This is the philosophy of the rule of law and democracy.

China Needs Institutional Entrepreneurs

Today, China needs both idea entrepreneurs and political entrepreneurs. The reason is China must transform from an authoritarian society to a liberal society founded on the rule of law and democracy. This is very challenging. In some sense, China is now disordered. Old norms are no longer widely accepted but new norms are yet to be established. Neither traditional Chinese culture nor Marxism are now believed in by the majority, let alone followed. The Chinese people are not happy with the current system. But their understanding of liberty, the rule of law, democracy, and private property is even worse than a hundred years ago. So they are very confused. Transition will necessarily bring about great conflicts of both ideas and interests. High-level political and leadership skills are needed to navigate during the transition.

During the first Axial Age, the East and West created civilization at the same time. However, during the second great age, China did not participate in the creation of new ideas. China's "Renaissance" was during the Song dynasty, but it did not lead us towards modernity, instead it revised ancient ways. The West's Renaissance did not intend to move back; it used ancient ways as an excuse to move forward. One hundred years ago, after the Opium War, and especially after the Jiawu War (Sino-Japanese War in 1894), we Chinese began to acknowledge this point and China began its enlightenment. The May Fourth Movement in 1919 was China's Enlightenment. Actually, before the May Fourth Movement we Chinese began to be enlightened by the introduction of ideas about liberty, constitutional government, and democracy. Regrettably, not long after the May Fourth Movement did this enlightenment end. We replaced "enlightenment" with "ideology" so our enlightenment was like half-cooked rice. When we started Reform and Opening in the late 1970s, we started a new enlightenment, but it only lasted about 10 years until 1989. We must acknowledge that the issues we face today are the same as 100 years ago. We need a new enlightenment. Not only should this happen, it will happen.

Enlightenment requires idea entrepreneurs, great liberal thinkers, to develop and use new viewpoints, new theories, and new values to persuade society that it can transform.

China also needs great political entrepreneurs to institutionalize new ideas. Political entrepreneurs are different from thinkers because thinkers do not need official positions, but political entrepreneurs must be in a position of leadership. People without a political position cannot possibly implement institutional changes. To become a good political entrepreneur, a person must have two basic characteristics: right ideas and strong leadership.

Unfortunately, China has reached a point where its politicians are drawn exclusively from the bureaucracy, whereas originally there was a split between the two institutions. Our top leaders now are called "civil servants." Our judges and justices are also defined as "civil servants." This is an absurd predicament. The bureaucracy follows carefully proscribed rules to ensure that mistakes are avoided, while great politicians should be interested in acting for the nation's destiny and future. Politicians must to some extent be of outstanding abilities, and are required to withstand the hardships of political competition. It is very unlikely to have great leadership with a bureaucratic training process.

Why should we worry about the bureaucracy training our politicians? The party secretary is the true head of all levels of governments, and the promotion ladder is strictly bottom-up hierarchical. Imagine that you were somehow to become the deputy head of a county government in China. How many steps away from becoming the county party secretary would you be? Five! And each step closer would require at least two years. If your luck was good, in 10 years you could become the party's county secretary. Once you hold this position, you have effectively monopolized power at that level and can undertake large-scale projects. But if you still want to progress up the political ladder, your next position should be a deputy mayor of a municipal government. Suppose you now become the deputy mayor. You are still five levels away from the city party secretary, which would require another ten years. Reaching the provincial party secretary from a deputy governor of a province is another 10 years. You can become a top national leader only after you hold the provincial party secretary for some years.

At the end of this 30-plus year process, we have only two possible results: those with courage and principles will have been knocked out, while those who have rid themselves of these attributes will have become thoroughly bureaucratized, and thus we are left with a nation of bureaucratized leaders.

That is why the leadership of the Hu-Wen regime was so weak. It was the first time in history of the Chinese Communist Party that top leaders came completely from the bureaucracy. It is understandable that they lacked a sense of mission, vision, and courage.

The system as it now exists is incapable of producing great leaders at precisely the time when we need great leaders for a transition to a constitutional and democratic system.

In the case of Taiwan, did their transition to democracy rest simply on possessing good fortune? Before his death in 1988, Chiang Ching-kuo recognized the importance of democratic institutions and began Taiwan's transformation. The first generation of mainland Chinese revolutionaries had the power to create a similar transformation, but failed to do so. Even Deng Xiaoping missed his opportunity to become mainland China's Chiang Ching-kuo. After 60 years, we are still waiting.

Of course, history is about contingency, and sometimes chance circumstances combine with a person who possesses principle, a sense of mission, courage, and the ability to lead. Owing to special historical circumstances, China's new leader appears to be a strong man, as he is not completely the product of our bureaucratic training system because of his special family background. We Chinese must therefore hold on to a sense of hope. It is because of this that I believe that the next ten years presents a window of opportunity. It is imperative that we do not miss the chance to reform, as future generations of leaders are unlikely to be as capable as today's if the current political system—especially the promotion system—are not changed.

What is uncertain is what kind of ideas the new leadership holds.

Democratization Is a Long and Slow Process

Lastly, I especially want to focus on Confucianism and democratic politics. There are many debates about Confucianism. My own opinion is Confucianism has people-oriented ("*mínběn*") ideas, but it does not have an institutional framework for democracy, so the social orders and ideal institutions in Confucianism place hope in wise rulers and virtuous ministers. That is unrealistic. Confucianism never had a "Heaven Reliant Sword" to restrain monarchs. Now it is clear that only if the government is restricted by law and power is bestowed by the people, can governments truly govern for the people. Mou Zongsan, a representative of Neo-Confucianism, said in the past, China had administrative democracy ("*zhíquán de mínzhǔ*"), but not political democracy ("*zhèngquán de mínzhǔ*").[7] Because there was no political democracy, administrative democracy could not be guaranteed unless wise rulers and virtuous ministers appear. Relying on the appearance of good emperors and chancellors is not viable. However, Confucian culture and democracy are not incompatible. Taiwan, Japan, and Korea have all been influenced by Confucian culture, but have all succeeded in implementing democratization. I agree with Mr. Mou's opinion.

The establishment of democracy in China will be a long and slow process. China's traditional system has three pillars: Imperial power, imperial examinations, and Confucian culture. Under the imperial authority system, the nation's land, the state, and the people are the private property of the emperor. This viewpoint has not changed completely at the present time. The West used to believe in this. Louis XIV once said "I am the State." In the end the West abandoned this idea. The state belongs to the people, sovereignty belongs to the people, and the people are free and rational. Now rulers can only serve the people to rule legally.

In ancient China, the Imperial Examinations System guaranteed the professional management of China. It was the world's earliest selection system to be implemented. The drawback was it attracted a large amount of top talent into the government. These people did not create value, they

[7] Mou Zongsan. 2006. *Zhengdao yu zhidao* (Political System and Governance). Guilin, China: Guangxi Normal University Press. P. 18.

only redistributed wealth, but they did not distribute it according to the logic of the market, only the logic of theft.

Lastly, there is Confucian culture.

In the short span of less than twenty years during the beginning of the last century, all three pillars of China's traditional system toppled. In 1905 the Imperial Examinations System ended. In 1911 the Xinhai Revolution overthrew the emperor. In 1919 the May Fourth Movement sidelined Confucianism. Now China has many issues that we must consider further. We must understand the systems of the past and the systems we need in the future. There is no need to rush. Today's Chinese are not at the same level as Westerners when it comes to understanding the rule of law, and we have also lost touch with our traditional sense of integrity. We overthrew the emperor but did not establish democracy. This was most likely related to our undue haste. We could have been more patient. The advancement of democracy happens step by step. On television we see Taiwanese legislators fighting, but two hundred years ago there were also fights in America's Congress, and some were worse. Democracy is a process that requires time and patience. We cannot rush the rule of law or democracy, nor can we believe that any small problem means failure. If one hundred years ago our forefathers had been more patient, perhaps China's democracy and rule of law would have been more advanced than it is today. After all, the Republic of China established in 1911 was the first republic in Asia!

CHAPTER 22

China Must Get Rid of Six Idea Traps

The key to transitioning China into a liberal society is whether China can succeed in its political reform. China is now bounded by following six wrong ideas, including: (1) China's Economic Success Comes from the China Model; (2) Economic Liberalization Can Continue without Political Reform; (3) The Status Quo Is Good for the Vested Interests; (4) State-Owned Enterprises Are the Cornerstone of the Chinese Communist Party's Ruling Power; (5) Power Comes from the Barrel of a Gun; and (6) An Unlimited Government Is Stronger than a Limited Government. If China cannot get out of these six idea traps, political reform will be impossible.[1]

* * *

China has made considerable progress in the past three and half decades in its transition to a market economy, even with the stagnation during the Hu-Wen regime. However, it still has a long way to go to become a democratic/liberal society. The key to transitioning China into a liberal society

[1] This chapter is excerpted from the author's paper "The Power of Ideas and Leadership in China's Transition to a Liberal Society", published in the *Cato Journal*, Vol. 35, No. 1 (Winter 2015): 1–40.

W. Zhang, *Ideas for China's Future*,
https://doi.org/10.1007/978-981-15-4304-3_22

is whether China can succeed in its political reform. The last three and half decades have been dominated by economic reform. Now a fundamental political reform is urgently needed. Establishing a rule of law and a democratic system should be the major targets of political reform. It may take another three decades, but the next decade under General Secretary Xi Jinping's regime will be crucial to start political reform. Whether or not China can succeed in its political reform also depends on ideas and leadership. In my judgment, China is now bounded by some wrong ideas and the bureaucratization of leadership.

I identify six traps of wrong ideas. If China cannot get out of these six idea traps, the political reform will be impossible.

Trap One: China's Economic Success Comes from the China Model

The argument embedded in the China Model School is that China has succeeded in the past three decades because it has created its own unique governance system, and it is this unique system that drove China's achievement in just three decades whereas it took the West 200 years to achieve. Therefore, China should continue its own model, rather than follow the West's model. As I mentioned earlier, the idea of the China Model School is wrong. The fast economic development in the past three and half decades was because China enjoyed a "late-comer's advantage," which is common to all other late-comers. Using the terminology of Hayek, the Chinese economy is a parasitic economy.[2] The West constructed the road; China just followed it. That China walked faster does not mean that its institutions are superior. As Hayek argued convincingly, the sciences, technologies, and managerial skills developed in free societies can be borrowed by unfree societies to support economic development. As such, the latter can even have faster growth rates for a limited period of time.

Just looking at most of the technologies Chinese companies use and the new products they massively produce, including the computer, mobile phone, car, airplane, internet, and so on, most of them are innovations of the Western free societies; they are not China's innovation. As the late-comer's advantages are diminishing over time, China's future

[2] Hayek, F. A. 2011 (1960). *The Constitution of Liberty*. Chicago: University of Chicago Press. P. 101.

development will crucially depend on its home-made innovation. Without fundamental changes in its political institutions, the late-comer's advantages will eventually turn into a curse.[3]

Trap Two: Economic Liberalization Can Continue Without Political Reform

The second prevalent wrong idea is that China's economic success in the past three decades shows that even without political democratization, economic liberalization and high growth are possible. This idea is wrong for two major reasons.

First, while the economic liberalization alone can provide considerable incentives for business activities and therefore economic growth in the early stage when the growth is mainly driven by the reallocation of the existing resources, as people have wealth to protect and innovation becomes crucial for growth, the rule of law becomes a necessity. Without the rule of law, property rights are always at risk of confiscation, and entrepreneurs would not have enough incentive to innovate, because innovations take a longer process and more uncertain compared to arbitrage activities. The massive immigration of Chinese entrepreneurs into foreign countries in the past decade signals the serious need for property rights protection, which can only be met under a system based on the rule of law.

Second, the Chinese government needs new legitimacy to rule the country. The legitimacy of the CCP's rule originally came from winning the bloody revolution. For a long time, the Chinese people have accepted this traditional legitimacy. However, this is no longer sufficient. According to the Chinese tradition, the legitimacy of the ruling regime also depends on the living condition of the ordinary people under the regime. Deng Xiaoping realized that the Communist Party could sustain its rule only when it let people achieve good standards of living. So, he launched the reform. In some sense he succeeded, as the Chinese Communist Party is still in power long after the Soviet Union and Eastern European communist regimes collapsed. Nevertheless, as the survival problem has been solved in China, the Chinese people are no longer satisfied with a comfortable material life. They

[3] This point was first raised by Xiaokai Yang in his lecture notes.

need dignity, freedom, and self-expression.[4] If the government cannot protect people's basic human rights, including the freedom of speech, press, and religion, its legitimacy will be seriously challenged. Even within the Communist Party, without some form of democracy, the legitimacy of its leaders would be questioned. This calls for political reform to build the rule of law and democracy. Only through such political reform, can the Chinese government gain its new and urgently needed legitimacy.

Trap Three: The Status Quo Is Good for the Vested Interests

A dominant idea among the ordinary people as well as among the elite is that the status quo benefits the vested interests groups at the expense of others. This idea seems to be reasonable on the surface. There are conflicts between the vested interests and others. But a deep analysis shows that this idea is not right. The existing system actually turns out to be good for nobody, even the vested interests. While the vested interests enjoy privileges, they do not have the basic human rights such as free speech and personal security, just like other ordinary people. Even though the privileges give them better opportunities to be wealthy and powerful for the time being, the lack of human rights implies that they are always at political risk—neither their personal freedom nor their property is secure. Under the current system, anyone can be arrested without going through a legal procedure, regardless of seniority.[5] The interesting thing is that the conflicts of interests among the ruling elites are actually much greater than that between the rulers and the ruled. Anyone can become the victim of the political power struggle. As a result, the vested interests are living in anxious situations. Not only those who are judicially sentenced for corruption and political reasons have lost their freedom. Even those senior officials who did not commit to any financial fraud feel like they are living

[4] Based on data of the World Value Survey, Inglehart and Welzel (2005) provide a very convincing argument for democratization as the survival value is overtaken by the self-expression value. R. Inglehart and Welzel. 2005. *Modernization, Cultural Changes, and Democracy: Human Development Sequence*. Cambridge, UK: Cambridge University Press.

[5] The Chinese Communist Party has the "*shuanggui* system" under which any Party member can be arrested by the CCP Discipline and Investigation Committee long before being prosecuted.

under house arrest. For instance, a retired minister could not even go abroad to visit his children and relatives without an official permit. So why would the vested interests think the current system is good for them but institutional reform would hurt them? The answer is that they are too ignorant. Once the vested interests realize where their true interests reside, they would more likely support, or at least less likely resist, political reform, even if they still want to retain their power. In the long-run, the rule-of-law system is better than the rule-of-man system even for the elite, as demonstrated by British history.[6]

Trap Four: State-Owned Enterprises Are the Cornerstone of the CCP's Ruling Power

One of the ideological barriers to privatization of the state-owned enterprises is that they are regarded as the economic cornerstone of the CCP's ruling power. This idea is also wrong. Historically, the Chinese Communist Party took power before it built its state sector, not the other way around. If it had relied on its control of a large state sector, it would never have had the opportunity to rule the country. The CCP won the war against the Nationalist Party not because of its assets but because of its ideas. Even 100 percent state ownership of the economy cannot guarantee the ruling of the Communist Party. The Soviet Union is a typical example. It collapsed when the state owned the whole economy. The CCP still holds its ruling power not because of the state economy but because of the rapid development of the private economy and the partial privatization of the SOEs in the 1990s. Today, because of the inefficiency and corruption of the state sector, SOEs have become a negative asset for the government. If the remaining part of the state sector can be privatized, the better economic performance might earn the CCP more public support.

Trap Five: Power Comes from the Barrel of a Gun

Mao Zedong once said that "power comes from the barrel of a gun." This idea has become a deep belief of the Communist Party. The absolute control of the military is regarded as the essence of the CCP's ruling authority,

[6] D. C. North, J. J. Wallis and B. R. Weingast. 2009. *Violence and Social Orders: A Conceptual Framework for Interpreting Recorded Human History*. New York: Cambridge University Press.

so any proposal to nationalize the military is strongly opposed.[7] However, if this idea was true, no political regime could have been overthrown, because the military forces were initially always in the hands of the ruling authority. Even the CCP could not have taken over power because in the 1940s the Nationalist Party's military force was much stronger than the Communist Party's. The Communist Party won not because of its gun power but because of the power of its ideas. Guns followed ideas. When ideas change, guns change hands. Many Chinese intellectuals turned to the Communist Party during the civil war after the anti-Japanese War, because they were dissatisfied with the dictatorship of the Nationalist Party and believed that the Communist Party would give them more freedom and democracy. The leaders of the Communist Party must realize that honoring its promise on freedom and democracy is more important than controlling the army.

Trap Six: An Unlimited Government Is Stronger Than a Limited Government

The sixth wrong idea is that an unlimited government is stronger than a limited government. This idea has been a doctrine of the Chinese government for a long time, and China's quick response to the global financial crisis seems to provide new support to it. The idea actually confuses authority with strength, and confuses strength with power. History has shown that a strong government is not an unlimited government, but a limited one. The reason is that a government can be strong only if it is trusted by its people. This can be well exemplified by the history of Great Britain.[8] Before the Glorious Revolution in 1688, the king's government was almost unlimited. For example, the king decided whether or not to repay the government debts on time. As a result, it was very difficult for the government to issue bonds to the public. After the Glorious Revolution, the British government changed into a limited government under the constitutional monarchy. With higher credibility of the bond contracts,

[7]According to the CCP's doctrine, the army should be controlled by the Party, not the state. Thus, the Chinese army is the Party's army, not the nation's.

[8]B. R. Weingast. 1997. "The Political Foundations of Limited Government: Parliament and Sovereign Debt in 17th and eighteenth Century England." In J. N. Drobak and J. V. C. Nye (eds.), *The Frontier of the New Institutional Economics*, 213–46. New York: Academic Press.

the capacity for the government to raise funds through bond issues dramatically increased. A truly strong government is one under the rule of law, rather than under the rule of man. Limited government and democracy are like the commitment made by the government to its people. With these commitments, people can then trust the government, and the government becomes strong as a result. If the Chinese government cannot transform itself into a limited government, then it cannot become a truly strong government.

PART IV

Liberty and the Future of China

CHAPTER 23

Will Economic Freedom Lead to Political Freedom?

The development of finance and the development of the market have brought us a lot of economic freedom. It has made us wealthier and made our lives better. However, the arrival of political freedom is not a matter of course or automatic. After people become wealthy, they pursue order, stability, and efficiency. They might be afraid of change. If we want true political freedom, then simply becoming more market-oriented is insufficient. We must put in a more arduous effort.[1]

* * *

In the Middle Ages, a theologian named Saint Augustine said humanity has three great evil desires. The first is the desire for money and wealth. The second is the desire for power, honor, and reputation.[2] The third is lust. Most of human history developed under the domination of these

[1] The original version of this chapter was written in October 2015.

[2] Herbert A. Deane. 1963. *The Political and Social Ideas of St. Augustine*. New York: Columbia University Press. PP. 44–56. Quoted from Albert Otto Hirschman. 2013. *The Passion and the Interests: Political Arguments for Capitalism before its Triumph*. Princeton, NJ: Princeton University Press. P. 9.

W. Zhang, *Ideas for China's Future*,
https://doi.org/10.1007/978-981-15-4304-3_23

three desires. From this perspective, what will be brought about from the development of finance or the logic of the market?

There are two points. First, the means in which desires are realized will change. When finance and markets are not developed, people pursue the desire for wealth primarily through plunder. I call this the "logic of theft." This is even more so the case for satisfaction of the desire for power. After finance and markets are developed, people satisfy their desire for wealth through exchange and cooperation to create value. We can understand lust from this perspective, as explained by Professor Zhiwu Chen in his book *The Logic of Finance, Part II.*[3] The development of finance separates love from marriage or child-rearing. This is a transformation of the way desires are realized.

Second, when finance is developed and the market mechanism functions well, people can use the desire for wealth to replace the desire for power. This point is extremely important. Throughout history, many disasters resulted from people's desire for power. Conquests led to a huge number of deaths. Satisfaction of this desire for power included both foreign conquest and ruling over the people domestically. A ruler will use force—not only limits on liberty but also murder—to make people listen to him and satisfy his own desire for power. After finance and the market are developed, people can pursue wealth and material well-being more freely. The relative value of the desire for power declines. Sima Qian (145-c. 90 BC) was a market liberal in the ancient Han dynasty.[4] He spoke of "the man with 1,000 coins being like a duke, and the man with 10,000 coins being as happy as a king." If we can reach this point, then people do not necessarily need to pursue official positions and power, nor do they need to plunder. If we compare countries where finance is developed and where it is not, this point is obvious.

From this perspective, the development of finance and the evolution of the market played a major role in people replacing crueler and more aggressive desires with more peaceful ones. The desire to make money is mostly realized through financial means and can be considered a peaceful

[3] Zhiwu Chen. 2015. *The Logic of Finance II (Jinrong de Luoji).* Imagist Books. Xi'an: Northwest University Press.

[4] Murray Rothbard said Sima Qian "was an advocate of laissez-faire". See Murray Rothbard. 2006 (1995). *Economic Thought Before Adam Smith: An Austrian Perspective on the History of Economic Thought.* Volume I. Auburn, Alabama: Ludwig Mises Institute. P. 26.

desire. People that like to make money and can make money generally do not like to fight. On the contrary, people without the ability to make money and who only desire power like to fight. Fighting is only good for a small group of people and the ruling class. It is bad for most of the common people. This viewpoint has a long history. Many Enlightenment thinkers, such as Montesquieu, Immanuel Kant, Adam Smith, and Frederic Bastiat, had brilliant analysis. I cannot help myself but to share their viewpoints.

Montesquieu said:

> Peace is the natural effect of trade. Two nations who traffic with each other become reciprocally dependent; for if one has an interest in buying, the other has an interest in selling; and thus their union is founded on their mutual necessities.[5]

Jean-François Melon, a close friend of Montesquieu, said:

> The spirit of conquest and the spirit of commerce are mutually exclusive in a nation.[6]

One hundred years ago, Norman Angell, a British journalist, wrote *The Great Illusion*. In *The Better Angels of Our Nature*, Steven Pinker described Mr. Angell's argument:

> *Plunder may have been profitable in primitive economies, when wealth lay in finite resources like gold or land or in the handiwork of self-sufficient craftsmen. But in a world in which wealth grows out of exchange, credit, and a division of labor, conquest cannot make a conqueror richer. ... In fact, he would make himself poorer, since the conquest would cost money and lives and would damage the networks of trust and cooperation that allow everyone to enjoy gains in trade.*[7]

[5] Quoted from Albert Otto Hirschman. 2013 (1977). *The Passion and the Interests: Political Arguments for Capitalism before its Triumph*. Princeton, NJ: Princeton University Press. P. 80.

[6] Quoted from Albert Otto Hirschman. 2013 (1977). *The Passion and the Interests: Political Arguments for Capitalism before its Triumph*. Princeton, NJ: Princeton University Press. P. 80.

[7] Quoted from Steven Pinker. 2011. *The Better Angels of Our Nature: Why Violence Has Declined*. New York, NY: Viking. P. 245.

I quoted these thinkers to prove the point that the development of finance and the market benefit peace. A large amount of recent research has proven the likelihood of war between two countries with market economies decreases significantly.[8] How we promote the opening of the country is extremely important. A closed off country is likely to become a warring country. An open country does not become willing to fight easily. Therefore, the cause for free trade is the cause for human peace!

Below, I want to emphasize the point about the relationship between economic liberty and political liberty. Professor Chen's book discusses the relationship between finance and the government. His analysis is brilliant. I will speak from another perspective. If finance brings us more economic freedom, then what type of relationship will there be between economic freedom and political freedom? There is no definite conclusion about this relationship in the history of thought. Here, I will share different scholars' views on this issue.

The optimistic view is economic freedom certainly leads to political freedom. Montesquieu differentiated between movable and immovable property. We know that financial assets are movable property, but throughout most of human history immovable property was dominant, even though we had currency. (Of course, movable and immovable property is relative, such as land, which can be collateralized and securitized.) I previously asked why do people want to go to war? Primarily, they wanted to seize immovable property. Montesquieu believed liquid assets, such as bills of exchange and other financial tools, could supplement the constitutional protection against despotism. The Jewish people invented bills of exchange. What was their reason for doing so? When Jews only had immovable property, despotic governments could easily persecute them. Bills of exchange allowed wealth to be easily transferred between nations. On this, Montesquieu said:

> *…and through this means commerce could elude violence, and maintain itself everywhere; for the richest trader had only invisible wealth which could be sent everywhere without leaving a trace. … In this manner we owe … to the avarice of rulers the establishment of a contrivance which somehow lifts commerce right out of their grip.*

[8] B. Russett and J. Oneal. 2001. *Triangulating peace: Democracy, Interdependence and International Organization*. New York: Norton.

> *Since that time, the rulers have been compelled to govern with greater wisdom than they themselves might have intended; for, owing to these events, the great and sudden arbitrary actions of the sovereign (*les grands coups d'autorité*) have been proven to be ineffective and ... only good government brings prosperity [to the prince].*[9]

Because financial assets can be concealed, are highly liquid, and are easily transported, it is difficult for rulers to exploit merchants. Only a benevolent government could collect taxes.

Scottish Enlightenment thinker Sir James Steuart had this to say:

> *The statesman looks about with amazement; he who was wont to consider himself as the first man in the society in every respect, perceives himself eclipsed by the lustre of private wealth, which avoids his grasp when he attempts to seize it. This makes his government more complex and more difficult to be carried on; he must now avail himself of art and address as well as of power and authority.*[10]

His view is the same as Montesquieu's. He put more emphasis on rulers being unable to use the arbitrary and brutal methods of the past after commercial society becomes more complex. Professor Chen's book also discusses a lot of related content.

These viewpoints discussed above tell us economic freedom will bring about political freedom because the marketization of the economy, especially the introduction of financial tools, makes traditional despotism bad governance. The influence of property on political liberty that Professor Chen emphasized is extremely important. If the people you want to criticize control your livelihood, then you cannot possibly have freedom of speech. There is a high degree of correlation between the freedom of speech as a political right and private property.

Of course, should we be this optimistic? As long as society has economic freedom, will we naturally have the political freedom we want? This is not certain. Here, I want to quote two more thinkers. Adam Ferguson said:

[9]Quoted from Albert Otto Hirschman. 2013 (1977). *The Passion and the Interests: Political Arguments for Capitalism before its Triumph.* Princeton, NJ: Princeton University Press. P. 72.

[10]Quoted from Albert Otto Hirschman. 2013 (1977). *The Passion and the Interests: Political Arguments for Capitalism before its Triumph.* Princeton, NJ: Princeton University Press. P. 82.

> *When we suppose government to have bestowed a degree of tranquility, which we sometimes hope to reap from it, as the best of its fruits, and public affairs to proceed, in the several departments of legislation and execution, with the least possible interruption to commerce and lucrative arts; such a state … is more akin to despotism than we are apt to imagine…*
>
> *Liberty is never in greater danger than it is when we measure national felicity … by the mere tranquility which may attend on equitable administration.*[11]

Perhaps ensuring tranquility, order, and efficiency is the main defense of authoritarianism.

Alexis de Tocqueville believed citizens focusing entirely on pursuing their own private interests made it possible for a "clever and ambitious man to seize power." He warned those who wanted "law and order" for the sake of a more favorable commercial environment:

> *A nation that demands from its government nothing but the maintenance of order is already a slave in the bottom of its heart; it is the slave of its wellbeing, and the man who is to chain it can arrive on the scene.*[12]

These two men had the same concern. In simple terms, when people have more material possessions, they fear losing those material possessions. They instinctively resist changes, especially political changes. Ferguson and de Tocqueville came to this realization centuries ago and they inspire us today.

In summary, the development of finance and the development of the market have brought us a lot of economic freedom. It has made us wealthier and made our lives better. To a certain degree, economic freedom challenges the political system and will incentivize people to require political freedom. However, the arrival of political freedom is not a matter of course or automatic. After people become wealthy, they pursue order, stability, and efficiency. They might be afraid of change. If we want true political freedom, then simply becoming more market-oriented is insufficient. We must put in a more arduous effort.

[11] Quoted from Albert Otto Hirschman. 2013 (1977). *The Passion and the Interests: Political Arguments for Capitalism before its Triumph.* Princeton, NJ: Princeton University Press. P. 121.

[12] Quoted from Albert Otto Hirschman. 2013 (1977). *The Passion and the Interests: Political Arguments for Capitalism before its Triumph.* Princeton, NJ: Princeton University Press. P. 123–124.

Indeed, some Chinese entrepreneurs I know strongly oppose political liberalization simply because they worry about social turmoil which might be brought about by political liberalization.

The question these entrepreneurs do not answer is: Is it possible to have a sustained market system, without political freedom and rule of law system? I doubt it. When the government power is not restricted by the rule of law, it is unlikely that rights related to making money will be protected.

CHAPTER 24

The Anti-Corruption Dilemma

The real dilemma of anti-corruption is how to deal with the stock of corruption, or the corruption that has already happened. If there is no break from corruption of the past, then anti-corruption cannot possibly succeed. However, if we want a firm break from the past, ordinary people might disapprove. This is the dilemma! Whether we can get out of this dilemma depends on the wisdom and courage of our leaders, and the rationality and patience of ordinary people.[1]

* * *

Anti-corruption will be the greatest challenge for China's leaders over the next 10 years. The Report to the Eighteenth National Congress of the Communist Party of China stated the issue of corruption could "cause the collapse of the Party and the fall of the state." Can anti-corruption save the party? I believe it will be determined to a large degree by how we fight corruption.

The real dilemma of anti-corruption is how to deal with the stock of corruption, or the corruption that has already happened. If there is no

[1] The original version of this chapter was written in December 2012.

W. Zhang, *Ideas for China's Future*,
https://doi.org/10.1007/978-981-15-4304-3_24

break from corruption of the past, then anti-corruption cannot possibly succeed. If the measures are excessively strong, then at best a lack of government officials will cause the government to be in a state of paralysis. At worst, government officials will revolt, and reform will not progress. However, if we want to totally forgive the past, ordinary people might disapprove. This is the dilemma! Whether we can get out of this dilemma depends on the wisdom and courage of our leaders, and the rationality and patience of ordinary people. Wu Si, a scholar of history and influential commentator, Li Yongzhong, a deputy director of the Chinese Academy of Discipline Inspection and Supervision, and other scholars have proposed conditional amnesty, which I will echo here. Actually, I also discussed this issue 10 years ago.

Let us first examine China's corruption over the last 10 years. From the macro perspective, what has changed? Two changes have been most important. The first is the transition from wealth-creating corruption to wealth-destroying corruption. In the 1980s and 1990s, so-called "corruption" to a large degree involved private citizens redeeming their rights from the hands of government bureaucrats. This caused resources to be used more efficiently. Resources that originally could only be utilized by state-owned enterprises could now also be used by private enterprises. They created tremendous value and drove economic growth.[2] However, this is not the kind of corruption we see today. Instead, government officials are abusing their power to seek rent. Rights that had been given to private citizens are being taken back, which causes resource allocation to be less efficient. Corruption in the 1980s and 1990s was associated with institutional reform. In the process of reform, some rights were released from the hands of government. Therefore, in a sense, corruption also drove China's market-oriented reforms. However, corruption over the last 10 years is associated with institutional retrogression. Corruption has become more serious, and the system becomes less and less market-oriented. Corruption in the 1980s and 1990s was businesspeople bribing government officials. Corruption over the last 10 years is government officials bribing other government officials. Of course, bribes paid to government officials by businesspeople still exists, but at this point might not be as important. This is the first characteristic.

[2] See Weiying Zhang. 2015. *The Logic of the Market; An Insider's View of Chinese Economic Reform*. Washington, DC: Cato Institute. P. 130–133.

The second characteristic is as the strength of anti-corruption activities increases, the severity of corruption also increases. Using Baidu, I searched for articles that included the Chinese word for "anti-corruption." There were 11,900 articles in 2003. There were 76,200 articles in 2004. There were 73,330 articles in 2005. There were 106,000 articles in 2006. The number of articles reached 246,000 in 2010 and 861,000 in 2012. There is a similar growth trend for articles on people.cn. Since the 16th National Congress of the Communist Party of China, more than 70 provincial-level bureaucrats have left office due to corruption or corruption-related issues. Having seven or eight provincial-level cadres arrested every year, on average, is rarely seen in any country throughout history. It should be said that the strength of anti-corruption activities is increasing. However, our corruption is more and more severe. For example, four successive heads of transportation for Henan Province left office due to corruption. The first person left office in 1997 for accepting bribes worth ¥300,000. The fourth person was arrested in November of 2011 for accepting bribes worth ¥30,000,000. That is an increase of 100 times over 14 years. Of course, this is a special example. However, based on my observations, this example might represent the basic trend of change in the severity of corruption.

Both the new generation of leaders and the last generation of leaders put extreme focus on anti-corruption activities. Scholars and high-level officials have proposed various anti-corruption measures. These measures can be summarized as the following points. First, more supervision to increase the probability corrupt behavior is discovered. As we know, if one hundred people are corrupt and only one person is caught, then the deterrent is very low. If fifty or sixty are caught, then the deterrent will be greater. Second, there must be freedom of the press. Only with freedom of the press can the public supervise the government. Third, the strength of punishment must be increased. In other words, it must make the corrupt officials that accept bribes feel scared. Fourth, increase the legal wage of government officials. One reason officials are corrupt is their nominal wages are too low, so they have no choice but to subsidize themselves with other income. Fifth, government officials must disclose their wealth. This point has been discussed often recently. Sixth, through ideological work, the morality of officials can be increased. Seventh, reduce the power of government departments. Currently, the government is too powerful. If we can decrease approval requirements, decrease government resource allocation, reduce the government's power to set industrial policy, and reduce the government's power to interfere in the economy, then corruption will decrease significantly. Eighth, truly implement democracy and the rule of law.

It should be said that these measures already encompass all the anti-corruption measures we can implement. If we established a completely new government, or the scale of the government was limited, or the current issue with corruption was not serious, then these methods would effectively inhibit corruption. If a newly created government had more strict supervision, if punishments were a little heavier, if the press was a little more free, if the government was a little less powerful, and if we had democracy and the rule of law, then I believe corruption would not be as serious as it is. However, we must implement anti-corruption activities on the foundation provided by the current government. Some measures might sound good but are very difficult to implement. For example, high salaries for government officials is not practical in a government that is already so large and powerful. Provincial-level bureaucrats are a very small proportion of the overall total, yet more than 70 have been arrested over the last 10 years.

Under these circumstances, the effectiveness of the measures described above is very limited. The most important reason that they are limited is because existing corruption has already reached a relatively severe degree. For example, the People's Republic of China only has 34 provincial-level capital cities, but more than a dozen provincial-level capital city party secretaries have been dismissed for corruption. On a percentage terms, this is a very high number. People might doubt these numbers, but my feeling is that they are conservative. Officials might not have accepted cash bribes, but they have received a watch or a painting as a gift, or they obtained favorable terms on the purchase of a house, or their children received assistance when they studied overseas. According to the existing standards, there is very little that can be detected. We see it exposed on the Internet. We also see a very interesting phenomenon. The public hates corruption, but only in an abstract way. Whenever a specific person gets in trouble for corruption, many people actually express sympathy. They ask: "How can that person be so unlucky?" This type of contradiction in the psychology of the public represents the concept of fairness in human nature. If many people behave in an illegal way, but only a few are punished for it, then people will believe this is unfair. People will increase their tolerance for this type of behavior.

There are two types of mechanisms for punishing corruption. The first is the administrative and legal mechanism. The second is the reputation mechanism or public opinion mechanism. In the past, a person would be arrested for corruption and serve time in prison. This is a legal punishment. At the same time, that person's colleagues would look down on him or her. This is a reputational punishment. However, today, it seems different. After a corrupt bureaucrat is sentenced, in contrast, he receives more sympathy. People provide support for his wife and children. This might reflect that the corrupt bureaucrats arrested for corruption are only a small percent of corrupt bureaucrats. Also, they likely are not the most seriously corrupt people.

Therefore, the most critical issue is how we deal with the stock of corruption. There are two ways of thinking. One way of thinking is to quantify the actions of the past, then pursue each one. The other way of thinking is to only focus on new activity and let bygones be bygones. Of course, we can still discuss their precise meaning.

The experience of the last 10 years has shown that anti-corruption campaigns that focus on the past appear vigorous, but compared to the prevalence and severity of corruption, it cannot fundamentally resolve the issue.

Over the last 10 years, anti-corruption measures have not truly formed a deterrence. Many bureaucrats are corrupt, but it is just like buying lottery tickets. Some have bad luck and get caught. A more serious issue is that fighting corruption perhaps has turned into a tool for power struggles. Whether or not you are arrested might not depend on the severity of your corruption, but instead on your obedience. In this way, the corrupt bureaucrats that are removed are not actually the most corrupt bureaucrats. I personally know of a case with a relatively clean bureaucrat that offended the party secretary. He was sentenced to four years in jail for so-called bribes that even included birthday money his close friend gave to his children. Based on my knowledge, similar cases are not rare. This type of power struggle has a "strike first" characteristic. Striking first becomes the corrupt bureaucrat's optimal strategy. Further, this type of anti-corruption measure might have made corruption more serious. It is like killing someone to keep a secret, then having to kill people that know about the murder. There is a similar problem with corruption. If you do not have enough money to pay off your superiors, then there will not be anyone around to protect you. However, if your corruption is big enough to allow you to pay off a lot of people, then you actually become safe.

Another issue is the fight against corruption in public opinion. We can see that since the 18th National Congress of the Communist Party of China, this has played a major role. Especially on Weibo or WeChat, where each person becomes part of the media, it has had a certain effect on exposing corruption. However, we must also acknowledge there are many issues with the fight against corruption on Weibo. One issue is potential violations of human rights. A lot of information on Weibo is irresponsible. Individual privacy rights are easily violated. Another problem is that the fight against corruption on Weibo can also become a tool for power struggles, as I mentioned previously.

We must pay special attention to the prevention of possible violence caused by the fight against corruption on Weibo. Regardless if you are clean or not, as soon as the media says you are not clean, sometimes it is difficult to defend yourself. With the current situation, because so few bureaucrats are clean, no one is willing to speak on behalf of others. As long as a person is exposed by the media, he will be pushed to answer by his superiors. This might constitute a miscarriage of justice. Additionally, sometimes this violates the spirit of the rule of law. In the recent Lei Zhengfu incident, the scandalous pictures were taken deceptively.[3] The evidence was obtained illegally, but now the legality of the procedures that obtain evidence is not considered in the fight against corruption. From the long-term perspective, this does not benefit the establishment of a rule of law society.

Of course, we can imagine a bigger storm in the fight against corruption. However, how big can it get? If we really made it big, then bureaucrats will be terrified and try to sabotage the reforms. They might even form an alliance of corrupt bureaucrats. Because corruption is as common as it is, there is certainly a network of bureaucrats that will protect others in order to protect themselves. Therefore, bureaucrats might unite to resist anti-corruption measures. In the end, the government will be paralyzed. When the government is paralyzed, the fight against corruption cannot continue. Nor can a paralyzed government reform.[4]

[3] Lei was the party secretary of Beibei District, Chongqing Municipality. He was arrested after nude photos of him and a woman were leaked. He was sentenced to 13 years in prison in 2012 by the First Middle Court of Chongqing.

[4] Government officials often say there is "no action" today under Xi Jinping's anti-corruption campaign.

On the other hand, most of the money for buying and selling government favors comes from enterprises. Almost all corruption can be traced back to entrepreneurs as a group. Currently, some entrepreneurs do not have a sense of safety. One reason is they do not have confidence in the future. They fear that a so-called Chongqing-style "attack against organized crime" will occur. Instead of an attack on organized crime, there was arbitrary deprivation of private property. Another reason is they are worried about activities in the past, including bribery. This causes private entrepreneurs, and even state-owned enterprise officials, to emigrate. No one is truly willing to make a bigger bet on the Chinese economy, let alone innovate. At that point, the unemployment rate will increase, and the public's dissatisfaction will increase. Therefore, this is a bigger challenge for the government.

Another question is: Who will fight the corruption? If we acknowledge that corruption is as common as it is, then overall, it is very possible that the bureaucrats that fight corruption are not necessarily clean. How daring will their fight against corruption be? The deeper they get into the issue, the more likely they are to implicate themselves. Therefore, I believe that the probability of strong anti-corruption activities is very limited. If implementation is forced, perhaps the price to be paid is too great.

Therefore, another option is to not look backward, but instead only look forward. As I mentioned earlier, this is the conditional amnesty Wu Si and Li Yongzhong proposed. According to Wu Si's viewpoint, conditional amnesty can be used in exchange for bureaucrats' support for democratic reforms. Li Yongzhong believes looking into activities of the past will make the problem bigger. Of course, I believe they are only proposing a basic way of thinking. Specific measures require further research. Actually, there have been many experiments globally, including in Hong Kong. In almost every developed or undeveloped country or region that had serious corruption, the same problems were faced in the process of fighting corruption.

My own opinion is the 18th National Party Congress should be the cutoff point. Bureaucrats that were not corrupt after the 18th National Party Congress should not be punished. For bureaucrats that continued to be corrupt after the 18th National Party Congress, they should be held accountable for past and future activity. This way, it is not so easy to get a pass. At the same time, we should initiate disclosure and registration of personal wealth for government officials, then examine any part that exceeds reasonable income. It can either be confiscated or kept after paying a tax. However, I believe we must maintain the principle that if you do not tell the truth, you should be punished. For example, if you have 10 houses, but you only report two, then the other eight should be confiscated. Government officials will risk more by not telling the truth. Of course, we could also implement voluntary disclosures, where the officials that do not disclose must leave the government. At the same time, we must reinforce the anti-corruption measures that I mentioned earlier, such as reducing government power and strengthening supervision through public opinion. In the long run, we must establish a rule of law society and democratic system. Of course, under the condition the power of government officials is restrained, the compensation of government officials should be reasonably increased.

However, this kind of measure faces enormous challenges. The first challenge is to resolve the dissatisfaction of the public (including clean government officials). The public will believe this is relatively unfair. Why do the corrupt ones get exempt? This dissatisfaction is totally understandable. The second challenge is making this policy credible. Any policy that is not credible will be ineffective.

First, let us look at getting the understanding of the people. We must tell people that the goal of the fight against corruption is the establishment of a clean, effective government. We are not fighting corruption for the sake of fighting corruption. If we keep executing more people and arresting more people, but the government is still as corrupt in the future as it is today, then we can say we have not been successful. Actually, conditional amnesty is like insolvent firms undergoing bankruptcy protection. Even from the creditors' perspective, exempting a portion of the debt to allow the company to survive is better than total collapse. Of course, humanity has a weakness. We often focus on procedure but forget the goal. Similarly, we work in order to live happily, but we often sacrifice our happiness to make money. We want to avoid a similar problem in the process of fighting corruption. We cannot only focus on procedures but forget about our goal. We should also note that the past is complicated. An irrational system is the primary reason corruption became commonplace. When we see local people sympathizing with officials that have been arrested, it is because they feel these people were competent, but the incompetent people have not been arrested.

I also believe that if we have a comprehensive design, after the policy has been implemented for one or two years, the public will recognize the benefit. When people see that corruption has decreased significantly and government services have improved, then they will better understand the benefit of this policy. Of course, this requires the public to be patient.

How do we resolve the issue of credibility? I am afraid relying on a document with the government's letterhead is not workable. Due to frequent changes in government policy, a law passed by the National People's Congress is much more credible than a document on government letterhead. Therefore, I recommend going through the legislative process in the National People's Congress to ensure the credibility of this policy. At the same time, we can try trial programs. We can select a few counties or cities to experiment in, then expand it to the entire country.

I call this type of conditional amnesty policy "rational forgiveness." Forgiveness is one of the great virtues we humans have. Christianity speaks of atonement. Buddhism has the story of a butcher that lays down his knife to become a buddha. Chinese also have a culture of forgiveness. However, I say that it is rational forgiveness because it is not unprincipled forgiveness, not forgiveness for the sake of forgiveness, not forgiveness to display magnanimity. Rationality requires us to be detached from our status, identity, and interests when evaluating a type of transformation or policy. We must learn to empathize. Rationality also requires us to consider the viability of a policy, not just our subjective desires. Rationality also requires us to be forward looking, not backward looking, when implementing a transformative policy. We should not be too entangled in history's old accounts.

After Nelson Mandela became president of South Africa, Archbishop Desmond Tutu wrote a book titled *No Future without Forgiveness*. I want to add the sentence: No future without rationality. If we cannot rationally deal with the corruption issue we currently face, and if China's fight against corruption cannot escape the dilemma I spoke of previously, then we will be permanently locked in the corruption trap. As such, China's future cannot possibly be bright!

CHAPTER 25

There Is No China Model

The current conflict between China and US is not just a trade conflict, but more so a conflict of value systems and institutions.

The China model view is factually false. China's high growth over the last 40 years came from marketization, entrepreneurship, and three hundred years of Western technology accumulation, not the so-called "China Model." Using the "China Model" to explain the success of the last 40 years is detrimental to China's future development.[1]

* * *

The background of the trade conflict between China and the United States is not just a conflict between these two countries. It is a conflict between China and the Western World, including countries without a serious trade deficit with China, such as the European Union and the United Kingdom. This is not just a trade conflict, but more so a conflict of value systems and institutions. This issue is much more deeply rooted and is

[1] The original version of this chapter was written in October 2018.

W. Zhang, *Ideas for China's Future*,
https://doi.org/10.1007/978-981-15-4304-3_25

more difficult to adjust with technical measures. To understand this issue, we must start from the perspective of understanding the world and China's economy. First, we must understand the way the West considers issues. Second, we must correctly understand ourselves.

Understanding the World: Interests and Values

When I say understand the world, I am referring to the way Westerners view the world. The first question to answer is: Are the interactions between countries relationships of interests or relationships of values?

A common viewpoint is international relations are relationships of interest, so conflicts of interest are the source of conflicts between nations. However, contemporary international relations, especially after the end of World War II, have changed to include both relationships of interest and relationships of values. Interactions among nations not only focus on vital interests, but also right and wrong. This is the same for interactions among people. When values conflict with interests, values often dominate. This is the progress humanity has made over the last 100 years. The relationship between the United States and Egypt is an example. The Mubarak government's policy of maintaining peace in the Middle East was in the interest of the United States. Therefore, despite being a dictator, his relationship with the United States has always been harmonious. However, during the subsequent revolution, the values advocated by the revolutionaries were aligned with the values advocated for by the United States. Even if interests are harmed, the U.S. government had no choice but to stand with the revolutionaries instead of helping Mubarak suppress the revolution. Furthermore, many wars in the history of the Western world, including conflicts between the Islamic world and the Christian world or Protestant countries and Catholic countries, are a mix of conflicts of interests and value conflicts.

Understanding the World: The Three Values of the West

So-called values are in simple terms people's understanding of justice, good, and evil. There are three important values in the Western World: Human rights, racial equality, and early-comers helping late-comers.

The view on human rights can be traced back to English thinker John Locke's view that human rights are superior to state sovereignty. This influenced the contemporary Western World's nation state concept. Before that point, the so-called "nation" referred more to a ruling group or family, so one family such as the House of Habsburg could rule over many countries. Many current international conflicts involve views on human rights. The West believes matters related to human rights are not internal affairs. This is the moral and legal foundation of the United Nation's deployment of peacekeeping forces to stop ethnic genocide.

The view on racial equality was gradually established after World War II. It was precisely the guidance of this view that caused Europe—and especially Western Europe—to have no choice but to accept refugees, even though it led to a series of problems.

Early-comers helping late-comers is also a viewpoint that formed after World War II. Under this viewpoint, countries at different levels of development join international organizations under asymmetric conditions. From the beginning, China benefited as a developing country. After Reform and Opening, China became the largest recipient of aid from the World Bank. China also obtained preferential treatment when it joined the World Trade Organization as a developing country. On the contrary, the United States, as the leader of the world, bears a large cost. About one-fifth of United Nations funding comes from the United States. The Trump administration's pursuit of "reciprocity" is based on China's changed level of development. Whether or not China is still a developing country is an important debate.

Understanding the World: The West's Understanding of Peace

The Western World believes trade, democracy, and international organizations are the cornerstone of world peace.[2] This is the lesson we have learned from three hundred years of history. Trade aligns the interests of nations. Democracy moderates the ambitions of rulers. International organizations promote dialog to resolve misunderstandings and conflicts between nations.

[2] B. Russett and J. Oneal. 2001. *Triangulating Peace: Democracy, Interdependence and International Organization*. New York: Norton. Also see Michael Shermer. 2015. *The Moral Arc: Now Science and Reason Lead Humanity toward Truth, Justice and Freedom*. New York: Henry Holt and Company. P. 126–138.

French Enlightenment thinker Montesquieu said that the natural role of commerce is to bring about peace. Frederic Bastiat, a Nineteenth century French liberal, said: “Where goods cross borders, armies do not. Where goods do not cross borders, armies do.”[3]

German philosopher Immanuel Kant developed the theory of democratic peace.[4] This is now a deeply rooted concept in the West. In a book published in 2001, Bruce Russett and John R. Oneal, two American political scientists, studied hundreds of wars in the 19th and 20th centuries. They found the likelihood of democratic countries going to war was low. When one of two opposing countries is non-democratic, the likelihood of going to war is one-times higher than the average. When both countries are democracies, the likelihood of a conflict declines by 50%. After adding a market economy and international trade, the likelihood of a conflict reduces. When they controlled for variables representing democracy, relative military might, hegemony, and economic growth, they found that countries with high levels of trade dependence in a given year were less likely to be involved in a military dispute the next year. A country that is open to the world is less inclined to military conflicts. In other words, democratic peace only occurs when both countries are democratic, whereas trade works when either of the countries is a market economy.[5] In terms of world peace, trade is more important than democracy!

Understanding China’s Economy: China’s Accomplishments Over 40 Years

Whether or not we understand China’s thousands of years of history, we only need to truly consider China’s history over the last 40 years.

No one denies China’s rapid economic growth and increase in living standards over the last 40 years. However, the understanding and explanation are contested. Currently, the “China Model Theory” and the “Universal Model Theory” are two explanations of China’s growth over

[3] Quoted from Michael Shermer. 2015. *The Moral Arc: Now Science and Reason Lead Humanity toward Truth, Justice and Freedom*. New York: Henry Holt and Company. P. 126.

[4] Immanuel Kant. 1983 (1795). “The Perpetual Peace: A Philosophical Sketch.” in Ted Humphrey (trans.), *Perpetual Peace and Other Essays*. Indianapolis: Hackett.

[5] Michael Shermer. 2015. *The Moral Arc: Now Science and Reason Lead Humanity toward Truth, Justice and Freedom*. New York: Henry Holt and Company. P. 127–128.

the last few decades. The former believes China's economic growth benefited from a unique China Model, referring to a powerful government, huge state-owned enterprises, and wise industrial policy. The latter believes the reason for China's amazing success was the same as for the rise of Great Britain, the rise of France, the rise of Germany and Japan after World War II, and the rise of the Asian Tigers. It was based on the power of the market and on creativity and risk-taking represented by entrepreneurship. China also utilized the technology accumulated by developed Western countries over the last 300 years. In my paper titled "The Three Industrial Revolutions as I Experienced Them," I summarized how China—within 40 years after Reform and Opening—experienced the three industrial revolutions the Western World experienced over 250 years. The late-mover's advantage meant we took fewer detours. We could directly enjoy the technologies others paid a tremendous price to obtain through experimentation.

Not only does the China Model conflict with reality, it will produce a terrible consequence for China's future.

Understanding China's Economy: Is There the So-Called China Model?

According to the Marketization Index Report compiled by the Beijing National Economy Research Institute, China's overall marketization index increased from 4.01 in 1997 to 8.19 in 2014. The marketization index declined some after the four-trillion yuan stimulus policy in 2009. Nevertheless, there is significant difference in degree of marketization between regions. Zhejiang Province, Guangdong Province, and Jiangsu Province rank highest in the degree of marketization. Eastern China ranks above Central and Western China. When we compare regional gross domestic product growth rates, we find Eastern China's GDP growth rate was always higher than Central and Western China before 2007. After 2007, Western China's growth rate ranked the highest, followed by Central China, and Eastern China's growth rate was lowest. A series of studies have shown the degree of marketization and GDP growth rates are negatively correlated among various provinces and municipalities over the last five to 10 years.

From this can we conclude there is a "Western China Model"? Are Western China's institutions and policies superior to Eastern China's? Should Eastern China be required to imitate Western China? The answer is no. The reason is very simple. Western China's marketization reforms started late, so it had a "late-mover's advantage." Eastern China's degree of marketization in 1997 and 2001 surpassed Western China's degree of marketization in 2006 and 2014 respectively. When we use marketization data from the Beijing National Economy Research Institute and economic growth data from the China Statistical Yearbook, we find that the "change" in marketization index is positively correlated with gross domestic product growth over the last 10 years and the last 40 years. This reveals the problem of the "China Model." Marketization is a dynamic and gradual process. We cannot infer a causal relationship based on economic performance at a certain point in time.

Additional empirical evidence can be used to confirm the positive relationship between marketization and economic growth. Empirical evidence related to the proportion of state-owned sector employment or state-owned industrial assets and per-capita gross domestic product or growth rates shows—without exception—regions with a higher state-owned sector grow slower. Regions where the state advances and the private sector recedes are less successful than regions where the private sector advances and the state recedes.

Most of China's growth over the last 40 years depended on arbitrage opportunities provided by technological late-mover advantage. Chinese entrepreneurs and Western firms could depend on arbitrage to make money. As arbitrage opportunities are shrinking, future development must rely on innovation more and more.

Economists use three metrics to measure innovation: Research and development intensity, patents, and the proportion of new product sales. These correspond to the input stage, intermediate stage, and output stage. In terms of these three metrics, China has made decent progress over the last 10 years, although there is a significant regional difference. Cross-regional analysis shows these three innovation metrics are positively correlated with the degree of marketization and privatization, but negatively correlated to the proportion of public sector employment or the number of government agencies per 10,000 people. In regions with a higher proportion of firms, employees, or industrial assets in the state-owned sector, the ability to innovate is lower. In regions with a higher proportion of private or foreign firms, the ability to innovate is higher.[6]

[6]Weiying Zhang. 2019. "The China model view is factually false." *Journal of Chinese Economic and Business Studies*, 17 (3): 287–311. https://doi.org/10.1080/14765284.2019.1663696.

Understanding China's Economy: Consequences of the "China Model"

The evidence described above shows that the "China Model" is seriously out of touch with reality. China's growth over the last 40 years came from marketization, entrepreneurship, and three hundred years of Western technology accumulation, not the so-called "China Model."

Using the "China Model" to explain the success of the last 40 years is detrimental to China's future development.

First, self-deception leads to self-destruction. Blindly emphasizing the unique China Model will lead to stronger state-owned enterprises, expanded government power, and dependence on industrial policy. This will lead to a reversal of the reform process and eventually the economy will stagnate.

Second, misleading the world leads to confrontation. The "China Model Theory" makes China different in a way that alarms the Western perspective. It must lead to conflict between China and the West. The unfriendly international environment we face today is not unrelated to certain (Chinese and foreign) economists' misunderstanding of China's success over the last 40 years. From the Western perspective, the so-called "China Model" is "state capitalism," which is incompatible with fair trade and world peace. We must remember Hayek's following warning:

> *While facts alone can never determine what is right, ill-considered notions of what is reasonable, right and good may change the facts and the circumstances in which we live; they may destroy, perhaps forever, not only developed individuals and buildings and art and cities (which we have long known to be vulnerable to the destructive powers of moralities and ideologies of various sorts), but also traditions, institutions, and interrelations without which such creations could hardly have come into being or even be recreated.*[7]

Imagine seeing a person without an arm running very fast. If you conclude his speed comes from missing an arm, then you naturally will call on others to saw off an arm. That will be a disaster. This is the meaning of Hayek's warning.

Economists must not confuse "in spite of" with "because of."

[7] Hayek, F. A. 1988. *The Fatal Conceit: The Errors of Socialism*, Edited by W. W. Bartley III. Chicago: University of Chicago Press. P. 27–28.

CHAPTER 26

China Needs to Overcome Its Resentment Complex

Resentment breeds the pride and xenophobia of national exceptionalism. It nourishes new national sentiments. Through 40 years of Reform and Opening, China has not only achieved tremendous success with economic development, but also greatly increased its international status. However, the Chinese people's resentment towards the West does not seem to have declined because of this. The resentment makes it difficult for Chinese people to accept universal values, but easy to go from inferiority to arrogance. For its own interest, China must overcome its resentment complex.[1]

* * *

Since the Opium War, Chinese have resented the West. Understanding this point is extremely important for understanding today's Sino-U.S. relationship.

Of course, resentment is not unique to Chinese. In contemporary world history, many late-rising nations have resented the countries that developed earlier.

[1] The original version of this chapter was written on August 2018.

W. Zhang, *Ideas for China's Future*,
https://doi.org/10.1007/978-981-15-4304-3_26

Reality's Inequality Breeds Resentment

Resentment is simply envy, jealously, and hate mixed together. In *Nationalism: Five Roads to Modernity*, American historian Liah Greenfeld tells us the term resentment was created by Nietzsche, then later defined and developed by German philosopher Max Scheler. It refers to a state of mind caused by suppressed, indescribable jealousy and abomination (survival jealousy). Greenfeld pointed out, in the formation of modern nations, less-developed countries always want to learn from and imitate advanced countries. On the one hand, the imitator views the imitated as more superior (otherwise there would be no need to imitate). On the other hand, mutual contact often highlights the inferiority of the imitator, so the usual reaction is resentment.[2]

Specifically speaking, two social conditions produce resentment. The first condition is the imitators' belief they are essentially comparable to the imitated. They are equal in theory, and thus can be mutually interchangeable (that is, catching up is possible). The second condition is the imitators also feel they are unequal. Regardless of the individual temperament and psychological structure of group members, the existence of these two conditions creates a tendency toward group resentment.

Greenfeld further pointed out resentment creates an impulse to resist external values, which may eventually lead to "value re-evaluation." This means value standards change. Values that were originally supreme are degraded, replaced by concepts that even had a negative connotation originally. Based on self-respect, a society with a rich historical and cultural legacy cannot totally accept all outside values. Resentment often causes elements of the local tradition opposite from the outside values to be deliberately cultivated. They might counterbalance the outside values. Alternatively, something might be portrayed as similar to outside values, but "existed much earlier" locally, in order to achieve psychological balance. Resentment breeds the pride and xenophobia of national exceptionalism. It nourishes new national sentiments.

[2] Liah Greenfeld. 1992. *Nationalism: Five Roads to Modernity*. Boston: Harvard University Press. P. 16–17.

The Nation State as a Modern Concept

Throughout human history, ethnic identity has existed, but the "nation state" is an entirely new concept. Over a long history, the nation was the ruler's private property. People commonly identified with a royal family or religion, but not a nation state. In medieval Europe, one king served as the king of two or more kingdoms, like how one person might serve as the chairman of more than one corporation today.

According to Greenfield's research, England is perhaps the first modern nation state in human history. Starting in the seventeenth century, it began to take shape with the core concepts of citizenship, liberty, and sovereignty of the people. This national concept was inherited by the formation of the United States of America in the late eighteenth and early nineteenth century. Compared to England, nation state identities in other countries like France, Russia, and Germany formed relatively late. This process occurred in France in the eighteenth century, Russia in the second half of the eighteenth century, and Germany in the late eighteenth century and early nineteenth century. Compared to the civic nationalism of England and the United States, Russian and German nationalism could be called ethnic nationalism, while France was somewhere in between.[3]

During the formation of the modern nation state, social, political, and cultural elites played a dominant role. The nobility was the key group in England, France, and Russia. Bourgeois intellectuals were the key group in Germany. The concepts of these elites became the genetics of national concepts.

The French Resentment Complex

France was the first nation to have a resentment complex. Over a few centuries before the eighteenth century, France was the superpower of Europe. It was even the protector of Catholicism. After the death of Louis XIV, France had already lost its status in Europe. England suddenly rose up and held a central role. In the latter half of the eighteenth century, when the national concept was introduced from England, the French discovered the English had surpassed them in many areas, even though France still had outstanding scientists, philosophers, and writers. French

[3] Ibid. P. 14.

national patriotism is displayed as a strong desire to restore the dominant position usurped by England and regain the glory of France.

There are two ways to ensure France's status and glory. The first is to implement liberal reforms to turn France into a country like England. The second is to weaken the power of England. Enlightenment thinkers like Voltaire and Montesquieu supported the first approach. They were not resentful. They believed France had the ability to implement the things learned from England, and easily surpass its competitors. However, this task was much harder and took longer than expected. Pro-British emotions gradually gave way to anti-British emotions. French aristocrats and intellectuals were convinced France was basically comparable to England, but France was indeed inferior. England's superior position damaged their national pride and bred resentment against the West (England).

French aristocrats and intellectuals misappropriated English values, but also re-evaluated them. For example, concepts like democracy, liberty, and equality were given entirely different meanings than in England. They replaced equality with "consistency." They replaced liberty with "sovereignty" and "general will (*volonté générale*)." They replaced the individual with "the collective." They paved the road for despotism and egalitarianism.

Resentment towards the English caused the French to have an instinctive hatred for money, commercial activities, and capitalism. In the French view, England is a greedy nation. An unjust, greedy, and corrupt nation dominated by commercial interests is not suitable for French imitation.[4]

In foreign relations, the goal of the French often is not to make France stronger, but instead weaken England at all costs. From the French perspective, bad news for the English is good news for the French. Support among French elites and the public for the American War for Independence was partially based on love of liberty and favorable opinions of the American people, but more so based on aversion to the English. American separation from British rule assuaged French anger. However, Louis XVI did not foresee the financial difficulties caused by the war igniting the French Revolution, eventually leading to his own death on the guillotine.

[4] Ibid. P. 177–184.

The German Resentment Complex

Resentment had a greater impact on the German nation. The German nation appeared in the late eighteenth century. After the Napoleonic Wars, it took root. France caused the appearance of German nationalism. At that time, however, England had already experienced the Industrial Revolution, whereas Germany was still not even a unified country. Not only was it behind England, it was humbled even by France. The middle class and intellectuals learned Enlightenment ideas such as reason, political liberty, and individual equality from "advanced" Western nations (England and France). Even though some reformers regarded France as an example to follow, their national pride was damaged.

By the start of the nineteenth century, with a stronger sense of national identity, German resentment also grew stronger. The "Western world" (Britain and France) became the embodiment of evil. The "dirty, shameless, and undisciplined" French were considered the "natural and traditional" enemies of Germany. The English were generally no better than the French, and their freedoms had little value. According to Friedrich List, the founder of the German Historical School, the English sought to monopolize the entire world's manufacturing ability and use its financial, technological, and naval advantage to make the world dependent on it. Therefore, Germany should not be hoodwinked by the road to liberalization propagandized by the English; but instead allow the state to dominate the economy and achieve leapfrog development. German nationalism became state-led "ethno-nationalism."

As the West became equated with capitalism, German resentment towards the West (England, America, and France) became resentment towards capitalism. As they turned their eyes inwards, German intellectuals discovered aspects of German life that embodied Western values, such as social classes, trade, industry, cities, and science. However, they also understood these factors were necessary if Germany wanted to surpass the West someday. Therefore, they had to maintain an ambiguous attitude towards all these things. However, Jewish people that represented these non-German values became scapegoats. Napoleon's liberation of Jews further stimulated German hate for Jewish people. They were mixed with the French, so anti-Jewish behavior became anti-French patriotism. This bred German anti-Semitism and led eventually to Hitler's massacre of six million Jews. Karl Marx, born into a Jewish family himself, concentrated his resentment toward capitalism, and private property became the source of all evil. Resentment might be the reason there is a bigger market for Marxism in continental Europe than in England, or in less-developed countries than in advanced countries.[5]

The Russian Resentment Complex

The Russian nation was also formed with resentment against the West. Peter the Great initiated and drove Russia's Westernization. Initially, Russians envied the West. They treated it as an absolute and unquestionable role model. They optimistically thought they could mimic Western countries to get on an equal footing, and then surpass them. Peter the Great's Westernization reforms certainly increased Russia's international status and gave Russians a sense of pride.

However, Peter the Great's reforms never made Russia truly equal to the West. The Russians were perplexed by the gap between Russia and Western role models. The West's superior position made them unhappy. Making the West a role model inevitably led to self-contempt and a sense of inferiority. The fire of resentment burned in their hearts.

Resentment gave birth to cultural relativism. When Russians began searching for their own special characteristics, they re-evaluated Western values. Because Russia is unique, it is incomparable to the West. Therefore, the West is an unsuitable role model for Russia, so Russia should take its own path. The West became the object of ridicule, and Russians that praised the West were ridiculed. Even Peter the Great's Westernization reforms were considered shameful to Russians.

However, totally rejecting the West is impossible. Russia did not have the capital to rival the West. Western acknowledgement of Russia was also a necessary condition for national pride. Because it was impossible to surpass the West, Russia's nationalist elite defined Russia as the alternative to the West. They still used Western standards to evaluate Russia but reinterpreted the standards so that Russia was better than the West in each aspect. Russia had an advantage for every corresponding Western defect. For every advantage the West had, Russia also had the same advantage. "Rationality" as a value was maintained, but it became closer to the concept of spirit as explained by Georg Wilhelm Friedrich Hegel. The implied creativity and autonomy of individuals was rejected. They acknowledged

[5] Ibid. P. 372–395.

"liberty" and "equality" were virtues but refused to recognize the Western system was the true embodiment of these virtues. Western liberty and equality were not true liberty and equality. True liberty is inner freedom and is not related to the law. Westerners have the right to liberty yet live in true slavery. Russians did not have liberty in a legal sense but lived in true liberty. Russian elites invented "the people." They defined "the people" as an ethnic aggregate. The Russian national spirit existed in "the people" but only the educated elite could reveal it. The vanguard elite know what "the people" wanted, but the public did not. Naturally, the former had the right to command the latter.[6]

Therefore, the Russian nationalism that formed out of resentment is racist, collectivist, and authoritarian. Perhaps this helps explain the reason Russia became the first socialist country.

Resentment induces Russians to frantically prove their worth. Again and again, they actively or passively confront the West, but each time they are humiliated. The same drama is still on show today.

Japan counts as a rare non-colonized country that imitated the West, but is not very resentful. The reason is Japan has always been an imitator. When Japan abandoned its imitation of other Asian countries (particularly China) and began imitating Europe, it simply switched its teacher. There was no harm to Japan's self-esteem. Surpassing its original teacher gave it a sense of pride. Before the Pacific War, the United States became the object of Japan's resentment. The result was a fiasco for Japan.

The Chinese Resentment Complex

Chinese civilization has thousands of years of history, but the Chinese national identity formed recently. We could say Westerner's ships and cannons gave birth to the Chinese national identity. "China" as a nation state appeared in the eyes of the Chinese. Before entering the twentieth century, the Chinese were loyal to the successive rulers of territories or the emperors and courts of the people in those territories, but not a sovereign nation. Changing dynasties or territorial division were the affairs of the rulers and had little impact on the commoners, similar to changing leadership or business combinations or separations have little impact on the average employee. From the public's perspective, they are the subject of

[6] Ibid. P. 250–262.

whoever sits on the throne. There is no difference between a Han emperor, a Khitan emperor, a Jurchen emperor, a Mongolian emperor, or a Manchu emperor. For this reason, they could not possibly have a definite "Chinese" concept.

With the arrival of Westerners, especially after the Opium War, the Chinese national identity awoke. The object of loyalty gradually transitioned from the imperial court and emperor to the nation and the country (although this transformation was not completed). During the formation of the Chinese nation-state identity, China's political and intellectual elite of the late nineteenth century and early twentieth century were the driving force. They aroused the Chinese people's sense of national crisis and shaped their national consciousness. However, similar to the nobility in France and Russia and the intellectual elite in Germany, China's political elite and intellectual elite resented the West from the beginning. From the perspective of a nation with thousands of years of civilization and a center-of-the-world viewpoint, resentment is a natural reaction to suddenly discovering a foreign civilization is more advanced. The Chinese elite's feelings toward the West are a combination of jealousy, envy, and hatred. On the one hand, they introduced Western values such as a republican form of government, democracy, liberty, individual rights, reason, and science to China. On the other hand, they also selectively absorbed or rejected Western values based on China's original political and cultural concepts. National pride and resentment made most of them instinctively reject Western values. Accepting all of them was impossible. If possible, they tried to find alternatives from the local culture or other inferior countries.[7]

The Chinese resent Russia due to territorial issues but hold relatively little resentment due to differences in development stage. Perhaps this is one of the reasons the Chinese in the end chose to "take the Russian road." Of course, the Russian road appeared to be more suitable to China's national conditions. Russia is backwards, so it took a unique path. If that path led to rapid prosperity, then the Chinese could wash away their national humiliation and restore glory to their country. For this reason, taking the Russian road had minimal impact on the Chinese self-esteem, but the expected benefit was large.

[7]Jin Guantao and Liu Qingfeng. 2008. *Studies in History of Ideas: The Formation of Important Modern Chinese Political Terms*. Hong Kong: The Chinese University of Hong Kong.

The formation of national identity was extremely important for China's modernization. It gave the Chinese a specific objective for which to strive. However, resentment in the process of forming the Chinese national identity also brought about a series of consequences, including:

First, the Chinese national concept is still ethnic, not civic. We are "Chinese" because we are all "descendants of the Yellow Emperor," not because we are all citizens with equal rights in a sovereign country. This type of national concept brings about certain issues for the governance of the country, because not all Chinese people are descendants of the Yellow Emperor. This type of national concept makes it difficult for China to attract foreign immigrants. No matter how long a foreigner works or lives in China, that person will never be acknowledged as a Chinese person.

Second, state sovereignty are greater than human rights, and power takes precedent over rights. Chinese nationalism formed between national "strength" and "salvation." Thus, national utilitarianism and collectivism are inevitable. Its emphasis is on the country and the collective above all else. Any violation of individual rights in the name of national interests and collective interests is justified. Even today, most Chinese still hold the view that "having a country means having a home" and "the small rivers are full when the big river has water." These statements are not logical. Further, the country is equivalent to the government. The government is equivalent to government officials. Therefore, the power of bureaucrats always has preference over the rights of individuals. This makes implementing the rule of law difficult.

Third, there is an emphasis on exceptionalism and a negation of universality. Exceptionalism is an antidote to resentment. It negates the possibility of comparison and negates advantages and disadvantages. Exceptionalism maintains self-esteem. This is the reason all resentful nations like exceptionalism, including China. Exceptionalism also allows us to directly reject universal values or to act counter to international norms.

Fourth, we imitate technology but refuse to imitate institutions. Not long after the Opium War, the Chinese began to acknowledge their own backwardness in science and technology. Out of necessity, the Westernization Movement was launched. Even today, however, "Chinese values for the body and Western learning for use" is still the leading thought on China's transformation. As long as the "body" is our own, we have no humility for using Western knowledge. This is like how scientists do not humble themselves in front of engineers. We always search through traditional culture to find values that counterbalance the West. We believe the Western concept of governance are no better than the ideas our ancestors proposed long ago.

Fifth, capitalism, democracy, and liberty are opposed. The Chinese equate capitalism, liberty, and democracy with the Western world. Acknowledging these things is equivalent to acknowledging the West is superior to China in these aspects, which is too undignified for the Chinese. Therefore, China cannot implement capitalism, liberty, or democracy. In China, there is no equivalent to Jews in pre-war Germany, so resentment is focused on people that make money! Even if China needs a market economy, it can only be a "socialist market economy with Chinese characteristics," essentially different from capitalism.

Sixth, self-sufficiency is emphasized. China must establish an independent and complete industrial system. We must have everything the West has. Food must be self-sufficient. All important products related to the "national economy and people's livelihood" must be produced ourselves because the West is unreliable and is prepared to suffocate us at any moment. The denial of export privileges against ZTE by United States Secretary of Commerce Wilbur Ross in April of 2018 is claimed as proof of this.

Seventh, there is a market for "conspiracy theories" in China. China is constantly a victim of Western conspiracies. The reason China is backwards is not because we are unintelligent, but because Westerners are too crafty. It is Western deceptions that halt our development, not our system or culture. Foreign help for China is certainly some other scheme.

Eighth, praising us is fine, but criticizing us is not. The Chinese are especially sensitive to criticism. Chinese criticism of China is bad enough. Foreign criticism of China is even worse. Chinese should not criticize China because "a son should never shun his mother's looks and a dog should never shun his owner's poverty." Criticizing your own country is "unpatriotic." Foreigners cannot criticize China, because that will harm the Chinese's self-esteem. Foreigners who criticize China must be anti-Chinese forces, whereas foreigners who flatter China must be friends. But as everyone knows, flattery often comes with ulterior motives.

Ninth, international relations are discussed in terms of gain and loss, not right and wrong. Sometimes, even like and dislike supersede gain and loss. Bad news for the West is good news for China. Anything the West supports, we must oppose. Anything the West opposes, we must support. If a conflict occurs between a Western country and a non-Western country, most Chinese hope the former loses and the latter wins. This is not because we like the latter, but because we abhor the former. For this reason, some Chinese cheered the September 11 attacks. Many Chinese rooted for Saddam Hussein. Of course, if the United States and Japan came into conflict, we would stand with the U.S., because our enmity towards the Japanese is deeper than our enmity towards Americans.

Tenth, resentment makes the Chinese hold back a sigh of relief, waiting for the opportunity to get ahead. It is easy to go from inferiority to arrogance. When the country gets a little bit richer and stronger, it immediately has an upstart mentality.

The Opium War was almost 180 years ago. Through 40 years of Reform and Opening, China has not only achieved tremendous success with economic development, but also greatly increased its international status. However, the Chinese people's resentment towards the West does not seem to have declined because of this. Resentment among Chinese immigrants to other countries seems to be even deeper. Recent concepts such as the "China Model" or "Four Great New Inventions" embody this resentment. If the "China Model" can spread throughout the world, then not only can China regain its long-lost superior status, but also can wash away the century of humiliation it cannot bear to look back on. What a pleasant thing this is!

The degree of resentment is an inverse measure of a nation's level of development and maturity. The day when the Chinese people's resentment fades might be the start of China's true rise!

For its own interest, China must overcome its resentment complex.

CHAPTER 27

Reform Philosophy Must Transition from Utilitarianism to Rights-Priority

Though the Chinese did not invent utilitarian philosophy, China has long had utilitarian traditions. China's economic reform in the past few decades has also been guided by utilitarianism; economic growth is everything and can justify anything. Because of this, some basic human rights are frequently violated during reform.

To establish a true market economy, China's reform philosophy must transition from utilitarianism to rights-priority. Otherwise, the marketization process can be easily reversed in the name of efficiency and stability, and rule of law principles cannot be sustained.[1]

* * *

Until now, we could say China's reforms were utilitarian reforms. The basic philosophy of utilitarian reforms is that society's greatest "good" is economic development, in particular gross domestic product (GDP) growth. The standard for evaluating any policy is whether it benefits economic development and GDP growth. Anything that benefits GDP

[1] The original version of this chapter was written in July 2014, as the keynote speech given by the author on July 4, 2014 at the Second Annual Bund Summit on International Finance, co-hosted by the Shanghai Financial Association and the Yabuli China Entrepreneurs Forum.

W. Zhang, *Ideas for China's Future*,
https://doi.org/10.1007/978-981-15-4304-3_27

growth is good. Anything that is harmful to GDP growth is bad. For GDP growth, we can even disregard people's basic rights and dignity.

The Chinese did not invent utilitarianism. More than 200 years ago, Jeremy Bentham, an English philosopher, developed the doctrine of utilitarianism, which was used to guide reforms in England's legal system. John Stuart Mill, a disciple of Bentham, further developed it and made it the philosophical foundation of the entire field of economics.[2] Utilitarianism includes both individual utilitarianism and social utilitarianism. Individual utilitarianism means each person seeks to maximize his or her own utility function. Social utilitarianism means maximizing so-called "social welfare." The basic characteristic of social utilitarianism is using the legitimacy of ends to justify the legitimacy of means. Consequentialism is the standard for evaluating anything. In other words, if my end is good, my means can be fair or foul, regardless of whether this end is "for economic growth," "in the national interest," or "for social welfare."

In many situations, utilitarian economics defends the market economy. However, it treats the market as an instrument for efficient resource allocation. When the market is considered to benefit efficiency and maximize so-called "social welfare" it defends the market. As soon as the market is considered to harm efficiency, it advocates for government intervention in the market. Examples of these "market failure" conditions are so-called "market monopolies," "externalities," and "information asymmetry," in each of which government interventions can be justified by efficiency. Utilitarianism's support for private property and liberty is similar.

Utilitarian standards for whether humanity's activities are legitimate or not might be inappropriate. These standards might harm basic rights. For example, assume there is a group of people in a society most people dislike. According to utilitarian standards, killing them can increase total social welfare ("the greatest happiness for the greatest number of people"). However, can we believe doing so is legitimate? In reality, utilitarian standards can be used to violate any individual's rights in the name of

[2] For a critical review of Bentham and Mill's utilitarianism, see Murry Rothbard. 2006 (1995). *Classical Economics: An Austrian Perspective on the History of Economic Thought*. Volume II. Auburn, Alabama: Ludwig von Mises Institute. Chapters 2 and 3. For a more comprehensive review of utilitarianism, see Will Kymlicka. 2002. *Contemporary Political Philosophy: An Introduction*. Second Edition. Oxford and New York: Oxford University Press. Chapter 2.

so-called "national interests," "collective interests," or "societal interests." Such examples are countless throughout the history of the world.

In contrast to utilitarianism is another standard of justice I call "rights-priority." As individuals, each of us have innate basic rights. These basic rights cannot be taken away from us for any reason. The legitimacy of ends does not justify the legitimacy of means. Rights-priority has a long history of traditions. It developed from Stoicism in ancient Greece. German philosopher Immanuel Kant's theory of freedom proposed more than 200 years ago is a type of rights-priority theory. Although there are significant differences between them, John Rawls' theories on liberty and justice, Robert Nozick's theories on self-ownership, Murray Rothbard's theories on natural rights, and F. A. Hayek's theories on liberty and evolution can all be encompassed in rights-priority philosophy.[3]

Rights-priority's defense of the market is based on people's moral rights, free nature, and dignity. The defense is not based on efficiency, or at least it is not solely based on efficiency. Rights are superior to utility.

Even though the Chinese did not invent utilitarian philosophy, China has always had utilitarian traditions. The First Emperor of Qin's "enrich the nation and strengthen the army" policy was utilitarian. Prioritizing of the state over individuals is utilitarianism. The planned economy was utilitarian. It took the nation's economic development as the criteria for every policy. The planned economy also provided a legitimate reason to expropriate private property and deny individual liberty. After Reform and Opening, we no longer believed the planned economy was an effective means to develop the economy, so we transitioned to a market economy. However, both the rejection of the planned economy and the embrace of the market economy were utilitarian. Even today, this way of thinking has not changed. "Everything for growth" and "stability overwhelms everything else" are classic examples of utilitarianism. Every policy is evaluated based on whether it benefits economic growth (efficiency) or social stability. Whether these policies violate our basic rights is not considered. For economic growth, China needs large-scale construction projects to build roads, industrial parks, and commercial plazas. The buildings that currently stand must be demolished, so the demolition is justified. The

[3] Most of rights-priority philosophies can be classified as "libertarianism". For a comprehensive view of libertarianism, see Will Kymlicka. 2002. *Contemporary Political Philosophy: An Introduction*. Second Edition. Oxford and New York: Oxford University Press. Chapter 4. For a review of Rawls's "Liberal Equality", see ibid. Chapter 3.

method used to demolish these buildings is unimportant. Ruthless means used to relocate the occupants of the buildings being demolished have caused misfortune for many people. This is done in the name of national economic development. Even if the objective is right, does this objective justify everything done during the process of relocation and demolition?

Similarly, when "stability overwhelms everything else," we might disregard basic rule of law principles and people's rights. Some people have even said such things as, "If we do not execute so-and-so, there will be chaos under the heavens." Can we consider this a legitimate reason to sentence a person to death?

Society cannot be without justice, but utilitarianism and rights-priority understand justice differently. Utilitarianism speaks in terms of benefit and cost, not right and wrong. Rights-priority speaks in terms of right and wrong, not benefit and cost. Justice for rights-priority means respect for basic rights. These basic rights cannot be negated for utilitarian purposes. The One Child Policy can explain this point. The purpose of the One Child Policy is population control. This sounds legitimate because overpopulation and limited resources mean we will not be able to develop or have a good life. Can we negate the basic right to reproduction, or even use inhumane methods to force abortions, and still be consistent with basic justice? Obviously, utilitarianism is incompatible with freedom.

We can also consider how society should view democracy. Is democracy a means or an ends? To utilitarianists, democracy is only a means, so people's debates center around whether democracy benefits economic development. If it benefits economic development, it is good. If it harms economic development, it is therefore bad, so we cannot use it. Utilitarianists of China often use India as an example to prove democracy is undesirable, because India's democratic system has not brought about economic prosperity. However, from the rights-priority perspective, democracy is not only a means, but also an ends. Democracy is a way for people to exercise their rights. Democracy is about the legitimacy of power.

Utilitarianism provides an excuse for the government to interfere with the economy. According to utilitarian theory, the government can concentrate power to do big things. This is advantageous for short-term economic growth and responding to economic crises. For example, when the Global Financial Crisis happened in 2009, China relied on the power of government to quickly implement strong stimulus policies. However, from the rights-priority perspective, if government intervention harms basic individual rights, then it is illegitimate. Interventionist policies cannot be endorsed just because the "efficiency" of government action is higher.

Utilitarianism has harmed social morals. The One Child Policy provides one more example. Recently, a professor returned home from abroad to teach at a university in south China. The professor was fired subsequently for having a second baby. What caused the dean of his school to make this type of decision? The department responsible for the One Child Policy notified the dean the policy had veto power over the school's advanced unit qualifications. If the professor was not fired, the school would not receive the qualifications.[4]

Here is one more merciless example. A married couple had an unplanned pregnancy, but the woman's health could not handle an abortion. At five or six months of gestation, their colleagues told the couple the work unit's annual bonus would be withheld due to the trouble caused by them. Under pressure from her colleagues, the woman's only choice was to risk her life to undergo an abortion. When a society favors certificates, medals, and bonuses over human life, I believe it will be hard for this kind of society to have a good social morality.

For utilitarian purposes, such as growth or stability, we will also limit people's right to speak. The freedom of speech is the most basic right. If we limit the freedom of speech for growth or stability, then people in the media will lack professional ethics. The media will become corrupt, which also leads to corruption in academia. Similarly, if we disrespect rule of law principles and negate judicial independence, then judges will lack professional ethics, which will lead to judicial corruption. The reason is simple. No one could take responsibility for someone else's decision. When you write something that is not the free expression of your own thought or when you make a judgment that is not based on the law and your conscience, it is impossible for you to take responsibility.

Limits on the freedom of speech might lead to society's moral degradation. We should recognize the serious moral consequences of utilitarianism.

Of course, the reason utilitarianism is prevalent has certain historical reasons both inside and outside of China. According to the modernization theory of Ronald Inglehard, people's survival values took priority

[4] See Zhang Pinghui's article titled "Guangzhou professor fired for alleged breach of the one-child policy" in the December 13, 2013 edition of the *South China Morning Post.*

throughout the transition from traditional societies to agricultural and industrialized societies.[5] For collective survival, individual rights were suppressed, and sometimes people were willing to accept this suppression. Under conditions of extreme poverty, for survival, people might voluntarily give up their own liberty and dignity. When I lived in the countryside, some people had nothing to eat, so they intentionally committed a crime in order to get sent to jail. After they got out of jail, they returned home and had nothing to eat, so they continued to commit crimes. However, after entering the post-industrial society, the value of individual rights, autonomy, and self-expression became more important. The well-known Maslow's hierarchy of needs also told us this. As society changes, traditional survival value is gradually replaced by the value of self-expression. At this point, continuing to evaluate our policies solely based on utilitarian standards is—in my belief—incompatible with humanity's progress.

This is the transformation we must face today. Regardless of whether we are considering issues or setting policies, China's reforms must transition from utilitarianism to rights-priority. Humanity has certain basic values. These basic values must take priority over any utilitarian consideration. We cannot negate them for any reason, even growing GDP or maintaining stability. Of course, we can use utilitarian standards to perform a cost-benefit analysis for choices that involve material interests. However, we cannot use utilitarianism to weigh matters involving people's basic rights and dignity. The legitimacy of our policies cannot only be based on whether they benefit economic development or increase efficiency. This is similar to why we cannot make a judgment on prostitution based on whether it makes money.

The importance of the private economy is now widely recognized. Currently, however, this recognition is very utilitarian. In debates about whether public ownership or private ownership is better, our standard in the past was to ask which type of ownership system benefited economic development. I believe this is insufficient. We cannot understand the value of private enterprises solely from the perspective of benefiting economic development. If we understand it from this perspective, we might repudiate private enterprises at any time, or even nationalize them. In any event,

[5] Ronald Inglehard. 1997. *Modernization and Postmodernization: Cultural, Economic and Political Change in 43 Countries.* Princeton, NJ: Princeton University Press.

some people can always find a reason to say privately owned enterprises harm economic development.

We should view privately owned enterprises from a new perspective. We should acknowledge the freedom to start a business, the freedom to innovate, and the freedom to exchange are humanity's basic rights. This includes engaging in the financial industry. We cannot deprive them for any other reason.

Utilitarian considerations cannot establish a true market economy. With utilitarianism, as previously stated, at any time we can say the market harms economic development or social stability, and thus repudiate it. The market is not just a tool for GDP growth. The market is a pathway for humanity to realize self-value and pursue excellence. If we respect people's basic rights and give each person equal liberty, then a market economy will appear naturally. On the contrary, if our systems and policies disrespect people's basic rights and liberties, then even more reform measures cannot establish a true market economy system, and marketization process can be easily reversed any time in the name of efficiency and stability. The rule of law principle cannot be sustained.

CHAPTER 28

Pursuit of Liberty Is a Duty

China's contribution to world innovation over the past 500 years was basically zero. The problem obviously involves China's system and institutions. The basic characteristic of China's systems is limitations of liberty. This stifles creativity and entrepreneurship. Can China rewrite its innovation history over the next 50 or 100 years? The answer depends to a large degree on whether China can walk along the path started by Deng Xiaoping to steadily increase the Chinese people's freedom. Only with freedom can the entrepreneurship and creativity of the Chinese play a full role.

Therefore, advancing liberty is the duty of every person that cares about China's destiny. More so, it is the mission of every Chinese![1]

* * *

The Chinese civilization is one of the world's oldest civilizations and is also claimed as the only ancient civilization to last to the present day. Brilliant discoveries were made in ancient China that made important contributions to human progress. However, in modern times (the past 500 years), China has lacked inventions. Allow me to use numbers to prove this point.

[1] The original version of this chapter was written in July 2017.

W. Zhang, *Ideas for China's Future*,
https://doi.org/10.1007/978-981-15-4304-3_28

Charles Murray, an American scholar, wrote a book titled *Human Accomplishment: The Pursuit of Excellence in the Arts and Sciences, 800 B.C. to 1950.*[2] He listed 161 major technological inventions between 400 B.C. and 1950 A.D., of which China has seven, or 4.3% of the total. All these seven inventions occurred before 1500 A.D. In the two-thousand years leading up to 1500 A.D., there were 10 major inventions, including the abacus, the rudder, paper, gunpowder, stirrups, and canal locks. This means China accounted for 70% of major inventions in history, with the last one occurring between 1041 and 1048 A.D. when Bi Sheng invented movable type. Of the 151 major inventions that came after 1500 A.D., none of them were invented by Chinese.

Jack Challoner compiled a more authoritative and complete account.[3] He listed 1001 major inventions that changed the world between the Paleolithic Age (2.5 million years ago) and 2008 A.D. China contributed 30 inventions, or 3% of the total. All these 30 inventions occurred before 1500 A.D. There were 163 major inventions before 1500 A.D., meaning China accounted for 18.4%, of which six inventions (including movable type, the chain drive, the clock tower, the cannon, fireworks, and land mines) were from the Song dynasty. The last invention of China was in 1498 when the toothbrush was invented. This was the only major invention from the Ming dynasty. Among the 838 inventions in the 500 years after 1500 A.D., none of them came from China.

Economic growth is the continuous appearance of new products, new technologies, and new industries. Traditional societies only have a few industries such as agriculture, metallurgy, ceramics, and handicrafts, of which agriculture dominates. Today, how many industries do we have? According to the United Nations' set of nested categories of exports, there are 97 two-digit industries, 1222 four-digit industries, and 5053 six-digit industries. The list keeps growing. These new industries were created by entrepreneurs over the last 300 years. Every new product can be traced back to its origins. Among these numerous new industries and products, which new industries or major products were invented by Chinese? None!

[2] Charles Murray. 2007. *Human Accomplishment: The Pursuit of Excellence in Arts and Sciences, 800 B. C. to 1950.* HarperCollins.

[3] Jack Challoner. 2009. *1001 Inventions that Changed the World.* New York: Barron's Education Series, Inc.

The automobile industry was created by Karl Benz, Gottlieb Daimler, and Wilhelm Maybach in 1880s Germany. After a series of technological progress, we have the variety of automobiles we see today. Albernathy, Clark, and Kantrow (1984) found that between 1900 and 1981, there were more than 600 major innovations in the automobile industry.[4] China is currently the largest producer of automobiles. However, if you write a history of technological progress in the automobile industry, you will come up with a list of thousands of inventors. That list will include German, French, British, Italian, American, Belgian, Swedish, Swiss, and Japanese names, but no Chinese names!

Even in traditional industries that China was advanced in before the seventeenth century, such as metallurgy, ceramics, and textiles, none of the major inventions over the last 300 years came from us Chinese.

I want to emphasize the difference between pre- and post–1500 A.D. In general, the number of major inventions in China is misleading.

Before 1500 A.D., the world was separated into different regions, and each region was isolated. Technological progress was slow, and diffusion was even slower. Even if a new technology appeared in one region, it had a minimal impact on other places. The contribution to humanity was extremely limited. For example, Cai Lun invented papermaking in 105 A.D., but China's papermaking technology only entered the Islamic World after 751 A.D. Three hundred years passed before it was transmitted to Western Europe. When I attended elementary school, I had to practice characters on a "dirt disk" because paper was unaffordable.

After 1500 A.D., the world began to integrate. Not only did the speed of technological innovation increase, but the speed of technological dispersion also became more rapid. As soon as a new technology appeared in one region, other regions quickly adopted it. This had a major impact on the overall progress of humanity. For example, Germans invented the automobile in 1886, but by 1900, France became the largest producer of automobiles. After another 15 years, America replaced France as the largest producer of automobiles.[5] By 1930, the automobile penetration rate

[4] William J. Abernathy, Kim B. Clark, and Alan M. Kantrow. 1984. *Industrial Renaissance: Producing a Competitive Future for America.* New York: Basic Books.

[5] Vaclav Smil. 2005. *Creating the Twentieth Century: Technical Innovations of 1867–1914 and Their Lasting Impact.* Oxford and New York: Oxford University Press. P. 134–139.

reached 60% in America. The continuous appearance and diffusion of new technology is the reason the speed of human progress increased rapidly over the past 300 years.

For this reason, after 1500 A.D., innovation was truly comparable between countries. Who was superior and who was inferior could be seen at a glance. China's lack of inventions that can be entered into the history books over the past 500 years means our contribution to human progress was basically zero. This is far worse than our ancestors!

I also want to emphasize the issue of population scale. Some countries are large and others are small, so simply comparing which country has more innovations is unconvincing.

In theory, given other conditions, the larger a country's population is, the more innovation there is and the faster technological progress is. Additionally, the relationship between innovation and population is exponential, not a simple proportional relationship. For example, if the population of one economy is twice as large as another economy, then the latter's innovation should be more than double the former's innovation. There are two reasons for this. First, knowledge has substantial economies of scale and spillover effects in production. When two ideas collide, they can produce a third and fourth idea. Second, knowledge is not exclusive in its use. (This is an important conclusion of endogenous growth theory.)

Ten thousand years ago, the melting glaciers separated the world into three large regions: (1) Afro-Eurasia; (2) The Americas; and (3) Oceania. Afro-Eurasia had the largest population, followed by the Americas. Oceania had the smallest population. After 1500 A.D., as these three worlds began to re-connect, we discovered Afro-Eurasia was the most developed, followed by the Americas. Oceania was the most primitive.[6]

In the 1930s, Swiss-born American biologist Max Kleiber discovered animal's metabolic ratio was the positive three-fourths power of body weight, and thus unit weight energy consumption is scaled to the negative one-fourth power.[7] For example, a cow weighs 1000 times larger than an American marmot (groundhog), but the energy consumed is only 178

[6] Michael Kremer. 1993. "Population Growth and Technological Change: One Million B.C. to 1990." *The Quarterly Journal of Economics* Vol. 108, No. 3 (Aug., 1993), pp. 681–716.

[7] Quoted from Steven Johnson. 2010. *Where Good Ideas Come From: The Natural History of Innovation*. New York: Riverhead Books. P. 8–9.

times larger. The unit energy consumption is 0.178 times larger, the heart rate is 5.6 times slower, and the lifespan is 5.6 times longer.

More than ten years ago, British-born physicist Geoffrey West and his research team discovered urban life also follows the negative one-fourth power scaling rule. If one city's population is 10 times larger than another city's population, then energy consumption, road area, and other public utilities will be only 5.6 times greater in the larger city. The per capita rate is 0.56 times. This is caused by economies of scale. However, innovation (patents, research and development expenditures, the number of inventors, and the number of people employed in science and technology) follows the positive one-fourth power scaling rule. If one city's population is 10 times larger than another city, then the total amount of innovation is 17.8 times the smaller city. The per capita rate is 1.78 times.[8]

From this perspective, China's contribution to world innovation is disproportionate to its population size. China's population is four times the size of America's population, 10 times the size of Japan's population, 20 times the size of Great Britain's population, and 165 times the size of Switzerland's population. According to the knowledge creation power scale rule, China should be 5.6 times more innovative than America, 17.8 times more innovative than Japan, 42.3 times more innovative than Great Britain, and 591 times more innovative than Switzerland. The per capita rate should be 1.4 times, 1.8 times, 2.1 times, and 3.6 times, respectively. Even using simple arithmetic scale, China's contribution to innovation should be four times greater than America, 10 times greater than Japan, 20 times greater than Great Britain, and 165 times greater than Switzerland.

The reality is China's contribution to world innovation over the past 500 years was basically zero. Forget about comparing ourselves to America or Great Britain, we cannot even get a fraction of Switzerland. The Swiss invented surgical forceps, electronic hearing aids, plastic surgery, liquid crystal displays, etc. The anti-counterfeiting ink used by the People's Bank of China to print renminbi banknotes is Swiss technology. Between 60–70% of flour produced in China is processed using Swiss-based Bühler Holding AG's machines.[9]

[8] L. Bettencourt, J. Lobo, D. Helbing, C. Kuhner and G. B. West. 2007. "Grown, Innovation, Scaling and the Pace of Life in Cities." *Proceedings of the National Academy of Sciences* 104, no. 17 (2007): 7301.

[9] James Breiding. 2012. *Swiss Made: The Untold Story behind Switzerland's Success.* Profile Books.

Where did the problem arise? Is there a problem with Chinese genetics? Of course not! Inventions of ancient Chinese, the achievements of overseas Chinese, and modern tests of intelligence all prove the average intelligence of the Chinese are at least not lower than the global average.

The problem obviously involves our system and institutions. This includes our economic system, political system, education system, cultural concepts, behavioral norms, etc. The basic characteristic of China's systems is limitations of liberty. This stifles creativity and entrepreneurship. Satisfying material and spiritual needs through commercialized innovation becomes impossible.

In its own history, the Chinese were most innovative in the Spring and Autumn period and Song dynasty. This is no accident. These two time periods were also the two most free periods in China's history.

After 1500 A.D., the Western world continued to move toward freedom and the rule of law, but we did the opposite.

I must emphasize liberty is an inseparable whole. When the mind is not free, action cannot be free. When speech is not free, thought cannot be free. Without liberty, creativity is impossible. Let me explain this point with an example.

Today, handwashing before meals and after going to the bathroom is common. However, Ignaz Semmelweis, a Hungarian physician, in 1847 was the first to propose handwashing in obstetrical clinics. He offended his peers and lost his job. He died in a mental hospital at the age of 47. Semmelweis' views were based on his research of "childbed fever." The hospital he was at had two maternity clinics. One serviced upper-class mothers cared for by professional doctors and nurses. The other relied on midwives to service the general public. He discovered deaths due to "childbed fever" were three times higher in the clinic with professional doctors. He believed the reason was doctors did not wash their hands between performing autopsies and deliveries. However, Semmelweis' views contradicted the prevailing scientific theory at the time. He also could not give an acceptable scientific justification for his discovery.

Today, most urbanites shower daily. However, between the Middle Ages and the early twentieth century, the prevailing hygiene theory in Europe believed putting the body in water was unhealthy, or even dangerous. Only barbarians would do such a thing. Queen Elizabeth I of England strangely bothered to take a bath once a month, and she was a veritable clean freak compared to her peers. Before the age of seven, Louis XIII, the King of France, had not taken a bath.[10]

How did human hygiene habits change? This is related to the invention of the printing press.

In the 1440s, Johannes Gutenberg, a German entrepreneur, adapted a wine press to invent the movable-type printing press. Within a 50-year span, the printing press had spread to 250 cities in Europe, the total number of the published books was between 15 and 20 million.[11] With the spread of inexpensive printed books, more and more people began reading. Many people suddenly discovered they were "farsighted." (Farsightedness is common, but most people did not realize it because they never read.) This led to explosive growth in demand for glasses. One hundred years after Gutenberg invented the printing press, thousands of eyewear manufacturers appeared in Europe. Glass came to represent advanced technology. This set off a revolution in optical technology.

In the 1590s, Dutch spectacle-makers, father and son Hans and Zacharias Janssen, put a few lenses together and discovered this magnified the size of the things observed. Thus, the microscope was invented. Robert Hook, an English scientist, discovered cells under the microscope, which initiated a scientific and medical revolution. Humanity began exploring the microscopic world. Less than 20 years after the appearance of the microscope, a cluster of Dutch spectacle-makers (including Hans Lippershey) invented the telescope. In less than one year, Galileo Galilei improved Hans Lippershey's design to create a telescope that was ten-times more powerful. In January 1610, Galileo used his telescope to observe four of Jupiter's moons. This was the first true challenge to Aristotelian cosmology. Human exploration of space began from that point. In 1668, Isaac Newton invented the first working reflective telescope.[12]

Early microscopes had low resolutions until the 1870s. Carl Zeiss, a German spectacle-maker, produced a new microscope based on precise

[10] Steven Johnson. 2014. *How We Got Now: Six Innovations That Made the Modern World*. New York: Riverhead Books. P. 136–138.

[11] Ian Goldin and Chris Kutarna. 2016. *Age of Discovery: Navigating the Risks and Rewards of Our New Renaissance*. St. Martin's Press. Chapter 2, Section 2.

[12] Steven Johnson. 2014. *How We Got Now: Six Innovations That Made the Modern World*. New York: Riverhead Books. P. 20–25.

mathematical formulas. With the help of this microscope, German physician Robert Koch and others observed the spread of disease came from bacteria that the naked eye cannot see, proving Ignaz Semmelweis' views were correct. From this, microbiology and bacteriology were born. The establishment of microbiology and bacteriology gradually changed humanity's hygienic practices.[13] This led to a huge increase in life expectancy.

Imagine if Johannes Gutenberg's printing press was prohibited, or if he was only allowed to print material approved by the church or the state. Reading would not become that common, demand for spectacles would not be as great, the microscope and telescope would not be invented, microbiology would not be established, and we could not drink pasteurized milk. Humanity's life expectancy would not have increased from 30 years to 70 years. Space exploration would be even more of a fantasy.

China's economic success over the past 30 years has attracted worldwide attention. We are extremely proud of it. Even though this is the result of Deng Xiaoping's Reform and Opening, it is also the result of the Western World's liberalization over the past 300 years. China's achievements over the past 30 years were built upon technological innovations accumulated over 300 years in the West. Reform and Opening allowed us to enjoy more liberty, but also gave us the opportunity to enjoy the result of other people's liberty. We are engaged in arbitrage, not innovation. We built a small attic on a tower built by others. We have no reason to be arrogant.

Isaac Newton spent 30 years discovering gravity. I spent three months understanding the law of universal gravitation. If I announce I covered the same distance in three months that Newton covered in 30 years, you should laugh. If I laugh at Newton, then you should feel that I am hopeless.

We often say China has 7% of the world's arable land but supports 20% of the world's population. We should ask how China accomplishes this. Stated simply, we use a lot of fertilizer. China uses 200 kilograms of fertilizer per hectare of arable land, and five of the most intensively cultivated provinces exceed 300 kilograms. This is six times higher than the United States. The Chinese get 80% of their protein from food crops. Nitrogen fertilizer provides 60% of China's food crop nutrients. Therefore, roughly half of the nitrogen in China's food comes from inorganic fertilizers.[14] Without fertilizer, half of China's population would starve.

[13] Ibid. p. 140–142.

[14] Vaclav Smil. 2005. *Creating the Twentieth Century: Technical Innovations of 1867–1914 and Their Lasting Impact*. Oxford and New York: Oxford University Press. P. 197.

Where did the production technology of nitrogen fertilizer come from? More than 100 years ago, German scientist Fritz Haber invented a production process for synthetic ammonia, and Carl Bosch used it for large-scale production. After U.S. President Nixon visited China in 1972, the first business between China and the United States was an order for 13 of the largest, most modern synthetic ammonia and urea production equipment, of which eight came from Kellogg.

Over the next 50 or 100 years, can China write the world's history of innovation to make up for the past 500 years? The answer depends to a large degree on whether we can walk along the path started by Deng Xiaoping to steadily increase the Chinese people's freedom. Only with freedom can the entrepreneurship and creativity of the Chinese play a full role. This will turn China into an innovative country.

Therefore, advancing liberty is the duty of every person that cares about China's destiny. More so, it is the mission of every Chinese!

CHAPTER 29

Without a Market for Ideas, China Has No Future

The so-called market of ideas is the equal freedom to express competing scholarship, viewpoints, speech, and faiths.

Social change and human progress are driven by new ideas. Changes in institutions and policies do not happen without changing ideas. Without a market for ideas, the appearance and transmission of new ideas is difficult, so all of society is deprived of the source of change.[1]

* * *

In the last years of his life, Nobel Prize-winning economist Ronald Coase mentioned the importance of the market for ideas on China's future reforms.[2] We should take his warning seriously.

The so-called market of ideas is the freedom to express equally competing scholarship, viewpoints, speech, and faiths. It includes the free competition to both create and accept ideas. It means that there are no administrative or legal restrictions on what can and cannot be researched or expressed.

[1] The original version of this chapter was written in March 2014.

[2] Ronald Coase and Ning Wang. 2013. *How China Became Capitalist.* New York: Palgrave Macmillan. P. 196–197.

W. Zhang, *Ideas for China's Future*,
https://doi.org/10.1007/978-981-15-4304-3_29

It also means that everyone has the right to choose any kind of theory or viewpoint. Different theories can only dominate the market by means of reason. No one has the right to force people to accept a kind of viewpoint or theory.

Why is the market for ideas important? Simply put, because social change and human progress are driven by new ideas. Changes in institutions and policies do not happen without changing ideas. Without a market for ideas, the appearance and transmission of new ideas is difficult, so all of society is deprived of the source of change.

Traditionally, economists and many other social scientists understood social change as the result of games between interests. They believed that social change happened because some type of interest (the beneficiaries of change) overcame another type of interest (the old system or old policy's vested interests). Or, it happened because the rulers and policy makers acknowledged that the benefits outweighed the costs. This interest is often understood as material interests or political power. We should say that this understanding contains a bit of truth because an indisputable fact is people's choices are determined by interests. As David Hume pointed out more than 200 years ago, however, "though men be much governed by interest; yet even interest itself, and all human affairs, are entirely governed by opinion."[3] The perception of a person's interests itself depends on his or her beliefs. Viewpoints are not just the means in which people obtain their interests.

Historical analysis and actual observations show that in many circumstances, social change happens not because one type of interest triumphed over another interest, but because an idea triumphed over an interest. Alternatively, a (new) idea replaced another (old) idea, or one type of ideology replaced another type of ideology. Many times the victory of some type of interest is actually the victory of some type of idea. For example, the victories led by the Chinese Communist Party of the New Democratic Revolution and the Socialist Revolution were not victories of the interests of the proletarian class over the interests of the bourgeoisie and landowner class, but instead were victories of Marxist-Leninism over other ideologies. As the leader of these revolutions, the Chinese Communist Party is

[3] Hume, D. ([1742] 1987). "Whether the British Government Inclines More to Absolute Monarchy, or to a Republic." In E. F. Miller (ed.), *Essays, Moral, Political and Literary*, Part I, Essay VII. P. 51. Indianapolis: Liberty Press.

considered the "vanguard" of the working class. However, the majority of those people were not farmers or workers; instead they were born into the elite class in the traditional society. The reason they sought revolution was because they accepted the ideas of Marxist-Leninism and believed that "taking the Russian road" was the best choice for Chinese society.

How come in the twentieth century the planned economy could become the system used by countries accounting for one-third of the world's population and exist for such a long period of time? It was the result of changes in ideas. The planned economy is the product of an idea. After the "Cultural Revolution," China was in a state of serious crisis. The imperative to change was recognized by all, but as for how to change was something that itself required ideas. The reason Deng Xiaoping initiated the market-oriented Reform and Opening was because he recognized the planned economy could not resolve China's issues. We had to give the people more liberty so they could direct their own incentives and motives to bring the role of the market into play. The reason China's Reform and Opening could be so successful is because in the 1980s leaders like Deng Xiaoping, Hu Yaobang, Zhao Ziyang, Wan Li, and others had the right ideas. However, in the end, especially after 2003, I believe there are problems with our ideas. Therefore, we can see the retreat or stagnation of reform initiatives is related to ideas.

This also means ideas can be both good and bad. If we accept a bad idea, perhaps it will bring about a disaster for humanity. If we accept a good idea, human progress will be faster, standards of living will be higher, and society will be more harmonious.

The problem is there is no *a priori* standard or authoritative judgment to rely on that separates correct and incorrect ideas. It is said putting things into practice is the only standard for examining the truth. However, examining the truth through practice can only be done after the fact, whereas ideas must be forward-looking. If an idea is not forward-looking, then change cannot happen. When a new idea is first proposed, it could not have possibly been put into practice before that point. A major challenge faced by humanity is our lack of *a priori* knowledge about the correctness or incorrectness of ideas. This is the reason we need the market of ideas. Determining whether an idea is correct or not can only be done by examining it in the market of ideas.

I do not mean to say the result of competition in the market of ideas will always be correct ideas, but if we want to reduce the possibility of incorrect ideas winning out, the only way to do so is to have free competition in the market for ideas.

From the point a new idea is proposed to its eventual application is similar to what economists call the process of "roundabout production." This process has three stages: Production, dissemination, and application.[4] At the higher end of the production stage are a small number of scholars, philosophers, and thinkers. Their role is to create new ideas, so we call them "idea entrepreneurs" or "thought institutional entrepreneurs." Even if it is indisputable some new viewpoints are initially proposed by average people, without scholars turning those ideas into theories, grassroots viewpoints are not likely to become a force for social change. Public intellectuals, media professionals, publishers, and educators are the intermediates in this process. Their function is to disseminate ideas. They select the ideas created by thinkers to organize them in a way the masses can understand. Then they disseminate these ideas to statesmen and the common people, thus changing the social consensus. F. A. Hayek called them the "secondhand dealers" of knowledge.[5] On the other end of this process are political figures and practitioners. Their role is to initiate change so new ideas become law and policy. I call these "implementation institutional entrepreneurs" (or "political entrepreneurs").

Of course, this process is interactive. Theorists do not pull theories out of the air. The issues faced by policy makers and the "will of the people" reflected by public media and public intellectuals are often the basis for theorists proposing new theories and ideas.

In reality, perhaps some people assume all three roles concurrently, or two of the three. However, conceptually and logically, these three roles are different. Also, in reality, in most circumstances, these roles are held by different people. The reason is there are conflicts between these roles. For example, practitioners must focus on the feasibility of policy and reaching balance between interests. This means sometimes they must say one thing and mean another, but if theorists and thinkers place excessive focus on

[4]For an analytical framework of the process of idea markets, see Waye A. Leghton and Edward J. Lopez. 2013. *Madman, Intellectuals and Academic Scribblers: The Economic Engine of Political Change*. Stanford, CA: Stanford University Press. P. 131–134.

[5]F. A. Hayek. 1949. "The Intellectuals and Socialism." *University of Chicago Law Review* 16;3(1949), 373.

"feasibility" and balance between interests, they cannot possibly produce a real theory. The reason a theory is a theory is because when it is first proposed, it is "unrealistic" and not acknowledged by the majority. As said by Hayek, "If politics is the art of the possible, political philosophy is the art of making politically possible the seemingly impossible."[6] Therefore, it is generally said outstanding political scientists cannot possibly be good statesmen, and *vice versa*. Confucius could only be an "uncrowned king" but not a monarch. Plato's "philosopher king" could only exist in his book *The Republic*, but not in the real world.[7]

Yet, the basic principles of the market for ideas are suitable for these three stages.

In the production stage of ideas, the basic principles of the market for ideas are academic freedom and freedom of thought. Academic freedom and freedom of thought mean scholars must be at liberty to undertake academic research in any area. Except for the limits of academia itself, when exploring and expressing academic viewpoints, scholars should not have any other restrictions. Any interference in academic freedom damages the market for ideas. Academic freedom also means equality between academic viewpoints, so that no scholarship or theory has the power to maintain monopoly status using political power. Otherwise, academic freedom does not exist.

In the dissemination stage of ideas, the basic principle of the market for ideas is viewpoints can be freely disseminated, while at the same time, existing viewpoints, customs, laws, and policies can be freely criticized. Of course, each person must take responsibility for his or her own speech.

In the application stage of ideas, the basic principle of the market for ideas is the formation and implementation of public policy should undergo extensive debate and criticism. Major legislative revision should be determined by referendum. Under probable circumstances, changes to law and policy should be a step-by-step evolutionary process. It should allow people many means to make selections instead of relying on constructivism led by a central authority. "Taking measures suited to local conditions" and "crossing the river by feeling the stones" are examples of applying the principles of the market for ideas in practice.

[6] F. A. Hayek. (2011 (1960)). *The Constitution of Liberty*. Chicago: University of Chicago Press. P. 180–181.

[7] Frederick II (1712–1786), also known as Frederick the Great, the ruler of the Kingdom of Prussia from 1740 until 1786, might be one of few exceptions. He sought to embody the Platonic ideal of a "philosopher king." Mao Zedong also sought to be a "philosopher king," but he was absolutely not a success.

Throughout history, humanity has enjoyed the benefits brought about by the market for ideas, but also suffered the disasters created by obstructing it. The free market for ideas during the Spring and Autumn period, the Warring States period, and Wei-Jin-Northern-Southern dynasty period created the magnificent Chinese civilization. The First Emperor of Qin's Burn Books and Bury Scholars Campaign, the Emperor Wu of Han's policy of dismissing other schools of thought besides Confucianism, and the Qing Dynasty's Literary Inquisition are all examples of interventions into and violation of the market for ideas. These are all related to the long-term stagnation of Chinese society. In the West, the monopoly status of the Catholic Church in the Middle Ages was a major obstruction to scientific and social progress. It was precisely along with the development of the market for ideas during the Renaissance that science and art flourished. People's ideas began to change, which eventually led to the Industrial Revolution. The tremendous progress of humanity over the last two hundred years was without a doubt the result of competition in the market for ideas.

We as humans cannot avoid making mistakes, but with the market for ideas, humanity can at least avoid making mistakes that lead to disaster. For example, as mentioned above, the planned economy was an idea. Putting this idea into practice in China widened the gap between China and developed countries. It caused loss of wealth or even life for hundreds of millions of people. We can imagine if during that time there was a market for ideas, so scholars and media professionals could freely express their opinions, then there certainly would have been people opposed to the planned economy. It would not have been put into practice for so long, nor would it have caused so much harm. Early on, when rural cooperatives and people's communes were created, some economists opposed them. They were quickly suppressed and were unable to speak up again. We can even imagine when people's communes were created and the Great Leap Forward was implemented, if localities were allowed to at least determine whether or not to implement them and for how long, some local officials would have resisted, so it is likely that tens of millions of people would not have starved to death. This example also proves the importance of the implementation segment of the market for ideas.

China's Reform and Opening benefited from the market for ideas. A leader like Deng Xiaoping was important, but many of his ideas came from the ideas of economists and other theorists. Without an atmosphere of relative freedom within economic circles during the end of the 1970s and the 1980s, the "Planned Commodity Economy" could not possibly have been written into the decision of the Third Plenary Session of the Twelfth Central Committee of the Chinese Communist Party, nor could the "Socialist Market Economy" have been written into the decision of the Third Plenary Session of the Fourteenth Central Committee. China's Reform and Opening could not have succeeded as much as it did.

A classic example of this I experienced personally was the price system reform. Before 1984, the imperative of price reform was recognized by both economists and bureaucrats. Even high-level leaders referred to the price issue as a roadblock to reform. The reason price reform could not move forward was because at that time the mainstream viewpoint was prices in a socialist economy must be set by the government, and the government had the ability to determine rational prices. The reason prices were not rational was because when the government set prices, it did not respect the "Law of Value." As long as prices were set according to the Law of Value, the price system would be rational. In April 1984, I finished writing *Taking Price Reform as the Center of Economic System Reform* (*Yi Jiagge Gaige wei Zhongxin Daidong Zhengge Jingji Tizhi Gaige*). In it, a basic viewpoint is rational prices cannot be determined by the government, so the only option for price reform was gradual liberalization of price controls via the dual-track system. Considering price reform from the perspective of liberalization was a completely new concept. In September 1984, my idea was introduced to the Mount Mogan Conference. First it was accepted by many participating economists, and then through the efforts of conference organizers, it was accepted by the government's high-level leadership. This led to a breakthrough in the price reform and had a major impact on the overall economic system reform. We can imagine if the organizers of the Mount Mogan Conference had decided beforehand participants could only discuss how to adjust prices, and not discuss how to liberalize prices (because it could be suspected of "advocating the capitalist free market"), then no valuable opinions on price reform could have come out of that conference. Price reform at least would have been delayed for a considerable amount of time.[8]

[8] For a detailed analysis of China's price reform process, see Weiying Zhang, Chapter 12 "China's Price Reform', in *The Logic of the Market: An Insider's View of Chinese Economic Reform*. Washington DC: Cato Institute. P. 235–263. For the original version of my paper on the dual-track price reform, see P. 265–282 in the above book.

After 30 years of reform in China, compared to the product market and factor market, the market for ideas has developed the slowest. Some may say even without a market for ideas, China has experienced an economic miracle, so from this we can see the market for ideas is not important. The mistake this viewpoint makes is it ignores the fact economies without a market for ideas can also benefit from the market for ideas in other countries. Without Professors Hayek, Friedman, and Coase, I do not believe our reforms would have been as successful as they were. These economists' ideas were products of a free market for ideas.

Just as economic development has the "late-mover's advantage," the market for ideas does, too. In an open society, any country can benefit from the ideas and viewpoints developed in other countries. Without a doubt, introducing ideas is much harder than introducing technology and products. Implementing new ideas must interact with interest structures, social structures, cultures, customs, and systems. Human nature has the inertia to resist new ideas. This means when the ideas developed in Western countries are applied in Chinese society, they must undergo a process of "Sinification." This is the responsibility of Chinese scholars. The decision of the Third Plenary Session of the Eighteen Central Committee established the basic direction of reform. It specifically mentioned the "modernization of the system of national governance and governance ability" as political system reform objectives. Without the debates among different academic viewpoints in the market for ideas, however, people will have different understandings of the meaning of "modernization of the system of national governance and governance ability." A basic consensus would be impossible. Without a basic consensus, reform cannot progress smoothly.

In the short-term, during any social change, perhaps the ideas of the political leadership are very important. However, in the long-term, perhaps the ideas of the common people are more important. No political leader can act in violation of the majority's beliefs for long. Large social transformations are the affairs of the whole people; they cannot only be the affairs of a small elite. Both the formation of political leaders' ideas and the changes in the views of the masses are the result of the operation of the market for ideas. Without a market for ideas, China has no future!

Index[1]

[1] Note: Page numbers followed by 'n' refer to notes.

W. Zhang, *Ideas for China's Future*,
https://doi.org/10.1007/978-981-15-4304-3

The manufacturer's authorised representative in the EU is Springer
Nature Customer Service Centre GmbH, Europaplatz 3, 69115 Heidelberg,
Germany. If you have any concerns regarding our products, please
contact ProductSafety@springernature.com

Printed and bound by CPI Group (UK) Ltd, Croydon, CR0 4YY
30/09/2026
02225460-0006